Transforming College Struggles Into Success Stories

Successful Academic Growth With Integrity

By,

James Edward Langley

DEDICATION

To my beloved wife, April,

This book is a testament to the unwavering support and boundless encouragement you have bestowed upon me throughout this journey.

Your belief in my dreams has been the guiding light that fueled my determination and sustained me through the challenges.

In moments of doubt, your words of encouragement echoed, propelling me forward with renewed vigor.

Your understanding and patience created a space where creativity could flourish and aspirations could take root.

Your sacrifices, both seen and unseen, have laid the foundation for the realization of this endeavor.

It is with immense gratitude and love that I dedicate this book to you, my confidante, my partner, and my greatest source of inspiration.

Thank you for being the wind beneath my wings and for standing by me with unwavering support.

This achievement is as much yours as it is mine, a shared journey that speaks volumes of the strength found in our partnership.

With all my love,

Jimi

PREFACE

The Rationale: Crafting a Comprehensive Guide

I decided to write this book after spending more than 14 years working in higher education. During that time, I had countless meetings with thousands of students, and I always took detailed notes about what they shared with me. Students often talked about what they felt was missing from their college or university experience and what they needed to succeed. These conversations made me realize there was a real gap that needed to be filled.

While working in higher education, I often found that the information students needed to answer their questions wasn't easy for them—or even me—to access. This made it clear to me that students needed a resource to help them navigate the challenges of college life. That's when I decided to create something that could serve as a guide, not just for students, but also for their parents, families, friends, and the professionals who support them.

This book is designed to be more than just a list of tips. It combines real data with practical advice to address the needs and wants of students. It offers strategies for academic success and explores topics that touch on both personal and professional growth. My goal is to provide a resource that helps students find their way through the complexities of college, so they can make the most of their experience and achieve their goals.

This book is a multifaceted endeavor that holds great value to me. This comprehensive guide aims to delve into the reasons behind embarking on such a project, which emphasizes the importance of having evidence-based insights, which addresses student requirements that offered success strategies, all in aiming to align everything with their personal and professional passions in an ethical manner.

Insights & Integrating Data

In writing this book, which is rooted in specific types of data along with integrating insightful analogies, I feel will bring credibility and reliability to its content. The book provides evidence that supports the claims, recommendations, and strategies presented. By incorporating research findings, trends, and patterns, the book ensures that the information is not only informative but also reflective of the current landscape.

Insightful analogies that identify certain student demographics allow me to tailor the content to the specific needs of diverse student populations. For example, analyzing learning preferences, technological adoption, and academic challenges provides insights that shape the book's content.

Student Needs and Wants: A Student-Centric Approach

A student-centric approach is foundational to the success of this book. Understanding the needs and wants of students ensures that the content is relevant, engaging, and genuinely beneficial. This approach involves considering factors such as learning preferences, challenges, and aspirations.

- Recognizing the diversity of student learning styles is essential. Whether students are visual learners, auditory learners, or kinesthetic learners, this book incorporate strategies and techniques that cater to different learning preferences.
- Identifying common challenges faced by students, such as time management, stress, and academic pressure, allows me to provide practical solutions. This book becomes a resource that not only imparts knowledge but also supports students in overcoming

hurdles.
- Acknowledging students' career aspirations and personal goals helps tailor the content to be more impactful. Whether addressing specific academic disciplines, career paths, or personal development, aligning with students' aspirations enhances relevance and resonance.

Success Strategies and Foci: Guiding Students Toward Achievement

This book is focused on success strategies serving as a guidepost for students navigating the academic landscape. By distilling key success principles and actionable strategies, this book empowers students to make informed decisions, set meaningful goals, and overcome challenges.

- Success strategies can include fostering academic resilience, helping students bounce back from setbacks, and instilling a growth mindset. The book becomes a source of inspiration and guidance, encouraging students to view challenges as opportunities for growth.
- Time management is a critical success factor in academic pursuits. This book provides practical time management strategies, productivity tips, and tools that students can integrate into their daily lives.
- Success is not solely defined by academic achievements but extends to personal and professional fulfillment. This book incorporates holistic success strategies that encompass well-being, interpersonal skills, and lifelong learning.

Personal and Professional Interests: Passion as a Driving Force

In writing this book I align it with personal and professional interests serving as a testament to my passion and commitment. I am genuinely invested in the subject matter, the authenticity and enthusiasm are palpable, creating a more compelling and impactful resource.

- Infusing personal experiences, anecdotes, and insights into this book fosters a connection with readers. Students are more likely to resonate with an author who shares their genuine experiences and perspectives.
- Writing a book based on personal and professional interests ensures sustained motivation throughout the process. My passion becomes a driving force, fueling the dedication needed to see this project through to completion I am writing about topics I am deeply passionate about; this book will become a valuable contribution to academic and professional discourse. It reflects my commitment to advancing knowledge and supporting the success of others.

A Holistic Approach to Educational Writing

In writing a book that integrates insightful analogies, incorporates students' needs and wants, provides supportive success strategies, and relates to students' personal and professional interests, is my holistic approach that adds depth, relevance, and authenticity to educational literature. By weaving together evidence-based insights, student-centric considerations, success-focused strategies, and a genuine passion for the subject, I am creating a comprehensive guide that not only imparts knowledge but also inspires and empowers students on their academic and professional journey.

Table of Contents

INTRODUCTION 1
   Why this kind of book? 1
   Student Resilience and Resource Utilization 6
FAMOUS QUOTES 10
CHAPTER 1 11
   Challenges Faced by Underrepresented Students 11
      Fostering Inclusive Campus Environments: Addressing Micro aggressions, Discrimination, and Racism 20
      Cultivating Diversity: Addressing the Lack of Representation in Curriculum and Faculty 23
      Bridging the Gap: Access to Resources and Support Services 25
      Breaking Down Financial Barriers: Economic Challenges 27
      Navigating Stereotypes and Stigmas: Understanding the Impact 30
      Ensuring Campus Safety: Navigating Concerns and Promoting Student Well-Being 32
      Fostering Inclusivity: The Imperative of Cultural Competency &Training for Faculty and Staff 35
      Breaking the Silence: Understanding the Impact of Alienation and Isolation 38
      Breaking Barriers: The Impact of Lack of Representation in Leadership Roles on Campus Policies 41
      Power of Student Voices as Catalysts for Change: The Transformative Power of Advocacy and Student Activism 44
   Student's Needs 48
   Student's Wants 53
   The Ethical Imperative 58

- Meeting Student Needs 63
- CHAPTER 2 68
- Strategies 68
  - P.A.S.S 68
  - Success Planning 72
- Focus Areas 81
  - Academic Factors 81
  - Advising 86
    - Maximizing Academic Advising 90
    - Purpose: Guiding Students Toward Success 92
    - Topics for Meaningful Discussions 98
    - Interpreting Information Received: Navigating Guidance for Informed Decision-Making 106
    - Key Takeaways: A Roadmap 114
  - Awareness of Learning Styles 118
    - Visual Learners 118
    - Auditory Learners 119
    - Kinesthetic Learner 121
  - Meeting with Professors 124
    - Clarification of Course Material 124
    - Feedback on Assignments 125
    - Discussion of Academic Goals 126
    - Building a Professional Relationship 127
    - Exploration of Research Opportunities 128
    - Preparation for Exams and Assessments 129
    - Understanding Course Expectations 130
    - Seeking Academic Advice 132
    - Addressing Personal Challenges 133

Enhancing Communication Skills 134
Navigating the Academic Load 136
Balance of Background Knowledge: Introductory vs. Extensive 140
Role of Reading 144
Effective Management: Reviewing Material 148
Imperative on Completion of Coursework 152
Igniting Passion for Learning: The Significance of Interest Level 156
Significance of Concentration: Understandings, Challenges, and Solutions 160
Preparing for Assessments: Expected & Unexpected Questions on Assessments 164
Navigating Worries of Failure: Interruption of Thoughts 168
Note-taking Skills: (From books and lectures, before & after class) 173
Follow-Through and Outcomes: The Impact of Good and Poor Intentions 177
Assurance of Learning Processes 182
Test Preparations 187
Role of Memory in Learning 192
"Cramming" Pros and Cons: Memorization vs. Understanding 196
CHAPTER 3 200
Institutional Detractors 200
Issues and Concerns 200
Concerns Regarding Various Campus Environments 204
   Physical Buildings and Locations 204
   Class Size, Class Quality, and Locations 206
   Adequate Study Facilities 208

  Campus Size 209

  Housing..210

  Student Demographics..211

  Campus Safety and Security 212

  Accessibility...213

  Environmental Considerations...214

  Impact on Students 215

Personal Detractors..216

 Issues and Concerns...216

  Overcoming Financial Stress..216

  Overcoming Time Management Challenges......................227

  Overcoming Homesickness..230

  Overcoming Health-Related Challenges............................233

  Balancing Personal and Academic Responsibilities..............236

  Overcoming Motivational Challenges 240

  Navigating Relationship Challenges 243

  Navigating Cultural Adjustment Challenges......................246

  Navigating Perfectionism Challenges 249

  Addressing Test Anxiety 252

  Addressing Unresolved Issues: Strategies for Resolution.....255

  Conquering Distraction Issues..258

  Building Confidence for Success..261

  Navigating Commitment Issues...264

  Navigating Employment Issues 267

  Navigating Family Issues 270

  Navigating Burnout 274

  Navigating Uncertainty: Career and Personal Goals...........277

CHAPTER 4..281

Agreements 281
   Strategic Agreements..281
   Implementing Agreements...284
   Action Steps 287
   Implementing Action Steps 289
   Empowering Student Achievement 292
Personal Interest Areas 296
   Role of Student Clubs: Definition, Purpose, and Relevance 296
   Guidance and Support: Mentoring 300
   Support and Connection: Family Involvement.......................304
   Building a Supportive Network: Friendships 307
Professional Interest Areas 310
   A Catalyst for Academic Success: Tutoring 310
   Shaping Success Beyond the Classroom: Professional Mentoring
  314
   Fostering Success through Interactive Learning: Workshops .318
   Nurturing Success through Knowledge Exchange: Seminars.322
   Cultivating Success through Collaborative Learning: Study Halls 326
CHAPTER 5...330
Understanding the Concept of Time Management 330
   Budgeting Time Management 334
   Formulas for Effective Time Budgeting.................................338
   S.M.A.R.T. (Overview)...342
   S.M.A.R.T. Goal Setting 346
   Guide for Effective Learning..349
   D.A.I.L.Y. Study Method 349
   BLOOM'S TAXONOMY...352

CONCLUSION 360
REFERENCES 364

INTRODUCTION

Why this kind of book?

Academic success and integrity are two cornerstones of a student's educational journey. In today's highly competitive world, where knowledge and skills play a crucial role in shaping one's future, the importance of academic success and integrity cannot be overstated. This book explores the symbiotic relationship between academic success and integrity, highlighting why both are integral to a student's overall success.

Academic Success: A Pathway to Personal and Professional Achievement

Knowledge Acquisition and Application:
Academic success represents the culmination of effective learning and is central to personal and professional development. Through coursework and academic engagement, students not only acquire critical knowledge but also develop essential cognitive skills such as critical thinking, problem-solving, and analytical abilities. This acquired knowledge becomes a valuable asset that students can leverage to excel both in their academic pursuits and in their chosen careers. As students delve deeper into their fields of study, they gain a more nuanced understanding of their disciplines, which enhances their ability to apply theoretical concepts in practical situations. This foundation of knowledge and skill application is crucial for achieving long-term success in both academic and professional environments (Brusilovsky & Millán, 2007).

Career Opportunities:
Achieving academic success significantly expands career opportunities by making candidates more attractive to employers. A strong academic record often signifies a person's ability to grasp complex concepts and apply them effectively, which is highly valued in the job market. Research has consistently shown a positive correlation between academic achievement and employment prospects, indicating that employers frequently regard academic success as a marker of potential job performance and capability (Borghans, Duckworth, Heckman, & Ter Weel, 2008). Furthermore, high academic achievement can open doors to advanced career opportunities, professional networks, and further educational prospects, all of which contribute to a robust career trajectory.

Personal Growth and Fulfillment:
Academic success plays a pivotal role in fostering personal growth and fulfillment. Achieving academic goals can lead to significant boosts in self-esteem, confidence, and overall sense of accomplishment. This sense of achievement motivates students to set and pursue higher goals, both academically and personally. The process of overcoming academic challenges and reaching milestones encourages perseverance, discipline, and self-efficacy. As students experience success and growth in their academic lives, these achievements often translate into greater satisfaction and a positive impact on various aspects of their lives, contributing to a well-rounded and fulfilling personal development (Schunk, 2003)

Integrity: The Ethical Foundation of Academic Success

Academic Integrity:

Academic integrity encompasses the ethical principles and values guiding student behavior within an academic context. This includes adhering to standards of honesty, fairness, and responsibility in various academic activities such as writing papers, taking exams, and conducting research. Upholding academic integrity is crucial because it ensures that students engage in genuine and ethical academic practices. This commitment to ethical behavior supports the credibility and value of the educational process by preventing dishonesty such as cheating and plagiarism, thereby fostering a fair and equitable academic environment (McCabe & Pavela, 2000).

The Importance of Upholding Academic Integrity:

Maintaining academic integrity is essential for several reasons, notably preserving the value of education and fostering genuine learning. By ensuring that grades and credentials are earned honestly, academic integrity upholds the legitimacy of educational achievements and protects the integrity of academic institutions. Additionally, engaging in academic integrity helps students genuinely master the material, as honest completion of assignments reinforces their understanding and skill development. This ethical behavior also prepares students for professional environments where integrity is critical, as unethical academic conduct can correlate with unethical practices in the workplace. Establishing a strong moral foundation through academic integrity is therefore pivotal for both personal and professional success (Gino et al., 2011).

Interconnectedness of Academic Success and Integrity

Ethical Learning:
The interconnectedness of academic success and integrity is exemplified through the concept of ethical learning. Success achieved through ethical means is more meaningful and sustainable, as it reflects a commitment to honest and principled behavior. When students learn the material, complete assignments, and perform well in exams with integrity, they not only achieve academic success but also embody ethical values. This approach to learning ensures that achievements are a true reflection of a student's capabilities and understanding, thereby enhancing the overall value and credibility of their academic success (Feldman & Klass, 2012).

Trust and Reputation:
Academic success grounded in integrity fosters trust and enhances reputation. Students who consistently demonstrate honesty and ethical behavior in their academic endeavors build a reputation for reliability and trustworthiness. This reputation can lead to increased opportunities and recognition in both academic and professional spheres. Additionally, students who uphold integrity are better prepared to face complex ethical dilemmas in real-life scenarios, as they have already developed a strong moral compass. This ethical foundation supports their ability to navigate challenges with integrity, contributing to their long-term success and respect in their chosen fields (Bowers & W.J., 1964).

Academic success and integrity are inseparable components of a student's success. Academic success provides the foundation for personal and professional achievement, while integrity ensures that success is achieved ethically and honestly. It is crucial for educational institutions to instill and promote academic integrity, as it not only upholds the value of education but also prepares students to lead ethical lives beyond the classroom. The synergy between academic success and integrity is a testament to the interconnectedness of ethical learning, trust, and lifelong success. Thus, students should recognize that achieving their academic goals with integrity is not only commendable but also an investment in a bright and ethical future.

Student Resilience and Resource Utilization

College life is often challenging, with academic, personal, and social hurdles that can overwhelm students. Yet, many students have demonstrated remarkable resilience by seeking and connecting with resources to overcome these challenges. We share anecdotal stories of students who initially struggled in college and the positive transformation that occurred when they tapped into available resources.

Overcoming Academic Challenges
Alex's Academic Resilience
- Alex initially faced academic difficulties due to a heavy course load. He was overwhelmed by the amount of coursework and struggled to keep up with his assignments. Feeling lost, he reached out to a professor for guidance.
- Solution: The professor directed Alex to the college's academic resource center, where he found tutoring services and study skills workshops.
- Transformation: With the support of tutors and improved study habits, Alex's grades improved significantly, and he regained his academic confidence.

Sarah's Journey to Success
- Sarah had difficulty balancing her academics with part-time work and family responsibilities. She felt isolated and overwhelmed.
- Solution: Sarah discovered the college's counseling center, which offered individual and group counseling to help students manage stress and anxiety.
- Transformation: Through counseling, Sarah developed effective time management skills and stress-coping strategies. She learned to prioritize her responsibilities

and successfully balanced her academic and personal life.

Navigating Personal and Emotional Challenges

Robert's Journey to Self-Acceptance
- Robert, a transgender student, struggled with self-acceptance and feelings of isolation when they first arrived at college. They faced difficulties in opening up to peers about their gender identity.
- Solution: Robert connected with the college's LGBTQ+ support group, where they found a safe space to share their experiences and connect with fellow students who understood their journey. They also attended workshops on gender identity and diversity.
- Transformation: Through the support of the LGBTQ+ group and educational workshops, Robert gained confidence in expressing their true self. They made close friends who respected their identity, leading to increased self-acceptance and a more positive college experience.

Sandy's Advocacy for LGBTQ+ Inclusivity
- Sandy, a bisexual student, noticed a lack of LGBTQ+ representation and awareness on her college campus. She felt that the curriculum and campus events were not adequately inclusive.
- Solution: Sandy decided to take action by starting an LGBTQ+ awareness campaign on campus. She collaborated with faculty, student organizations, and administrators to organize LGBTQ+ awareness events, diversity workshops, and inclusive curriculum initiatives.
- Transformation: Sandy's advocacy efforts led to positive changes on campus. The college became more LGBTQ+ inclusive, with improved representation in coursework and a more supportive environment for LGBTQ+ students. Sandy's activism not only

benefited her but also future generations of LGBTQ+ students at the college.

Kevin's Mental Health Recovery
- Kevin struggled with anxiety and depression, which affected his college performance. He had difficulty attending classes and completing assignments.
- Solution: Kevin reached out to the college's mental health services and related to a counselor.
- Transformation: With the support of counseling and access to mental health resources, Kevin learned to manage his mental health challenges. He regained his enthusiasm for learning and experienced a significant improvement in his academic performance.

Emma's Transition to College Life
- Emma found it challenging to adapt to college life and make friends. She often felt lonely and overwhelmed by the social aspects of college.
- Solution: Emma joined a student club dedicated to helping freshmen transition to college life. She also utilized the college's career services for guidance.
- Transformation: Through her involvement in the club and career services, Emma formed meaningful friendships, developed a support network, and gained valuable insights into her career path. Her newfound connections and sense of belonging improved her overall college experience.

Impact of Supportive Campus Resources
James's Financial Struggles
- James faced financial hardship that affected his ability to cover tuition and living expenses.
- Solution: James visited the college's financial aid office and explored available scholarships, grants, and work-study opportunities.

- Transformation: By accessing financial resources, James was able to alleviate his financial burdens, continue his education, and reduce stress. His academic performance and overall well-being improved significantly.

Maria's Language Barrier
- Maria, an international student, initially faced language barriers that hindered her academic progress.
- Solution: Maria sought out the college's language center, where she found language courses, conversation partners, and language tutoring.
- Transformation: With the support of language resources, Maria improved her English language skills and confidently engaged in class discussions. Her newfound language proficiency boosted her academic performance and integration into the college community.

These stories of students highlight the transformative power of connecting with college resources. Whether facing academic, personal, or emotional challenges, students who sought help and utilized available services were able to overcome their struggles and achieve academic success. These stories underscore the importance of creating a supportive and accessible environment in colleges, where students can access resources to navigate their college journey and ultimately thrive.

While these stories showcase the positive impact of resource utilization, it is crucial for your educational institution to continue providing comprehensive support to address the diverse needs of students, ensuring that all individuals can succeed in their college endeavors.

FAMOUS QUOTES

"Nothing can dim the light which shines from within."
— Maya Angelou

"Having light we pass it on to others."
— Wittenberg University

"With confidence, you have won even before you have started."
— Marcus Garvey

"The greatest gift is not being afraid to question."
— Ruby Dee

"The tragedy in life doesn't lie in not reaching your goal. The tragedy lies in having no goal to reach."
— Benjamin Mays

"Openness may not completely disarm prejudice, but it's a good place to start."
— Jason Collins

"Preservation of one's own culture does not require contempt or disrespect for other cultures."
— Cesar Chavez

"Injustice anywhere is a threat to justice everywhere."
— Nelson Mandela

"We may have different religions, different languages, different colored skin, but we all belong to one human race."
— Kofi Annan

CHAPTER 1

Challenges Faced by Underrepresented Students

Higher education is meant to be a pathway to personal and professional growth, but not all students have equal access to these opportunities. Underrepresented students in higher education face unique challenges that can hinder their academic success and limit future prospects. In this overview we will explore what it means to be an underrepresented student in higher education and the barriers they encounter. Later in the book we will delve into various ways of overcoming barriers.

It's important to note that the specific categories of underrepresented students can vary by region, country, and context. Educational institutions and policymakers often strive to address disparities by implementing diversity and inclusion initiatives, providing financial aid and scholarships, and offering support services to promote equal access and success in higher education for underrepresented groups.

In higher education, there are several categories or groups that are commonly considered when discussing underrepresented students. These categories represent demographic groups that have historically been marginalized or have limited representation within the educational system. The key categories to be considered for underrepresented students in higher education would typically include:

Definitions

Racial and Ethnic Minorities

Racial and ethnic minorities include individuals from racial and ethnic backgrounds that have historically been underrepresented in higher education. This category encompasses groups such as African Americans, Hispanic/Latinx, Native Americans, Asian Americans, and other minority populations. These groups often face systemic barriers that affect their access to higher education and their experiences within academic environments. The term highlights the disparities and challenges faced by these populations in achieving equal representation and success in colleges and universities (Loo & Rolison, 1986).

First-Generation College Students

First-generation college students are those whose parents or guardians did not complete a four-year college degree. These students typically navigate higher education without the benefit of familial experience, which can impact their understanding of college processes, academic expectations, and institutional support systems. This lack of a familial higher education background often results in challenges related to academic preparation, college navigation, and accessing resources, contributing to unique pressures and barriers (Ishitani & T.T., 2006).

Low-Income Students

Low-income students come from economically disadvantaged backgrounds and often face financial barriers to accessing and completing higher education. These barriers include high tuition costs, limited availability of scholarships, and the need to work while studying. Financial constraints can lead to increased student loan debt and may affect students' ability to focus on their studies, impacting their overall academic success and persistence (Hoxworth & L., 2007).

LGBTQ+ Students

LGBTQ+ students identify as lesbian, gay, bisexual, transgender, queer, or other non-heteronormative identities and may face unique challenges related to their sexual orientation or gender identity. Discrimination, lack of inclusive policies, and social stigma can adversely affect their mental health, academic performance, and overall campus experience. Ensuring a supportive and inclusive campus environment is crucial for their academic and personal well-being (Barton & A., 2008).

Students with Disabilities

Students with disabilities encompass individuals who have physical, cognitive, sensory, or learning impairments that may require specific accommodations to ensure equal access to educational opportunities. Challenges faced by these students can include navigating physical or digital barriers, obtaining necessary accommodations, and overcoming societal attitudes that may impact their educational experiences (Burgstahler, 2008).

Women in STEM (Science, Technology, Engineering, and Mathematics)

Women in STEM fields are often underrepresented in comparison to their male counterparts. Gender bias, stereotypes, and a lack of role models can discourage women from pursuing and persisting in STEM careers. Efforts to increase female participation in these fields include addressing these barriers and creating supportive environments that promote equity and inclusion (National Research Council, 2010).

Non-Traditional Students

Non-traditional students include older adults, veterans, and individuals returning to education after a significant hiatus. They often juggle multiple responsibilities, such as work and family obligations, alongside their studies. These additional responsibilities create unique challenges in managing time, balancing academic and personal demands, and accessing support services (Choy & S.P., 2002).

Minority Groups in Specific Fields

Certain minority groups may be underrepresented in specific academic disciplines or professions, such as law or medicine. This underrepresentation can result from systemic barriers, a lack of role models, and limited access to networking opportunities within those fields. Addressing these disparities requires targeted efforts to support and encourage minority students in these areas (Turner & Myers, 2000).

Religious Groups

Students from religious minorities may face challenges related to campus climate, including the accommodation of their faith practices and the potential for religious biases or misunderstandings. Ensuring that educational institutions are respectful and accommodating of diverse religious beliefs is essential for fostering an inclusive and supportive academic environment (Hancock & Canelas, 2017).

Students from Geographic Locations

Students from rural or underserved geographic areas may encounter unique challenges related to limited access to educational resources and institutions. These challenges include fewer local educational opportunities, lack of academic support services, and difficulties accessing higher education institutions due to distance. Addressing these issues is crucial for improving educational equity and access for students from these regions (Hurtado & DeAngelo, 2012).

Diversity in higher education has evolved over the years, reflecting societal changes and an increased awareness of the importance of inclusive educational environments. As colleges and universities strive to become more diverse, challenges persist, particularly for underrepresented students on predominantly white campuses. We delve into the background of diversity in higher education, highlighting trends in its evolution and the specific challenges faced by underrepresented students in predominantly white academic settings.

Historically, higher education institutions in the United States were predominantly homogenous, catering to a limited demographic. However, the latter half of the 20th century witnessed significant shifts, driven by civil rights movements and legislative efforts. Landmark decisions, such as Brown v. Board of Education in 1954, paved the way for desegregation, influencing higher education's landscape. Affirmative action policies in the 1960s and 1970s aimed to rectify historical inequities, fostering a more diverse student body.

Racial and Ethnic Diversity

The enrollment of underrepresented minority students in higher education has indeed increased over recent decades. For instance, data from the National Center for Education Statistics (NCES) reveal that the percentage of Black students enrolled in degree-granting postsecondary institutions grew from 10% in 1976 to 14% in 2019. This rise indicates progress toward greater racial and ethnic diversity within colleges and universities, driven by various initiatives aimed at broadening access and reducing educational disparities. However, despite these advancements, there is ongoing work needed to address the remaining gaps and ensure that the gains in enrollment translate into equitable educational outcomes and opportunities for all students (NCES, 2021).

Gender Diversity

The gender composition of college and university populations has also experienced notable changes. Women, once underrepresented in certain fields, now constitute a significant majority in some disciplines, such as health professions and social sciences (NCES, 2021). Despite progress, challenges persist for underrepresented students on predominantly white campuses. These challenges encompass various aspects, from academic to social, and have a profound impact on the overall student experience.

LGBTQ+ students in higher education often confront unique challenges that can impact their educational experience and overall well-being. These challenges may include navigating a campus culture that may not always be inclusive or accepting of their sexual orientation or gender identity, concerns about coming out to peers and faculty, and the potential for facing discrimination or microaggressions (Rankin, 2003).

Research indicates that LGBTQ+ students may also grapple with higher rates of mental health issues, such as anxiety and depression, compared to their heterosexual and cisgender peers (Kerr, Santurri, & Peters, 2013). To address these challenges, many universities and colleges have established LGBTQ+ resource centers, support groups, and inclusive policies to create more welcoming and affirming environments for LGBTQ+ students.

Campus Climate and Inclusion

Underrepresented students often encounter a challenging campus climate that can significantly affect their academic experiences and success. Issues such as microaggressions, discriminatory practices, and a lack of inclusive policies contribute to an environment that may feel unwelcoming or hostile. Research by Smith (2018) highlights that these factors can undermine students' sense of belonging and engagement, leading to lower academic performance and higher rates of attrition among minority students. Addressing these challenges requires comprehensive efforts to foster a more inclusive and supportive campus environment where all students feel valued and respected.

Lack of Representation in Curriculum and Faculty

The lack of representation in curriculum and faculty can significantly impact underrepresented students' academic experiences and success. When course materials and faculty do not reflect diverse perspectives and backgrounds, students may struggle to see themselves in their studies and feel disconnected from their educational environment. Garcia (2017) points out that the absence of diverse voices in both the curriculum and faculty ranks can hinder students' sense of belonging and limit their academic engagement. Ensuring that educational content and faculty demographics are more inclusive can enhance the academic experience and support the success of all students.

Access to Resources and Support Services

Disparities in access to essential resources such as counseling, mentorship, and academic support services can create significant barriers for underrepresented students. Johnson (2019) highlights that unequal access to these support services can adversely affect students' ability to successfully navigate the complexities of higher education. Without adequate support, these students may face increased challenges that impact their academic performance and overall well-being. Addressing these disparities requires targeted efforts to ensure equitable access to resources that support student success and retention.

Understanding the historical context and trends in diversity in higher education is crucial for addressing the challenges faced by underrepresented students on predominantly white campuses. Efforts to create truly inclusive academic environments by universities and others must consider the complex interplay of historical legacies, institutional policies, and societal dynamics. This overview sets the stage for review and discussion to have a deeper exploration of the specific concerns and potential solutions that can contribute to a more equitable higher education experience for underrepresented students.

Fostering Inclusive Campus Environments: Addressing Micro aggressions, Discrimination, and Racism

The campus climate plays a pivotal role in shaping the overall educational experience for students. A welcoming environment fosters a sense of belonging and contributes to academic success, mental well-being, and the holistic development of individuals. We delve into the significance of a welcoming campus climate, highlighting the challenges posed by microaggressions, discrimination, and racism that underrepresented students often encounter.

Importance of a Welcoming Campus Climate

A welcoming campus climate is foundational for creating an inclusive educational setting. A positive campus climate is linked to increased student engagement, retention, and overall satisfaction (Smith, 2018). It provides a sense of safety and acceptance, promoting a conducive atmosphere for learning and personal growth.

Instances of Microaggressions, Discrimination, and Racism

Despite strides toward diversity and inclusion, underrepresented students on predominantly white campuses still grapple with instances of microaggressions, discrimination, and racism. Microaggressions, often subtle and unintentional, contribute to a hostile climate for marginalized groups (Sue et al., 2007). Discrimination, whether overt or systemic, can manifest in various facets of campus life, from academic settings to social interactions. Racism, deeply rooted in historical contexts, persists in subtle and overt forms, impacting the mental health and well-being of students of color (Smith, 2018).

Instances of microaggressions, discrimination, racism, and bias based on sexual preferences persist in various social contexts, including education, the workplace, and everyday interactions. These manifestations can include subtle comments, stereotypes, or overt acts that marginalize individuals based on their sexual orientation. Such experiences contribute to feelings of exclusion and emotional distress among LGBTQ+ individuals (Nadal et al., 2011).

Additionally, institutional policies and practices may inadvertently discriminate against LGBTQ+ individuals, impacting their access to opportunities and resources (Grant et al., 2011). Efforts to combat these issues often involve education, awareness campaigns, and inclusive policies aimed at creating environments where people of all sexual orientations are treated with respect and dignity.

Addressing Challenges and Creating Change

Addressing these challenges requires a multi-faceted approach. Campus policies and practices must explicitly denounce discrimination and racism while actively promoting inclusivity. Educational programs on cultural competency can enhance awareness and sensitivity among students and faculty (Gonzalez, 2016). Moreover, establishing support mechanisms, such as counseling services and reporting systems for incidents of discrimination, contributes to creating a safer environment (Johnson, 2019).

A welcoming campus climate is indispensable for the success and well-being of underrepresented students on predominantly white campuses. By acknowledging and actively addressing instances of microaggressions, discrimination, and racism, institutions can foster a more inclusive environment that enables all students to thrive. Creating lasting change requires a commitment to continuous education, policy reform, and the cultivation of an atmosphere where diversity is not just acknowledged but celebrated.

Cultivating Diversity: Addressing the Lack of Representation in Curriculum and Faculty

The lack of representation in curriculum and faculty within higher education institutions poses significant challenges to fostering inclusive learning environments. We explore the consequences of the absence of diverse perspectives in course materials and emphasize the importance of cultivating a faculty that reflects the diversity of the student body.

Absence of Diverse Perspectives in Course Materials

A critical aspect of creating an inclusive learning environment is ensuring that course materials incorporate diverse perspectives. However, underrepresented students on predominantly white campuses often encounter curricula that overlook the contributions and experiences of diverse communities (Garcia, 2017). This omission not only limits students' exposure to a comprehensive understanding of various subject matters but also perpetuates a Eurocentric worldview that may alienate and marginalize students from diverse backgrounds.

Importance of Having a Diverse Faculty

The composition of the faculty plays a pivotal role in shaping students' educational experiences. A diverse faculty brings a variety of perspectives, experiences, and teaching styles into the classroom, enriching the learning environment for all students (Chang et al., 2014). Representation matters, as students benefit from seeing individuals who share their backgrounds in positions of authority and expertise. Moreover, a diverse faculty contributes to a more inclusive campus climate, fostering a sense of belonging and encouraging underrepresented students to pursue academic and professional goals (Garcia, 2017).

Addressing the Gap and Promoting Inclusivity

To address the lack of representation in curriculum and faculty, institutions must prioritize intentional efforts to diversify both. Incorporating diverse perspectives into course materials requires a curriculum review that ensures representation across various cultures, histories, and voices. Additionally, efforts to recruit and retain a diverse faculty should be supported through inclusive hiring practices and professional development opportunities (Garcia, 2017; Chang et al., 2014).

Addressing the lack of representation in curriculum and faculty is essential for creating an inclusive and equitable higher education experience. By recognizing the importance of diverse perspectives in course materials and the significance of a diverse faculty, institutions can contribute to a more enriching learning environment that prepares students to engage with the complexities of a global society.

Bridging the Gap:
Access to Resources and Support Services

Access to resources and support services is a critical determinant of academic success and overall well-being for all students. However, underrepresented students on predominantly white campuses often face disparities in accessing essential services such as counseling, mentorship, and academic support. We analyze the availability of these resources and examine how a lack of access disproportionately affects underrepresented student populations.

Counseling, Mentorship, and Academic Support

While colleges and universities strive to offer comprehensive support services, the availability of resources can vary, impacting underrepresented students. Counseling services are crucial for addressing mental health needs, but studies indicate that underrepresented students may underutilize these services due to stigma or cultural barriers (Johnson, 2019). Mentorship programs, which provide guidance and support, may also be lacking or not tailored to the unique challenges faced by underrepresented students (Johnson, 2019). Moreover, academic support services, including tutoring and study resources, may not sufficiently address the diverse learning needs of underrepresented students (Brown, 2018).

Impact of Limited Access on Underrepresented Students

The consequences of limited access to resources are profound for underrepresented students. Mental health disparities can contribute to higher stress levels, lower academic performance, and an increased risk of attrition (Johnson, 2019). The absence of tailored mentorship deprives students of valuable guidance in navigating the challenges of higher education and establishing professional networks. Academic support gaps contribute to disparities in learning outcomes, hindering underrepresented students from reaching their full academic potential (Brown, 2018).

Addressing Disparities and Enhancing Access

To address these disparities, higher education institutions must prioritize equitable access to resources and support services. Culturally competent counseling services, mentorship programs that consider the unique needs of underrepresented students, and academic support initiatives tailored to diverse learning styles are essential (Johnson, 2019; Brown, 2018).

Moreover, fostering a campus culture that destigmatizes seeking help is crucial for encouraging underrepresented students to utilize available resources. Addressing the disparities in access to resources and support services is integral to fostering an inclusive higher education environment. By recognizing the unique challenges faced by underrepresented students and implementing targeted initiatives, institutions can ensure that all students have equitable access to the support they need for academic success and personal well-being.

Breaking Down Financial Barriers: Economic Challenges

The pursuit of higher education is often hindered by financial barriers, with underrepresented students facing unique economic challenges. We delve into the economic hurdles encountered by these students, examining issues such as high tuition costs, disparities in financial aid, and the impact of scholarship availability.

Economic Challenges Faced by Underrepresented Students

High Tuition Costs

The rising cost of tuition presents a formidable challenge for underrepresented students, amplifying existing economic disparities and creating significant financial strain. As tuition fees continue to escalate, these students are often forced to take on substantial student loan debt, which can impact their long-term financial stability and exacerbate socioeconomic inequalities (Gomez, 2017). The burden of high tuition costs can limit access to higher education and contribute to increased dropout rates among underrepresented groups, as they may struggle to balance the financial demands of their education with other economic pressures. Addressing these challenges requires a concerted effort to make higher education more affordable and accessible, ensuring that financial barriers do not hinder academic success and career advancement.

Financial Aid Disparities

Despite the existence of financial aid designed to alleviate the burden of tuition, disparities persist, particularly affecting underrepresented students. Many students face challenges related to accessing information about available aid, navigating complex application processes, and encountering biases in the allocation of financial resources (Gomez, 2017). These issues contribute to an uneven distribution of aid, further intensifying the financial strain on underrepresented students and potentially impeding their ability to enroll in or complete higher education. To mitigate these disparities, there is a need for greater transparency in the financial aid process and more equitable distribution of resources to ensure that all students have an equal opportunity to succeed academically.

Scholarship Availability

The availability of scholarships specifically designed for underrepresented students remains a critical issue in addressing financial barriers to higher education. A lack of diversity in scholarship opportunities restricts access to financial support for these students, limiting their ability to pursue and complete their educational goals (Boggs, 2020). Scholarships play a vital role in reducing the financial burden of tuition and related expenses, yet insufficient funding and limited targeted opportunities can hinder the educational aspirations of underrepresented individuals. Expanding scholarship availability and ensuring that opportunities are accessible to diverse student populations are essential steps in promoting equitable access to higher education and supporting the academic success of all students.

Addressing Financial Barriers

Addressing the financial barriers faced by underrepresented students requires a comprehensive and multifaceted approach. Educational institutions must actively work to reduce tuition costs, enhance transparency in the financial aid process, and implement targeted scholarship programs to alleviate the financial challenges these students encounter (Boggs, 2020; Gomez, 2017). Policymakers also play a crucial role by advocating for policies that address systemic economic disparities and improve financial aid accessibility. By working together to create a more equitable financial landscape, we can help ensure that underrepresented students have the support they need to succeed academically and achieve their educational and career aspirations.

The economic challenges faced by underrepresented students in higher education demand urgent attention. By acknowledging and addressing issues such as high tuition costs, financial aid disparities, and scholarship availability, institutions can contribute to creating a more equitable educational landscape where financial barriers do not impede the pursuit of academic and career aspirations.

Navigating Stereotypes and Stigmas: Understanding the Impact

Stereotypes and stigma can significantly shape the experiences of underrepresented students in higher education. We explore the profound impact of stereotypes on these students, examining how pervasive societal beliefs can affect academic performance and mental health.

Impact of Stereotypes on Underrepresented Students

Academic Performance

Stereotypes rooted in cultural biases can lead to stereotype threat, where individuals from underrepresented groups fear confirming negative stereotypes about their abilities. This phenomenon can significantly undermine academic performance by increasing anxiety, reducing motivation, and creating a self-fulfilling prophecy that hinders cognitive function (Steele, 2010). Research has shown that when students are aware of stereotypes related to their academic abilities, they may experience heightened stress and distraction, which impairs their cognitive processes and academic outcomes (Sue et al., 2007).

Mental Health

The constant exposure to stereotypes can lead to significant mental health challenges for underrepresented students. These individuals may face stigmatization that exacerbates stress, anxiety, and a sense of isolation, ultimately affecting their overall well-being and academic success (Smith, 2018). The negative impact on mental health can create barriers to academic achievement and contribute to feelings of inadequacy and disengagement from their educational pursuits.

Addressing Stereotypes and Fostering Inclusivity

To mitigate the impact of stereotypes on underrepresented students, institutions must actively work to create inclusive environments that challenge and dispel biases. Implementing culturally competent education, incorporating diverse perspectives in curricula, and providing targeted support systems are crucial strategies for addressing stereotypes (Sue et al., 2007). Promoting positive role models and fostering a campus culture that values diversity can empower underrepresented students and enhance their resilience against stereotype threats, thereby supporting their academic and personal growth (Smith, 2018).

The impact of stereotypes and stigma on underrepresented students in higher education is a critical concern. By understanding the ways in which stereotypes affect academic performance and mental health, institutions can implement strategies to create inclusive environments that empower students to thrive despite societal biases.

Ensuring Campus Safety: Navigating Concerns and Promoting Student Well-Being

Campus safety is a critical aspect of the higher education experience, significantly influencing the well-being of all students. We address concerns about safety and security on campus, with a particular focus on incidents of racial profiling and campus policing, while referencing studies that explore the intricate relationship between campus safety and student well-being.

Concerns about Safety and Security

While colleges and universities strive to create safe and secure environments for all students, concerns about safety often persist, particularly for underrepresented groups. Racial profiling, which can occur through biased campus policing practices, contributes to an atmosphere of mistrust and unease among students of color. Such incidents can lead to significant mental health challenges, as students may experience heightened stress and anxiety about their personal safety (Lee, 2016). This ongoing apprehension can affect their academic performance and overall campus experience, as the lack of a secure environment can undermine their ability to engage fully in their educational pursuits.

Incidents of Racial Profiling and Campus Policing

Racial profiling involves targeting individuals based on their race or ethnicity, leading to unwarranted suspicion or harassment, which disproportionately affects students of color on college campuses (Lee, 2016). This practice not only exacerbates feelings of vulnerability and marginalization but also disrupts the campus climate, creating an environment where students may feel unsafe or unfairly targeted. Such experiences can contribute to a diminished sense of belonging and engagement within the academic community, thereby negatively impacting their overall college experience and academic success.

Relationship Between Campus Safety and Student Well-Being

The relationship between campus safety and student well-being is intricate and significant. Research has shown that a sense of safety is closely linked to overall student satisfaction, mental health, and academic success (Jackson, 2018). When students perceive their campus as a secure environment, they are more likely to experience positive mental health outcomes and engage more fully in their academic and social activities. Conversely, incidents of racial profiling and mistrust in campus policing can heighten stress levels and undermine students' sense of security, adversely affecting their well-being and academic performance (Jackson, 2018; Lee, 2016).

Addressing Concerns and Promoting Inclusivity

To effectively address safety and security concerns, institutions need to prioritize inclusive and culturally competent campus policing practices. This includes implementing training programs for law enforcement personnel to enhance their sensitivity to racial and cultural issues and fostering open lines of communication between students and campus police (Jackson, 2018). Additionally, creating a campus culture that actively challenges racial bias and discrimination is crucial for building a safer, more supportive environment for all students. Proactive measures such as community engagement initiatives and the establishment of clear protocols for addressing bias can contribute to a more inclusive and equitable campus climate (Lee, 2016; Jackson, 2018).

Ensuring campus safety is paramount for promoting the well-being of all students. By acknowledging concerns about racial profiling and campus policing and implementing measures to address these issues, institutions can create an inclusive and secure environment that supports the academic and personal growth of every student.

Fostering Inclusivity: The Imperative of Cultural Competency & Training for Faculty and Staff

Cultural competency training for faculty and staff is a crucial element in creating a truly inclusive higher education environment. We delve into the importance of cultural competency training, exploring its role in fostering inclusivity and referencing research on the effectiveness of such programs.

Importance of Cultural Competency Training

Cultural competency training is essential for equipping faculty and staff with the necessary skills and knowledge to effectively engage with a diverse student population. This type of training is particularly critical in predominantly white institutions, where underrepresented students may encounter specific challenges related to their race, ethnicity, or cultural background. Effective cultural competency training goes beyond mere awareness, aiming to develop faculty and staff members' abilities to adapt their teaching methods, communication styles, and support mechanisms to address the unique needs of a varied student body (Gonzalez, 2016). By fostering an environment of respect and understanding, this training helps educators create a more inclusive atmosphere that supports the academic and personal growth of all students, particularly those from marginalized or underrepresented groups.

Contributions to a More Inclusive Environment

Cultural competency training plays a vital role in fostering a more inclusive educational environment by addressing and dismantling stereotypes, reducing biases, and promoting mutual understanding among faculty and staff. This training encourages educators to become more aware of their own biases and the diverse cultural backgrounds of their students, leading to improved interactions and a more respectful campus climate (Wang et al., 2018). By enhancing faculty and staff's ability to navigate and appreciate diverse cultural perspectives, cultural competency programs contribute to a supportive and equitable learning environment. This, in turn, helps ensure that all students, regardless of their background, feel valued and respected, thus enhancing their overall academic experience and engagement.

Effectiveness of Cultural Competency Programs

Research indicates that cultural competency training can have a significant positive impact on faculty and staff behavior, attitudes, and practices. A study by Wang et al. (2018) revealed that faculty members who engaged in cultural competency programs reported a heightened awareness of diversity issues, improved communication with students from diverse backgrounds, and a greater preparedness to address cultural differences in their teaching practices. These programs foster a deeper understanding of cultural dynamics and enhance educators' ability to create a more inclusive and responsive learning environment, thereby improving student interactions and overall educational outcomes (Wang et al., 2018).

Addressing Implicit Bias and Enhancing Communication

Cultural competency training is instrumental in addressing implicit biases that may affect interactions between faculty, staff, and students. By fostering a shared understanding and language around cultural differences, these programs contribute to improved communication and relationships within the campus community (Gonzalez, 2016). Enhanced communication skills not only improve student-faculty interactions but also positively impact campus climate and overall student satisfaction. Effective training helps to mitigate the negative effects of implicit bias and promotes a more inclusive and supportive environment, benefiting both academic and personal aspects of student life (Gonzalez, 2016; Wang et al., 2018).

Cultural competency training for faculty and staff is indispensable for creating a supportive and inclusive higher education environment. By acknowledging the importance of such training and referencing research on its effectiveness, institutions can take significant strides toward cultivating an atmosphere that celebrates diversity and empowers all students to succeed.

Breaking the Silence: Understanding the Impact of Alienation and Isolation

Feelings of alienation and isolation among underrepresented students on predominantly white campuses are profound challenges that can significantly impact both mental health and academic success. We explore the experiences of alienation and isolation, delving into their psychological effects and referencing relevant studies.

Feelings of Alienation and Isolation

Underrepresented students often grapple with feelings of alienation and isolation in academic environments where they may be underrepresented or misunderstood. These feelings can arise from a lack of cultural representation in the curriculum, a shortage of diverse faculty and leadership, or experiences of being perceived as 'other' within the campus community (Smith, 2018). Alienation refers to a deep-seated sense of disconnection from the academic and social environment, while isolation typically reflects the absence of meaningful social connections and support systems. Both forms of disconnection can significantly impact students' sense of belonging and their overall campus experience, making it challenging for them to engage fully with their academic and social lives.

Impact on Mental Health

Feelings of alienation and isolation are closely linked to negative mental health outcomes, which can significantly impact students' overall well-being and academic performance. Research has shown that students experiencing these feelings are at a higher risk for stress, anxiety, and depression, which can undermine their ability to thrive academically and socially (Smith, 2018). Alienation often contributes to heightened stress levels, as students may feel unsupported and undervalued within the academic environment. The resulting mental health challenges can impede academic success by decreasing motivation, increasing absenteeism, and limiting engagement in campus activities, thus affecting students' ability to perform well academically (Johnson et al., 2020).

Impact on Academic Success

The feelings of alienation and isolation experienced by underrepresented students can profoundly affect their academic success. Students who feel disconnected from their campus environment are less likely to engage in academic and extracurricular activities, which can diminish their overall motivation and academic performance (Johnson et al., 2020). The lack of connection can hinder the formation of supportive peer networks, essential for academic success and personal growth. Alienation can also impede access to mentorship and academic resources, which are crucial for navigating the challenges of higher education and achieving academic goals. This diminished engagement and support can result in lower academic achievement and higher dropout rates among students who feel isolated (Johnson et al., 2020).

Psychological Effects of Social Isolation

Extensive research highlights the detrimental psychological effects of social isolation, including its impact on mental health and cognitive functioning (Cacioppo & Hawkley, 2009) found that prolonged social isolation is associated with increased stress responses, impaired cognitive abilities, and a heightened risk of depressive symptoms. Their work underscores the severe psychological toll that isolation can take, which is particularly relevant in higher education settings where social support is crucial for student success. Addressing social isolation is therefore essential for improving mental health outcomes and fostering a more supportive and inclusive educational environment (Cacioppo & Hawkley, 2009).

Mitigating Alienation and Isolation

To effectively mitigate feelings of alienation and isolation among students, institutions must implement comprehensive strategies that foster a sense of belonging and community. This includes developing inclusive policies, enhancing culturally competent support services, and ensuring diverse representation across all aspects of campus life (Smith, 2018). Mentorship programs and peer support initiatives are crucial in providing underrepresented students with meaningful connections and resources, helping them overcome barriers to engagement and success. By addressing these issues proactively, institutions can create a more supportive environment that enhances student well-being and academic achievement (Johnson et al., 2020).

Experiences of alienation and isolation among underrepresented students are critical issues that demand attention. By understanding the psychological effects and referencing studies on social isolation, institutions can take proactive measures to create inclusive environments that support the mental health and academic success of all students.

Breaking Barriers: The Impact of Lack of Representation in Leadership Roles on Campus Policies

The underrepresentation of individuals from diverse backgrounds in leadership roles within higher education institutions is a pervasive issue that extends far beyond mere numbers. We explore the underrepresentation of marginalized individuals in leadership positions and discuss the crucial importance of diverse leadership in shaping campus policies.

Underrepresentation in Leadership Roles

Despite the increasing diversity within student populations, there remains a notable gap in the representation of underrepresented individuals in leadership positions within academia. This disparity is evident across various levels, from department chairs to university presidents, and contributes to a perpetuation of institutional cultures that may inadvertently marginalize certain groups (Turner et al., 2008). The lack of representation among academic leaders can result in a lack of advocacy for the unique needs of underrepresented students and can limit the development of policies that promote equity and inclusion. Consequently, the absence of diverse perspectives in leadership roles can reinforce systemic biases and hinder progress towards a more inclusive and supportive academic environment.

Importance of Diverse Leadership in Shaping Campus Policies

Diverse leadership is crucial for developing inclusive campus policies that reflect the diverse needs and perspectives of all students. Research consistently shows that leadership teams with diverse members are better equipped to create and implement policies that address issues related to equity, diversity, and inclusion (Milem et al., 2005). Individuals from underrepresented backgrounds bring unique insights and experiences that contribute to more comprehensive and equitable policymaking. This diversity in leadership ensures that policies are not only designed to address the needs of the majority but also to accommodate and support marginalized groups, thereby fostering a more inclusive educational environment for all students.

Impact of Diverse Leadership on Organizational Outcomes

Research highlights the significant positive impact that diverse leadership has on various organizational outcomes within higher education. Institutions led by diverse teams often exhibit improved cultural competence, greater student satisfaction, and enhanced faculty-staff relations (Milem et al., 2005). Such leadership not only contributes to a more inclusive campus climate but also correlates with better overall institutional effectiveness. Diverse leadership teams bring a range of perspectives and experiences that can lead to more innovative solutions and more effective management practices, ultimately benefiting the entire academic community by fostering a more dynamic and supportive environment.

Addressing Underrepresentation and Promoting Diversity

Addressing the underrepresentation of underrepresented individuals in leadership roles requires intentional efforts to foster inclusive hiring practices, mentorship programs, and leadership development opportunities. Institutions must implement strategies to promote diversity at the leadership level, including targeted recruitment efforts and support for career advancement among underrepresented groups (Turner et al., 2008). By prioritizing diversity in leadership, institutions can better meet the needs of their diverse student populations and create a campus culture that values and celebrates differences. This commitment to diversity at the top levels of leadership not only enhances institutional effectiveness but also helps to ensure that all students feel represented and supported in their educational journeys.

The lack of representation in leadership roles within higher education institutions has far-reaching implications for campus policies and overall organizational outcomes. By acknowledging the importance of diverse leadership and referencing studies on its positive impact, institutions can take proactive steps to break down barriers, fostering a more inclusive and effective higher education environment.

Power of Student Voices as Catalysts for Change: The Transformative Power of Advocacy and Student Activism

Advocacy groups and student activism play a pivotal role in shaping the landscape of higher education by amplifying the voices of underrepresented students and championing positive change. We explore the transformative influence of student-led initiatives, emphasizing their capacity to bring about positive change on campus, and references case studies that highlight the impact of successful student-led movements.

Role of Advocacy Groups and Student Activism

Advocacy groups and student activism are powerful catalysts for social change within higher education, addressing a wide range of issues such as diversity, inclusion, and social justice. These movements engage in dialogue, mobilize peers, and collaborate with institutional stakeholders to foster more equitable and inclusive campus environments (Harper, Patton, & Wooden, 2009). Student activists often respond to systemic inequalities, discriminatory practices, and the need for inclusive policies, driving significant change through their efforts. This dynamic force bridges academic, political, and social realms, demonstrating its potential to reshape higher education by challenging existing norms and pushing for progressive reforms (Giroux, 2018). Through sustained activism, students play a critical role in transforming campus cultures and advancing broader social justice agendas.

Bringing About Positive Change

Student-led initiatives have demonstrated their capacity to effect positive change by raising awareness, challenging institutional norms, and advocating for more inclusive policies. Through protests, awareness campaigns, and open dialogues, students have influenced critical aspects of higher education, such as admissions practices, curriculum development, and campus climate (Harper, Patton, & Wooden, 2009). The passion and energy of student activists often lead to tangible shifts in institutional practices and priorities, making their involvement a crucial element in driving reforms. These efforts not only address immediate concerns but also lay the groundwork for sustained improvements in campus inclusivity and equity.

Case Studies on Successful Student-Led Movements

The Black Student Movement at the University of North Carolina at Chapel Hill, established in 1967, has a distinguished history of advocating for the rights and well-being of Black students. This organization has played a pivotal role in increasing campus representation, establishing cultural centers, and implementing diversity training, demonstrating the significant impact of student activism on institutional change. Similarly, the United Farm Workers' Grape Boycott in the 1960s and 1970s, although not confined to higher education, highlighted the power of student involvement in labor activism, contributing to improvements in working conditions for farmworkers (Patton et al., 2016). The #BlackLivesMatter movement on campus has also been influential, with students across the U.S. mobilizing to demand changes in curriculum, faculty diversity, and campus inclusivity. These movements underscore the capacity of student activism to drive meaningful change and address systemic issues.

Fostering Lasting Change and a Culture of Advocacy

Student-led initiatives not only address immediate issues but also foster a lasting culture of advocacy within higher education. By engaging with grassroots movements, institutions can benefit from diverse perspectives that lead to more inclusive policies and practices. Successful initiatives illustrate that student activism is a driving force for systemic change, challenging entrenched norms and inspiring a collective commitment to a more equitable future (Giroux, 2018; Raby & Valeau, 2018). Institutions that embrace and support student activism contribute to a vibrant campus culture that values continuous improvement and social responsibility, ultimately benefiting the entire academic community.

Advocacy groups and student activism are instrumental in driving positive change within higher education. By amplifying student voices and catalyzing movements, these initiatives challenge the status quo, pushing institutions to reassess policies and practices. The case studies presented underscore the impactful role that student-led movements can play in fostering a more inclusive and equitable higher education environment.

These groups are also indispensable forces in shaping positive change within higher education. By referencing case studies and acknowledging the transformative potential of these initiatives, institutions can recognize the value of student-led movements and actively engage in fostering environments that encourage activism as a catalyst for a more just and inclusive educational landscape.

Student's Needs

College education is a pivotal phase in a student's life, laying the foundation for their future careers and personal growth. While acquiring knowledge and skills is paramount, ethical considerations are equally important to shape responsible, morally conscious citizens. This book explores what college students typically need from their education, coupled with a focus on ethics and integrity. The information presented here is drawn from various academic sources, articles, and studies.

Academic Excellence and Ethical Integrity

For a college environment to truly foster academic excellence, it must provide a rigorous curriculum supported by high-quality teaching and robust resources, all grounded in ethical principles. Ethical guidelines are crucial for maintaining academic integrity, ensuring that both faculty and students adhere to standards of honesty and fairness (Davis, 2009). Professors are responsible for setting a precedent by upholding academic honesty in their work and interactions, while students are expected to follow codes of conduct that prevent academic dishonesty. This adherence to ethical standards not only supports the credibility of the academic institution but also cultivates an environment where intellectual rigor and personal integrity are paramount. By integrating ethical practices into every facet of education, institutions contribute to the development of responsible and conscientious citizens who are well-prepared to engage critically with complex global issues.

Critical Thinking and Ethical Decision-Making

Critical thinking is an essential skill for college students, as it equips them to navigate complex ethical dilemmas and make informed decisions. Paul and Elder (2014) emphasize that the ability to think critically and ethically is crucial for addressing real-world challenges. A college education should actively promote the development of these skills, providing students with the tools to evaluate information, analyze various perspectives, and apply ethical reasoning in their decision-making processes. By fostering an environment where critical thinking is emphasized, educational institutions enable students to approach problems with a thoughtful, ethical mindset, thus preparing them to tackle both personal and professional challenges with integrity.

Inclusive Education

Inclusivity is a cornerstone of a comprehensive college education, ensuring that students from diverse backgrounds feel welcomed and valued. Milem and Berger (1997) highlight that a diverse and inclusive environment enhances educational outcomes by promoting respect, empathy, and cultural awareness among students. An inclusive campus culture not only supports the ethical development of students but also enriches their educational experience by exposing them to a variety of perspectives and ideas. By actively fostering an environment where diversity is celebrated and all students have equitable opportunities, institutions contribute to the creation of a more just and understanding society.

Moral and Civic Education

College education extends beyond academic learning to encompass moral and civic education, aiming to develop students' sense of social responsibility and ethical leadership. Moore and Lewis (2001) argue that institutions should actively engage students in discussions about sustainability, social justice, and community involvement. By incorporating these themes into the curriculum and extracurricular activities, colleges help students understand their role in addressing societal issues and foster a commitment to ethical leadership. This holistic approach to education not only prepares students to contribute meaningfully to their communities but also reinforces the importance of ethical behavior in all aspects of life.

Access to Ethical Role Models

Having access to ethical role models is crucial for students' development of moral and ethical values. Doh and Kim (2018) discuss how professors and staff who exemplify ethical behavior positively influence students' understanding of ethics and integrity. These role models provide students with practical examples of ethical decision-making and behavior, which can guide them in their own academic and personal lives. By fostering an environment where ethical conduct is visibly practiced and valued, institutions enhance students' ethical awareness and contribute to their overall moral development.

Academic Support and Mental Health Services

Academic support and mental health services are essential components of a comprehensive college experience, particularly given the increasing concerns about student well-being. Carr (2016) emphasizes that institutions have an ethical responsibility to ensure students' holistic development by providing resources and counseling services that address stress, anxiety, and other personal challenges. By offering robust support systems, colleges help students manage their academic and emotional pressures, contributing to their overall success and well-being. This commitment to student support not only improves academic performance but also enhances students' quality of life during their college years.

Ethical Use of Technology

As technology becomes increasingly integrated into academic life, ethical considerations regarding its use are paramount. Velasquez (2015) highlights the importance of educating students about digital ethics, including responsible online behavior, data privacy, and the ethical implications of technology use. Colleges must incorporate these topics into their curricula to prepare students for the ethical challenges of the digital age. By promoting awareness of ethical issues related to technology, institutions ensure that students can navigate the digital landscape responsibly and with integrity.

Social and Environmental Responsibility

Colleges play a critical role in fostering social and environmental responsibility among students. McPherson and Egan (2008) argue that institutions should encourage student participation in community service and sustainable practices to nurture a sense of responsibility towards society and the environment. These experiences not only contribute to the development of ethical values but also prepare students to become proactive and responsible citizens. By integrating social and environmental issues into the educational experience, colleges help students understand their impact on the world and inspire them to contribute positively to their communities.

College students' educational needs encompass not only academic excellence but also ethical and moral considerations. Ethical integrity, critical thinking, inclusivity, and access to role models play a crucial role in shaping responsible, ethically aware citizens. Additionally, addressing mental health and digital ethics, as well as promoting social and environmental responsibility, are essential components of a holistic college education.

It is incumbent on colleges and universities to provide an environment that nurtures both intellectual growth and ethical development, preparing students to contribute positively to society and uphold the principles of integrity and ethics throughout their lives.

Student's Wants

The pursuit of higher education is a significant investment of time and resources for college students. To ensure that this investment aligns with the principles of ethics and integrity, it is essential to understand what college students want from their educational experience. We explore the expectations of college students concerning their education, couched in ethical and integrity-driven principles, and draw attention to the need for educational institutions to meet these expectations.

Academic Excellence

Academic excellence remains a fundamental goal for college students, who seek rigorous, engaging, and up-to-date educational programs that equip them with the necessary knowledge and skills for success in their chosen fields (Kuh et al., 2015). Students expect their institutions to uphold high academic standards and resist practices like grade inflation or unethical shortcuts that might undermine the value of their degrees. Maintaining academic excellence involves not only providing challenging curricula but also ensuring that assessment methods are fair and that students are held to consistent standards of performance. This commitment to academic integrity is essential for fostering a learning environment where students can genuinely develop their abilities and prepare for their future careers.

Personal Growth and Development

In addition to academic achievement, students seek personal growth and development throughout their college experience (Astin, 1993). They look for opportunities to engage in self-reflection, critical thinking, and the exploration of their own values and beliefs. This holistic approach to education supports the ethical principle of nurturing students' overall development, preparing them to be well-rounded individuals who are not only knowledgeable but also responsible and reflective. By fostering an environment that promotes personal growth, colleges contribute to students' transformation into ethical citizens who are equipped to navigate complex personal and professional landscapes with integrity and self-awareness.

Ethical Values and Character

A significant expectation for many college students is the development of ethical values and strong character traits, such as integrity, honesty, and accountability (Berkowitz & Puka, 2010). Students hope that their education will not only impart academic knowledge but also instill a sense of ethical responsibility. Colleges play a crucial role in this aspect by integrating ethical principles into their curricula and fostering a campus culture that emphasizes ethical behavior. This includes creating opportunities for students to engage in discussions about ethics and to witness ethical practices modeled by faculty and staff, thereby supporting their growth into principled individuals who value integrity in all aspects of life.

Inclusivity and Diversity

Students today increasingly expect their college experience to reflect inclusivity and diversity (Hurtado & DeAngelo, 2012). They value exposure to a variety of perspectives, cultures, and backgrounds, which enriches their educational experience and prepares them for a diverse world. Ethical colleges are tasked with actively promoting inclusivity, diversity, and cultural sensitivity, ensuring that all students feel valued and supported. This involves implementing policies and practices that foster an equitable environment, such as diverse faculty hiring, inclusive curricula, and supportive resources for underrepresented groups. By prioritizing these aspects, institutions create a learning environment where every student has the opportunity to thrive and contribute meaningfully to the campus community.

Practical Skills and Career Readiness

Beyond academic knowledge, college students expect their education to prepare them for successful careers by providing practical skills, real-world experience, and career readiness (Hart Research Associates, 2015). Students look for programs that offer internships, hands-on projects, and career services that support job placement and professional development. Ethical institutions ensure that their educational offerings are aligned with industry standards and prepare students effectively for the workforce. By integrating career readiness into the academic experience, colleges help students transition smoothly from education to employment, thereby enhancing their long-term career prospects and professional success.

Transparency and Honesty

Transparency and honesty are critical expectations for college students regarding institutional administration and communication (Carini et al., 2006). Students seek clear and accurate information about academic requirements, policies, and financial costs to make informed decisions about their education. Ethical institutions are committed to upholding a culture of transparency, ensuring that all communication with students is straightforward and truthful. This transparency helps build trust between students and the institution, contributing to a fair and equitable educational environment where students are fully aware of their responsibilities and opportunities.

Supportive Faculty and Staff

College students greatly value supportive faculty and staff who are genuinely invested in their success (Tinto, 2007). They seek educators, mentors, and advisors who provide personal connection, guidance, and encouragement throughout their academic journey. Ethical institutions prioritize the well-being and development of their students by fostering an environment of trust and respect. This involves not only supporting faculty and staff in their roles but also ensuring that they are accessible, responsive, and committed to the students' overall growth and achievement.

Civic Engagement and Social Responsibility

Many students aim to engage in civic activities and embrace social responsibility during their college years (Jones et al., 2013). They seek opportunities to contribute positively to their communities through service learning, volunteer work, and ethical leadership initiatives. Ethical colleges support this by promoting civic engagement and providing resources for students to get involved in meaningful community activities. By encouraging students to take part in social responsibility projects, colleges help them develop a sense of purpose and a commitment to making a positive impact on society, thereby reinforcing the importance of active citizenship and ethical behavior.

The need is to create an educational environment that aligns with ethics and integrity, colleges and universities must understand and meet the expectations of their students. This includes providing academic excellence, fostering personal growth, promoting ethical values and character, ensuring inclusivity and diversity, developing practical skills, maintaining transparency and honesty, offering support, and encouraging civic engagement. By incorporating these expectations into their mission and practices, educational institutions can not only meet the needs of their students but also contribute to a more ethical and responsible society.

The Ethical Imperative

College education is a transformative journey, providing students with knowledge, skills, and experiences that shape their future. However, a college education should not be limited to academic proficiency alone. It is imperative that colleges and universities prioritize ethics and integrity as fundamental components of their educational mission. We will explore what college students need and want from their higher education experience in terms of ethics and integrity.

Ethical Curriculum

To foster ethical development, colleges must design a curriculum that incorporates ethical discussions, critical thinking, and moral reasoning. An ethics-focused curriculum engages students in exploring complex moral issues and developing their ability to make principled decisions in various contexts. According to Flanagan & Miller (2019), students who participate in ethics-related coursework are more adept at recognizing and addressing ethical issues. This type of curriculum not only enhances students' understanding of ethical principles but also prepares them to navigate moral dilemmas they may encounter in their personal and professional lives. By integrating ethical theory and practice into diverse academic disciplines, colleges ensure that students are equipped with the skills needed to uphold ethical standards in their future endeavors.

Moral Role Models

Employing faculty who serve as moral role models is critical for fostering ethical development among students.

These faculty members should exemplify ethical behavior not only through their academic expertise but also through their personal conduct and character. Treviño and Youngblood (1990) highlight the significant impact of faculty as ethical role models, noting that students often look to their professors for guidance on ethical issues. When faculty members demonstrate integrity, fairness, and respect in their interactions with students and colleagues, they provide a powerful example of ethical behavior. This modeling helps students develop their own ethical standards and decision-making abilities, reinforcing the importance of moral conduct in both academic and professional contexts.

Ethical Decision-Making Skills

Developing ethical decision-making skills is a vital component of college education. Integrating ethics workshops, case studies, and real-world simulations into the curriculum allows students to practice moral reasoning and decision-making. Rest and Narvaez (1994) found that students who engage in these activities are more likely to exhibit ethical behavior in their personal and professional lives. By providing practical experiences where students must navigate ethical dilemmas, colleges help them build the competencies necessary for making responsible choices. These educational opportunities also prepare students to handle complex situations with integrity and confidence, ultimately contributing to their growth as ethical leaders and professionals.

Ethical Conduct Codes

Establishing and upholding clear ethical conduct codes is essential for fostering a culture of integrity on campus.

These codes articulate the standards for behavior expected of students, faculty, and staff, and outline the consequences for violations. Kish and Topolovec (2019) emphasize the importance of having well-defined conduct codes, noting that they play a critical role in shaping ethical behavior within the academic community. By creating a framework that promotes accountability and transparency, colleges ensure that ethical standards are consistently applied, thereby reinforcing the values of integrity and fairness across the institution.

Ethical Leadership Opportunities

Providing students with opportunities to engage in ethical leadership roles is crucial for their moral and ethical development. Student organizations, volunteer programs, and student government positions offer platforms for students to practice and demonstrate ethical leadership. Schaub and Jefferis (2018) found that students who hold leadership positions during their college years are more likely to exhibit ethical leadership in their careers. These experiences not only allow students to apply their ethical knowledge in real-world settings but also help them develop skills in decision-making, accountability, and responsibility. By fostering these opportunities, colleges contribute to the formation of future leaders who are committed to ethical principles and social responsibility.

Diversity and Inclusion

An inclusive and diverse environment is essential for students to develop empathy, cultural sensitivity, and respect for differences. Colleges should prioritize diversity and inclusion efforts to ensure that students are exposed to a wide range of perspectives and experiences (Milem, Chang, &

Antonio, 2005). By creating a campus culture that values and celebrates diversity, institutions help students understand and appreciate the importance of equity and social justice. This exposure not only enriches the educational experience but also prepares students to navigate and contribute to a diverse world. Inclusivity and diversity initiatives should be integral to all aspects of campus life, from recruitment and hiring practices to curriculum design and student support services.

Applied Ethics

Applied ethics is a crucial aspect of a comprehensive college education. Internships, service learning, and experiential education provide students with opportunities to apply their ethical knowledge in practical settings. Jacoby and Associates (1998) show that these experiences can significantly impact students' ethical development by allowing them to confront real-world ethical dilemmas and practice moral reasoning. By integrating applied ethics into the curriculum, colleges help students connect theoretical ethical principles with practical applications, enhancing their ability to make ethical decisions in their personal and professional lives.

Ethical Accountability

Colleges must hold themselves accountable for fostering a culture of ethics and integrity. This includes transparency in addressing ethical violations, prompt action in resolving issues, and alignment with the institution's stated ethical values (Mintz & Morris, 2011). Ethical accountability at the institutional level influences student behavior and contributes to a positive campus climate. By upholding high standards of ethical conduct and ensuring that all members of the academic community are held accountable, colleges reinforce the importance of integrity and transparency, thereby creating an environment where ethical behavior is both expected and respected.

College students need a holistic educational experience that prioritizes ethics and integrity. An ethical education goes beyond classroom learning and encompasses a commitment to developing ethical reasoning, practicing ethical leadership, and embracing diversity and inclusion. It is the responsibility of colleges and universities to ensure that students graduate not only with academic knowledge but also with the ethical foundation necessary for a just and virtuous society.

Meeting Student Needs

Higher education institutions play a pivotal role in shaping the academic, personal, and ethical development of students. In response to the evolving landscape of student expectations, it is crucial for colleges and universities to provide students with what they both want and need from a college education while upholding ethical and integrity-driven principles. We delve into the ways colleges should align their practices with student desires and requirements, all the while maintaining a strong ethical and integrity foundation.

Aligning Curricula with Student Interests and Career Aspirations

Colleges must ensure that their academic offerings are closely aligned with students' interests and career aspirations to foster academic excellence and practical skills development. When students pursue careers in specialized fields such as sustainable development, it is crucial for colleges to provide curricula that reflect these professional interests. Kaplowitz et al. (2013) emphasize that ethical colleges should offer comprehensive programs that integrate environmental ethics and sustainability principles. This alignment not only meets students' career goals but also upholds educational integrity by delivering on the institution's promises. By designing curricula that match students' career aspirations, colleges reinforce their commitment to providing valuable and relevant education, thus supporting students in achieving both personal and professional success.

Personalized Support and Mentorship

Providing personalized support and mentorship is essential for meeting the diverse needs of students and fostering an ethical campus environment. Kuh (2008) highlights that faculty, advisors, and staff should actively engage with students to understand their individual goals, challenges, and aspirations. This personalized approach not only supports students' academic and personal development but also reinforces the culture of integrity by demonstrating respect for each student's unique potential. By tailoring support and mentorship to individual needs, colleges create an environment that values students' contributions and fosters a sense of belonging and ethical commitment, thereby enhancing the overall educational experience.

Ethics Education and Ethical Leadership

Ethics education should be a core component of the college curriculum to help students develop strong ethical values and leadership skills. Treviño and Nelson (2020) argue that integrating ethics education into academic programs is essential for cultivating students' moral character and decision-making abilities. By engaging in ethics-related coursework and leadership opportunities, students can reinforce their understanding of ethical principles and apply them in various contexts. Schaub and Jefferis (2018) further suggest that participating in ethical leadership roles within the campus community helps students practice and embody these principles. This dual approach of classroom learning, and practical application supports students in becoming responsible leaders who uphold integrity in their personal and professional lives.

Inclusivity and Diversity

To meet students' expectations for inclusivity and diversity, colleges must actively promote a campus culture that embraces and celebrates differences. Hurtado and DeAngelo (2012) emphasize that an inclusive environment should involve diverse faculty and staff, resources for underrepresented groups, and inclusive events and activities. By fostering such a culture, colleges align with ethical values of social justice and equity, ensuring that all students feel respected and valued. Embracing diversity not only enhances the educational experience but also prepares students to thrive in a multicultural society, reinforcing the institution's commitment to fairness and respect for all individuals.

Transparency and Accountability

Maintaining transparency and accountability is crucial for meeting students' expectations and upholding institutional integrity. Mintz and Morris (2011) highlight that colleges should ensure transparency in administrative decisions, tuition costs, grading policies, and other key areas. This openness helps to build trust and ensures that students are treated fairly and with respect. By adhering to high standards of accountability, colleges demonstrate their commitment to ethical practices and reinforce their credibility. Transparent operations not only align with ethical principles but also contribute to a positive campus environment where students feel informed and empowered.

Career Development and Real-World Experience

Colleges must ensure that their programs provide practical skills and real-world experiences to prepare students for the workforce. Hart Research Associates (2015) points out that students expect their education to include opportunities such as internships, co-op programs, and hands-on projects relevant to their career goals. These experiences not only align with students' expectations but also uphold the ethical principle of providing value for their educational investment. By offering meaningful career development opportunities, colleges help students bridge the gap between academic learning and professional practice, thereby enhancing their employability and career readiness.

Civic Engagement and Social Responsibility

Encouraging students to engage in civic activities and embrace social responsibility is a key aspect of a holistic college education. Jones et al. (2013) argue that colleges should actively promote opportunities for students to contribute positively to their communities. This can include participation in community service, advocacy initiatives, and leadership in social justice efforts. By fostering civic engagement and social responsibility, colleges not only fulfill students' desires to make a meaningful impact but also support the development of ethical values and responsible citizenship. This commitment aligns with the broader goal of preparing students to be proactive and ethical contributors to society.

Colleges and universities must adapt and respond to the evolving expectations and needs of their students while maintaining a commitment to ethics and integrity. By aligning curricula with student interests, providing personalized support, offering ethics education, promoting inclusivity, maintaining transparency, and fostering career development, colleges can create an educational experience that not only meets students' needs but also upholds the principles of ethics and integrity. Ultimately, the alignment of education with these ethical values contributes to a more responsible and ethical society.

CHAPTER 2

Strategies

P.A.S.S.

Positive Activity for Successful Students

Developmental, Intentional, Interventions

Three words that best describe the philosophy students should have about successful educational endeavors.

Developmental

Cognitive development encompasses several critical areas essential for personal growth and academic success. One key aspect is problem-solving skills, which involve the ability to analyze complex situations, think critically, and devise effective solutions. Additionally, understanding one's moral compass and conceptualizing long-term goals is vital for navigating both academic and personal challenges. Developing a solid command of language is fundamental, as it impacts communication, academic performance, and the ability to express oneself clearly. Moreover, essential social, personal, and emotional development forms the foundation of effective interpersonal relationships and emotional well-being. The formulation of self-concept and identity, which includes understanding personal characteristics, behaviors, and socioeconomic status, is crucial for self-awareness and direction in life. This developmental process should be approached holistically, considering how each element interrelates and contributes to an individual's overall growth.

Personal characteristics and socioeconomic status significantly shape cognitive and emotional development. For example, individuals from varying socioeconomic backgrounds may face challenges and opportunities that influence their developmental trajectory. The understanding of self-concept and identity is further nuanced by these personal and social factors, which can affect one's approach to problem-solving and goal-setting. Therefore, educational and developmental interventions should be tailored to address these individual differences, ensuring that each person receives support that is responsive to their unique circumstances and needs (Kohlberg, 1981; Erikson, 1968).

Intentional

Intentionality in interactions within an academic setting requires a clear sense of purpose and direction. When engaging with other students, faculty, advisors, academic units, or administration, having specific goals helps to ensure that interactions are productive and aligned with one's broader objectives. Intentional behaviors involve performing deliberate actions with a clear end in mind, whether these actions are individual or part of a series of steps designed to achieve a particular outcome. By focusing on intentional interactions, individuals can avoid unintended consequences and ensure that their efforts are directed toward achieving their goals. This approach requires thoughtful planning and a strategic mindset, as each action or decision contributes to the overall performance outcomes.

Moreover, intentionality extends beyond mere action; it involves reflective practice and ongoing evaluation. For instance, when planning an academic or professional project, one must continuously assess whether their actions align with their intended goals and adjust strategies as needed. This proactive approach helps maintain focus and adapt to any changes or challenges. Ensuring that each action is deliberate and goal-directed not only enhances personal effectiveness but also contributes to a more structured and coherent approach to achieving one's objectives. This methodical and intentional behavior is essential for navigating complex environments and achieving long-term success (Locke & Latham, 2002; Bandura, 1997).

Interventions

Effective interventions should target specific areas such as feelings, behaviors, attitudes, and habits, addressing individual or systemic concerns. These interventions can occur at various levels, including interactions with individuals, groups, professors, advisors, mentors, academic units, departments, or administration. Whether addressing academic, behavioral, cognitive, environmental, or policy-related issues, interventions should be structured and proactive. For example, a proactive academic intervention might involve creating a support plan for students struggling with coursework. In contrast, a behavioral intervention might focus on changing unproductive habits through counseling or workshops. By targeting specific areas with tailored strategies, interventions can effectively address and mitigate challenges.

However, interventions often need to be reactive due to unforeseen or uncontrolled situations, such as sudden changes in a student's academic performance or personal circumstances. In these cases, being responsive and utilizing each challenge as a learning opportunity is crucial. This involves clearly defining the desired outcome of the intervention, showing respect and support, and demonstrating how the intervention can benefit everyone involved. Reflective practice and continuous feedback are essential to ensure that interventions are effective in the short term and contribute to long-term improvement and learning (Hollands & Kuk, 2015; Gordon & Habley, 2000).

Success Planning

Success planning in college is essential for students to achieve their academic and personal goals and begin preparing for their professional goals. It involves setting clear objectives, organizing resources, and making strategic decisions. The following general principles, supported by research and best practices, can help students navigate their college journey effectively.

Goal Setting and Clarity

Set clear, specific, and achievable short-term and long-term success goals (Locke & Latham, 2002). Having well-defined objectives will provide direction and motivation throughout your college experience. Setting clear and specific goals is a fundamental aspect of success planning, providing individuals with a roadmap to navigate their endeavors. As Locke and Latham (2002) highlight in their seminal work on goal-setting theory, setting well-defined and challenging goals can significantly enhance motivation and performance. Clarity in goal formulation helps individuals articulate their aspirations, fostering a sense of purpose and direction.

This is particularly crucial in success planning, where goals serve as milestones, enabling individuals to track progress and make informed decisions about their strategies. Research by Matthews et al. (2009) underscores the positive impact of goal clarity on goal attainment, emphasizing the importance of clearly defined objectives in successful goal pursuit. In essence, the relevance of goal setting and clarity lies in their ability to provide individuals with a structured framework, aligning actions with desired outcomes and enhancing the likelihood of achieving success.

Time Management

Develop practical time management skills to balance coursework, extracurricular activities, and personal life. Macan et al. (1990). Use calendars, planners, and time-blocking to prioritize tasks and meet deadlines. Effective time management is a critical component of success planning, playing a pivotal role in optimizing productivity and achieving desired outcomes. As Covey (1989) emphasizes in "The 7 Habits of Highly Effective People," managing time efficiently involves prioritizing tasks based on importance and aligning activities with overarching goals.

Time management facilitates allocating resources to high-priority activities, ensuring that energy and effort are directed toward tasks that contribute most significantly to success. Studies such as those by Britton and Tesser (1991) further underscore the link between effective time management and goal attainment, emphasizing how judicious use of time enhances one's ability to meet objectives. In the context of success planning, mastering time management allows individuals to balance competing demands, reduce procrastination, and maintain focus on strategic priorities, ultimately contributing to the realization of personal and professional goals.

Study Strategies

Utilize evidence-based study techniques, such as active learning, spaced repetition, and retrieval practice, to enhance your learning and retention (Dunlosky et al., 2013). The adoption of effective study strategies is crucial in the context of success planning and serves as a foundational element for academic and professional achievement. Drawing on cognitive psychology and educational research, Dunlosky et al. (2013) highlight the significance of evidence-based study techniques, such as self-testing, distributed practice, and elaborative interrogation, in enhancing learning outcomes.

By incorporating these strategies, individuals can optimize the encoding and retrieval of information, fostering more profound understanding and retention. Additionally, Hattie and Timperley (2007) emphasize the importance of metacognition and self-regulation in effective study strategies, allowing individuals to monitor their learning progress and adjust their approaches accordingly. In the realm of success planning, cultivating robust study habits not only contributes to academic excellence but also equips individuals with the skills necessary for continued personal and professional development.

Seek Support and Resources

Leverage available support services, including tutoring, counseling, and academic advising, to address academic challenges and personal well-being. Pascarella & Terenzini (2005). Seeking support and utilizing available resources are integral components of success planning, facilitating individuals in overcoming challenges and maximizing their potential. According to Bandura's social cognitive theory (1986), seeking support from mentors, peers, or professional networks can enhance self-efficacy—the belief in one's capability to succeed.

Moreover, research by Robbins et al. (2015) underscores the positive impact of social support on academic achievement, emphasizing the importance of interpersonal connections in navigating the complexities of educational and professional endeavors. Accessing resources, such as libraries, online databases, and skill development programs, is equally essential. Tinto (1993) identified that involvement in academic and social resources fosters a sense of belonging and engagement, positively influencing student persistence and success. In the context of success planning, the proactive utilization of support networks and resources contributes to a more comprehensive and resilient approach, increasing the likelihood of goal attainment.

Networking and Collaboration

Build relationships with peers, faculty, and professionals in your field of interest (Lichtenstein & Brewer, 2019). Collaboration can lead to academic and career opportunities. Networking and collaborations play a pivotal role in success planning by offering avenues for knowledge exchange, skill development, and broader opportunities. According to Burt (2005), social network ties can provide individuals with access to diverse information and resources, facilitating the acquisition of critical insights and support necessary for success.

Research by Perry-Smith and Shalley (2003) highlights the positive impact of collaboration on creativity and innovation, emphasizing how working with others can lead to novel solutions and enhanced performance. In the context of success planning, building a professional network allows individuals to tap into collective expertise, gain mentorship, and identify potential collaborators for mutual benefit. Furthermore, as suggested by Hansen (1999), effective networking enhances visibility within one's field, opening doors to new possibilities and increasing the likelihood of achieving personal and professional goals. Thus, incorporating networking and collaborations into success planning provides a dynamic and interconnected approach to navigating the complexities of various endeavors.

Critical Thinking

Cultivate critical thinking skills by questioning assumptions, analyzing evidence, and evaluating information (Paul & Elder, 2006). This skill is valuable in both academic and real-world decision-making. Critical thinking is a cornerstone of success planning, providing individuals with the cognitive tools to analyze information, make informed decisions, and adapt to changing circumstances. As Paul and Elder (2006) defined, critical thinking involves disciplined intellectual analysis, evaluation, and problem-solving.

Research by Abrami et al. (2008) emphasizes the positive correlation between critical thinking skills and academic achievement, indicating that individual's adept at critical thinking are better equipped to excel in their educational pursuits. In the professional realm, Ennis (2011) highlights the significance of critical thinking in the workplace, emphasizing its role in practical problem-solving and decision-making. Incorporating critical thinking into success planning ensures that individuals can navigate challenges with a discerning mindset, assess the validity of information, and make strategic choices aligned with their goals. In essence, the ability to think critically is a valuable academic skill and a key factor in achieving success across various personal and professional domains.

Adaptability

Embrace change and adapt to new situations, technologies, and challenges. Murnane & Levy (1996). The ability to adjust to unexpected circumstances is crucial for success. Adaptability is a crucial attribute in success planning, enabling individuals to navigate dynamic environments and respond effectively to unforeseen challenges. According to Martin and Osberg (2007), adaptability involves adjusting strategies and perspectives in the face of changing circumstances.

Research by Boyatzis (2018) underscores the importance of emotional and social intelligence, components closely linked to adaptability, in fostering personal and professional success. In a rapidly evolving world, the ability to adapt is essential for continuous learning and growth, as noted by Hargrove and Quick (2003). Success planning that incorporates adaptability ensures that individuals can pivot when necessary, learn from setbacks, and capitalize on emerging opportunities. By cultivating an adaptable mindset, individuals can proactively shape their trajectories, enhancing their resilience and increasing the likelihood of accomplishing long-term goals in the face of uncertainty and complexity.

Self-Care

Prioritize physical and mental health by maintaining a balanced lifestyle, including exercise, healthy eating, and stress management. Hunt & Eisenberg (2010). In the context of success planning, prioritizing self-care is paramount as it directly influences an individual's well-being, resilience, and sustained performance. Research by Diener et al. (2009) highlights the positive correlation between well-being and productivity, suggesting that individuals who engage in self-care tend to experience enhanced cognitive function and work-related outcomes.

Additionally, the work of Maslach and Leiter (2016) underscores the importance of preventing burnout through self-care strategies, emphasizing that maintaining physical and mental health is essential for long-term success. Incorporating self-care into success planning involves recognizing the value of adequate rest, nutrition, and stress management, as articulated in the work of Greenberg et al. (2016). By nurturing one's holistic well-being, individuals can sustain the energy and focus required for effective goal pursuit, ensuring that success is achieved not only in professional endeavors but also in maintaining a balanced and fulfilling life.

Financial Literacy

Develop financial responsibility by budgeting, managing student loans, and making informed financial decisions. Hilgert et al. (2003). Financial literacy is particularly critical for students in the context of success planning, serving as a foundational skill set that equips them for future financial independence and success. Research by Mandell and Klein (2009) suggests that financial education positively influences the financial behaviors of young individuals, including budgeting and saving practices.

With the rising costs of education, managing student loans and debt becomes crucial, as highlighted by Chen and Volpe (1998). Integrating financial literacy into success planning for students ensures they are well-prepared to make informed decisions about student loans, credit, and long-term financial goals. As students transition into the workforce, financial literacy provides them with the tools to navigate salary negotiations, retirement planning, and investment decisions, contributing to a more holistic approach to success in both academic and professional realms.

Reflection and Assessment

Regularly reflect on your progress, assess your strengths and weaknesses, and adjust your strategies accordingly Schon (1987). Self-awareness is key to continuous improvement.

By adhering to these general principles, college students can enhance their chances of success academically and personally. In the realm of success planning for students, incorporating reflection and assessment is paramount for fostering continuous growth and self-awareness. Research by Boud, Keogh, and Walker (1985) underscores the importance of reflective practices in education, stating that reflection enhances learning by encouraging students to critically evaluate their experiences and identify areas for improvement.

Through regular self-assessment, as advocated by Tinto (1993), students can gain insights into their strengths, weaknesses, and learning preferences, facilitating the development of effective study habits and strategies. Additionally, the work of Nicol and Macfarlane-Dick (2006) highlights the role of assessment in promoting deep learning, emphasizing the value of assessments that encourage students to reflect on their understanding and apply knowledge in real-world contexts. By integrating reflection and assessment into success planning, students can cultivate a proactive approach to their academic and personal development, ultimately enhancing their ability to navigate challenges and achieve their long-term goals.

Focus Areas

Academic Factors

Being overall prepared for academic success in college requires more than just academic prowess. It involves a holistic approach that encompasses various aspects of student life. Here are key considerations for college students to ensure their readiness for academic success.

Time Management and Organization

Effective time management is crucial for balancing academic commitments, extracurricular activities, and personal life. According to Macan et al. (1990), developing strong time management skills can significantly enhance academic performance and reduce stress. Utilizing tools such as planners, digital calendars, and to-do lists can aid in staying organized and ensuring that tasks are completed efficiently. These organizational tools help prioritize responsibilities and allocate time appropriately, allowing individuals to meet deadlines and maintain a balanced schedule. By implementing structured time management strategies, students can better manage their workload, improving productivity and reducing anxiety.

Goal Setting

Setting clear and specific academic and personal goals is essential for providing direction and motivation throughout the college journey. Locke and Latham (2002) emphasize that well-defined and achievable goals can enhance focus and drive by giving students a concrete sense of purpose. Specific goals help prioritize tasks and create a roadmap for success, making it easier to track progress and adjust as needed. By establishing short-term and long-term objectives, students can stay motivated and align their efforts with their overarching ambitions, ultimately fostering a more organized and goal-oriented approach to their educational and personal development.

Study Strategies

Adopting evidence-based study techniques is crucial for optimizing learning and retention. Dunlosky et al. (2013) highlight the effectiveness of active learning, spaced repetition, and retrieval practice in enhancing academic performance. Active learning involves engaging with the material through discussions and problem-solving, while spaced repetition focuses on reviewing information at increasing intervals to improve long-term retention. Retrieval practice, or testing oneself on the material, further reinforces learning by requiring active recall. By incorporating these strategies into their study routines, students can improve their understanding and memory of academic content, leading to better performance and success.

Academic Support

Available academic support services, such as tutoring, academic advising, and writing centers, can significantly enhance the learning experience and address academic challenges. Pascarella and Terenzini (2005) underscore the positive impact of such support on students' academic success and overall experience. These services provide personalized assistance and resources tailored to individual needs, helping students navigate complex academic requirements and improve their skills. Engaging with these support mechanisms not only helps in overcoming difficulties but also fosters a more enriching educational experience, contributing to greater academic achievement and personal growth.

Mental and Physical Health

Prioritizing mental and physical health is essential for maintaining overall well-being and achieving academic success. Hunt and Eisenberg (2010) emphasize the importance of a balanced lifestyle that includes regular exercise, a nutritious diet, adequate sleep, and effective stress management. Maintaining these health practices not only supports cognitive function and emotional stability but also enhances resilience and performance in academic and personal pursuits. By focusing on self-care, students can better manage the pressures of college life and maintain the energy needed for sustained success and fulfillment.

Financial Literacy

Developing financial literacy is crucial for managing student loans, budgeting, and making informed financial decisions. Hilgert et al. (2003) discuss how financial literacy skills contribute to financial stability and can alleviate stress related to financial management. By learning to budget effectively and manage debt, students can reduce financial anxiety and focus more on their academic and personal goals. Financial education empowers individuals to make sound decisions regarding their financial futures, ensuring a more secure and successful transition into adulthood.

Network and Collaboration

Building a network of relationships with professors, peers, and professionals can open doors to academic and career opportunities. Lichtenstein and Brewer (2019) highlight the benefits of networking and collaboration in enriching the educational experience and facilitating career advancement. Engaging with others in your field provides access to valuable insights, mentorship, and potential collaborations, which can enhance academic and professional development. By fostering these connections, students can leverage collective knowledge and opportunities to achieve their goals more effectively.

Critical Thinking

Cultivating critical thinking skills is vital for academic success and effective problem-solving. Paul and Elder (2006) define critical thinking as the disciplined process of analyzing information, questioning assumptions, and making informed decisions. These skills enable individuals to evaluate evidence, think logically, and approach complex problems with a clear, reasoned perspective. Developing strong critical thinking abilities enhances academic performance and prepares students for thoughtful decision-making in various aspects of life.

Adaptability

Embracing change and developing resilience are essential for navigating unexpected challenges and uncertainties. Murnane and Levy (1996) argue that adaptability is a crucial attribute for success, allowing individuals to adjust strategies and perspectives in response to evolving situations. The ability to adapt enables students to manage disruptions and capitalize on new opportunities, fostering a more dynamic and flexible approach to achieving their goals. Cultivating adaptability helps individuals remain effective and resilient in the face of change.

Self-Reflection

Regular self-reflection is crucial for continuous growth and success. Schön (1987) emphasizes the importance of reflective practice in enhancing learning and personal development. By regularly assessing progress, identifying strengths and weaknesses, and adjusting strategies, individuals can gain valuable insights into their performance and make informed improvements. Self-reflection fosters self-awareness and enables more effective goal-setting and problem-solving, contributing to ongoing success and personal growth.

In college, academic success goes hand in hand with personal development and well-being. By considering these holistic aspects and taking a well-rounded approach to preparation, students can enhance their readiness for academic success.

Advising

College advising is a critical component of higher education, guiding students in their academic and personal development. Ethical integrity is a foundational element of effective advising, ensuring students receive honest, transparent, and unbiased guidance. We explore the principles and best practices of college advising, focusing on ethical integrity.

Confidentiality and Privacy

Advisors are required to uphold strict confidentiality when handling students' academic and personal information, as outlined by NACADA (2017). Maintaining confidentiality ensures that sensitive information shared by students during advising sessions remains private, fostering an environment where students feel secure enough to discuss their concerns openly. This practice builds trust between students and advisors and contributes to a supportive and effective advising relationship. By respecting students' privacy, advisors create a safe space that encourages honest communication and helps address issues more effectively.

Non-Discrimination and Equity

Advisors should commit to principles of non-discrimination and equity, ensuring that all students are treated with respect and fairness, as emphasized by ACPA & NASPA (2015). This commitment involves addressing the diverse needs of students and fostering an inclusive advising environment where every student feels valued and supported. By upholding these principles, advisors contribute to a more equitable educational experience, essential for promoting student success and well-being. Ensuring advising practices are free from bias and discrimination helps create a fair and supportive academic community.

Informed Decision-Making

Advisors play a crucial role in empowering students to make informed decisions by providing accurate, unbiased information about academic programs, requirements, and potential outcomes, as highlighted by Ender and Winston (2015). Effective advising involves presenting clear and comprehensive information that helps students weigh their options and make choices aligned with their personal and academic goals. Advisors should prioritize the students' interests, ensuring that their guidance supports their aspirations rather than institutional objectives. This approach enables students to make decisions that are in their best interest and support their overall success.

Transparency and Honesty

Transparency and honesty are fundamental in the advising process, requiring advisors to provide clear and accurate information about academic policies, program requirements, and any potential challenges, as emphasized by NACADA (2017). Being transparent helps to build a culture of trust and integrity, allowing students to make well-informed decisions about their academic paths. Honest communication about potential obstacles and expectations ensures that students have a realistic understanding of their educational journey, which is essential for effective planning and successful outcomes.

Avoiding Conflicts of Interest

Advisors must disclose and manage any potential conflicts of interest to ensure that their advice is solely in the best interests of the students, as outlined by ACPA & NASPA (2015). By identifying and addressing conflicts of interest, advisors maintain the integrity of the advising process and ensure that their guidance is impartial and focused on supporting the students' needs. This practice helps to preserve trust in the advising relationship and ensures that students receive objective and reliable support in their academic and career decisions.

Professional Development

Continuous professional development is essential for advisors to stay updated on evolving academic policies, technological advancements, and best practices, as noted by Ender and Winston (2015). Engaging in ongoing learning and development allows advisors to enhance their skills and knowledge, ensuring they provide the most current and effective support to students. Staying informed about new developments and trends in academic advising enables advisors to offer relevant and high-quality guidance, contributing to better student outcomes and a more effective advising process.

Ethical Decision-Making

Advisors should be prepared to guide students in ethical decision-making and dilemmas, empowering them to navigate complex situations with integrity, as highlighted by Knefelkamp et al. (2011). Providing support in ethical decision-making involves helping students analyze their options, consider the implications of their choices, and make decisions that align with their values and principles. This guidance is crucial for fostering students' ability to handle ethical challenges effectively and ensuring that they make decisions that support their long-term success and personal growth.

College advising, grounded in ethical integrity, plays a vital role in students' academic and personal development. By upholding principles of confidentiality, non-discrimination, informed decision-making, transparency, and professional development, advisors can guide students ethically toward success in higher education and beyond.

Maximizing Academic Advising

Academic advising is crucial in a college student's journey, providing guidance and support. The approach to academic advising can be either prescriptive or developmental, each with its merits and limitations. College students should use academic advising based on their needs, preferences, and goals.

Prescriptive Advising

Prescriptive advising is a directive approach where advisors provide specific course recommendations and establish clear pathways to fulfill degree requirements. This model is characterized by its structured nature, offering students a detailed plan that outlines the exact courses needed to complete their degree efficiently. According to O'Banion (2013), prescriptive advising can significantly benefit students by providing a streamlined plan, which is especially useful for those with tight deadlines or who lack clarity about their academic goals. This approach can also reduce confusion related to course selection, allowing students to focus on their studies without the added stress of navigating complex academic requirements.

However, prescriptive advising has notable limitations. It can restrict students' opportunities for exploration within different academic fields, potentially hindering their ability to discover new interests or passions. Additionally, the one-size-fits-all nature of this approach may not cater to the diverse needs and career aspirations of all students, as it imposes a uniform path that might not align with individual goals or circumstances.

Developmental Advising

Developmental advising emphasizes holistic student development by focusing on self-exploration, goal-setting, and decision-making. This approach prioritizes helping students understand their values and long-term objectives to support their overall personal and academic growth. As Crookston (1972) suggests, developmental advising fosters personal growth by enhancing students' self-awareness, critical thinking, and decision-making skills. It allows advisors to offer tailored guidance that aligns coursework with students' individual interests, strengths, and future goals, providing a more personalized educational experience.

Despite its benefits, developmental advising presents some challenges. It often requires a substantial investment of time and effort from students and advisors, which can be demanding. Additionally, this approach may offer less structure than prescriptive advising, potentially making it less suitable for students who prefer or need a more structured and clearly defined academic plan.

Ultimately, the choice between prescriptive and developmental advising should be student-centered, considering the individual's preferences, academic progress, and career aspirations. A hybrid approach that blends both aspects can be effective for many students. King & Kerr (2018). A flexible advising system, in which advisors are prepared to adapt their approach to meet the unique needs of each student, can ensure that advising remains a valuable resource for academic success.

Purpose: Guiding Students Toward Success

Academic advising is pivotal in higher education, serving as a dynamic and essential component of the student support system. The purpose of academic advising extends beyond course selection, encompassing a range of activities aimed at guiding students in their educational journey, fostering personal and academic development, and facilitating the achievement of their academic and career goals.

Guiding Educational Planning

One primary purpose of academic advising is to assist students in developing a comprehensive educational plan that aligns with their academic and career goals. Advisors work closely with students to help them select appropriate courses, create a personalized academic roadmap, and ensure that their chosen academic path aligns with their long-term aspirations. According to Grites (2015), effective advising involves understanding each student's individual interests and career objectives to tailor an educational plan that supports their goals. This personalized approach helps students navigate their academic journey more effectively, providing a structured framework that facilitates timely progression toward their degree and career ambitions. By integrating students' career goals with their academic plans, advisors play a crucial role in ensuring that students make informed choices that align with their future professional aspirations.

In addition to course selection, advisors help students understand how various academic experiences, such as internships or research opportunities, fit into their broader educational objectives. This comprehensive planning helps students meet graduation requirements and enhances their preparedness for their chosen careers. Through ongoing dialogue and adjustment of the academic plan as needed, advisors support students in adapting to changing interests and goals, thereby reinforcing their commitment to achieving success both academically and professionally.

Facilitating Goal-setting and Career Development

Academic advisors are instrumental in helping students identify and articulate their academic and career goals. Through regular discussions and assessments, advisors guide students in aligning their educational experiences with their long-term aspirations, fostering a sense of purpose and direction. As noted by Creamer (2000), effective advisors engage in ongoing conversations with students to clarify their goals and assist them in developing actionable plans to achieve them. This process involves exploring students' interests, values, and career ambitions to help them set specific, achievable goals that guide their academic journey.

Advisors also facilitate the development of career-related skills and experiences by recommending relevant courses, extracurricular activities, and professional opportunities that align with students' goals. This proactive approach not only aids in setting clear academic and career objectives but also ensures that students are well-prepared for their future careers. By helping students make connections between their academic work and their career aspirations, advisors play a critical role in enhancing students' motivation and commitment to their educational paths.

Providing Information on University Policies and Procedures

Academic advisors serve as invaluable resources for students by providing essential information on university policies, procedures, and academic requirements. This role involves clarifying details about degree requirements, course prerequisites, and academic regulations to ensure that students successfully navigate their academic journey. Habley, Bloom, and Robbins (2012) emphasize that advisors help students understand complex institutional policies and procedures, which is crucial for maintaining academic progress and compliance with university standards. By offering guidance on these matters, advisors help prevent misunderstandings and ensure that students meet all necessary requirements for graduation.

Furthermore, advisors assist students in understanding how university policies impact their academic decisions and overall educational experience. This includes providing information on academic standing, withdrawal processes, and available resources for academic support. By being well-versed in university regulations and procedures, advisors empower students to make informed decisions, contributing to a more seamless and successful academic experience.

Supporting Personal Development

Beyond academic guidance, the role of academic advising extends to supporting students' personal development. Advisors act as mentors who offer valuable guidance on various aspects of student life, including time management, study skills, and stress management. As Nutt (2003) points out, this holistic approach addresses academic and personal challenges, helping students develop essential life skills contributing to their overall success. By fostering personal growth and well-being, advisors play a crucial role in ensuring that students are equipped to handle the demands of college life effectively.

Advisors also provide support during personal difficulty, offering a listening ear and helping students connect with appropriate resources. This support helps students build resilience and maintain the balance between their academic and personal lives. By addressing both academic and personal concerns, advisors contribute to a more comprehensive approach to student success, ensuring that students not only achieve their educational goals but also thrive in all areas of their lives.

Enhancing Student Engagement and Retention

Academic advising is pivotal in enhancing student engagement and retention by fostering a sense of connection to the institution. Advisors build strong relationships with students, creating a supportive environment that encourages them to stay committed to their educational goals and persist through challenges. According to Kuh, Kinzie, Schuh, Whitt, and Associates (2005), effective advising contributes significantly to student engagement by ensuring students feel valued and supported throughout their academic journey. This engagement is crucial for maintaining motivation and a sense of belonging, which in turn influences students' decisions to continue their studies.

Advisors also help students navigate obstacles and connect with campus resources, strengthening their engagement and persistence. By providing personalized support and encouragement, advisors contribute to a positive student experience that promotes retention and academic success. This supportive relationship helps students overcome challenges and remain focused on their goals, ultimately enhancing their educational experience and success.

Addressing Academic Challenges and Concerns

Academic advisors play a critical role in addressing academic challenges and concerns that students may encounter during their college experience. Whether dealing with academic probation, course difficulties, or changes in significant, advisors provide essential guidance and support to help students navigate these obstacles. Grites (2015) highlights that advisors assist students in understanding their academic standing, exploring options for improvement, and making informed decisions about their academic path. This support is crucial for helping students overcome difficulties and stay on track toward achieving their educational goals.

Additionally, advisors offer resources and strategies for managing academic challenges, such as tutoring services, study skills workshops, and referrals to other campus support services. By providing tailored advice and support, advisors help students address their specific concerns and develop strategies for success. This proactive approach ensures that students receive the help they need to resolve issues and continue progressing in their academic careers.

Promoting Lifelong Learning and Self-Reflection

Academic advising encourages students to adopt a lifelong learning mindset and engage in self-reflection, which are essential for continuous personal and intellectual growth.

Advisors guide students in exploring their academic interests, evaluating their learning styles, and fostering a commitment to ongoing development. Creamer (2000) emphasizes that advisors play a key role in helping students recognize the importance of self-reflection and continuous learning as they progress through their academic and professional lives. By promoting these practices, advisors help students develop the skills necessary for lifelong success and adaptability.

Self-reflection enables students to assess their progress, identify strengths and weaknesses, and adjust their strategies accordingly. This reflective practice enhances academic performance and prepares students for future challenges by encouraging them to think critically about their experiences and goals. Advisors support this process by providing feedback and facilitating discussions that help students gain insights into their learning and development.

The purpose of academic advising is multifaceted, encompassing educational planning, goal setting, information provision, personal development, engagement, addressing challenges, and promoting lifelong learning. By fulfilling these purposes, academic advising becomes crucial in supporting students on their journey toward academic success and personal growth.

Topics for Meaningful Discussions

Academic advising involves more than just course selection; it is a dynamic process that encompasses a wide range of topics crucial to a student's overall success and development. Effective advising discussions go beyond the immediate academic concerns, addressing personal and professional growth. Below are key topics for meaningful discussions in academic advising.

Career Exploration and Planning

Engaging in discussions about career exploration and planning allows advisors to help students align their academic choices with their long-term career goals. Advisors can facilitate conversations about various career paths, industry trends, and the skills necessary for different professions. By discussing potential internships, job shadowing opportunities, and networking strategies, advisors guide students in gaining practical experience and building connections in their fields of interest. According to Creamer (2000), these discussions help students understand how their academic pursuits translate into career opportunities, ensuring their educational experiences are relevant and beneficial for their future professional lives. Advisors also assist students in setting career-oriented objectives and identifying the steps needed to achieve them, providing a clear roadmap for career success.

Moreover, advisors play a critical role in helping students explore how their academic interests align with potential career trajectories. By providing insights into job market trends and advising on skill development, advisors support students in making informed decisions about their future careers. This proactive approach ensures that students are focused on their current academic achievements and preparing for their professional futures, enhancing their overall career readiness.

Major and Minor Selection

Advisors play a vital role in guiding students through selecting majors and minors that align with their interests, strengths, and career aspirations. Through thoughtful discussions, advisors help students evaluate their academic interests and explore how different fields of study can support their future goals. As Grites (2015) points out, these conversations are crucial for helping students make informed decisions about their academic paths, ensuring that their chosen majors and minors are well-suited to their personal and professional objectives. Advisors assist students in understanding the requirements and opportunities associated with various majors and minors, which helps them choose paths that are both fulfilling and strategically advantageous for their careers.

Additionally, advisors encourage students to consider how their academic choices impact their career prospects and personal development. By providing insights into the practical applications of different fields of study and discussing potential career outcomes, advisors help students make choices that align with their long-term goals. This support ensures that students select majors and minors that interest them and position them for success in their chosen careers.

Academic Progress and Goal Setting

Regular discussions about academic progress and goal setting are essential for maintaining students' motivation and ensuring their success. Advisors monitor students' achievements, identify challenges, and help them set realistic academic goals. As Habley, Bloom, and Robbins (2012) note, these ongoing discussions foster a sense of accountability and encourage students to strive for continuous improvement. Advisors work with students to review their academic performance, assess their progress toward meeting degree requirements, and adjust their goals to stay on track.

By setting specific, measurable, and achievable goals, students are more likely to stay focused and motivated throughout their academic journey. Advisors play a critical role in helping students break down larger objectives into manageable steps and providing support to overcome obstacles. This approach helps students achieve their academic milestones and builds their confidence and resilience, contributing to their overall success.

Study Skills and Time Management

Advisors are instrumental in helping students develop practical study skills and time management strategies to enhance their academic performance. By discussing organizational techniques, prioritization methods, and strategies for creating a balanced schedule, advisors provide students with tools to manage their academic responsibilities more effectively. Pauk and Owens (2017) emphasize that these discussions can significantly impact students' ability to stay on top of their coursework and maintain a healthy balance between their academic and personal lives. Advisors may offer practical advice on setting study goals, creating effective study environments, and utilizing time management tools such as planners and digital calendars.

Furthermore, advisors can help students identify and address specific challenges they may face in managing their time and studying effectively. By providing tailored strategies and resources, advisors support students in developing habits that contribute to their overall success. This proactive guidance helps students build skills that are crucial for their current academic performance and beneficial for their future professional lives.

Extracurricular and Leadership Opportunities

Advisors should explore extracurricular and leadership opportunities with students, highlighting the significance of a well-rounded college experience. Involvement in clubs, organizations, and leadership roles enhances personal and professional development and enriches the overall college experience. According to Kuh, Kinzie, Schuh, Whitt, and Associates (2005), engaging in extracurricular activities helps students develop a range of skills, including teamwork, communication, and problem-solving, which are valuable in both academic and professional settings. Advisors encourage students to pursue opportunities that align with their interests and career goals, fostering a deeper connection to the campus community and enhancing personal growth.

Involvement in leadership roles and extracurricular activities also provides students with practical experiences that complement their academic learning. Advisors can guide students in identifying opportunities that align with their goals and interests and in leveraging these experiences to build a strong resume and network. By promoting a balanced college experience that includes academic and extracurricular pursuits, advisors help students develop into well-rounded individuals prepared for future challenges.

Academic Resources and Support Services

Academic advisors play a crucial role in informing students about the academic resources and support services available. This includes guiding students to tutoring services, writing centers, and counseling resources to help them overcome academic challenges and enhance their learning experience. As Nutt (2003) emphasizes, advisors help students understand the range of resources and encourage them to seek assistance when needed. By making students aware of these services, advisors ensure they have access to the support necessary for academic success and personal well-being.

In addition to providing information about available resources, advisors assist students in utilizing these services effectively. This includes helping students understand how to make appointments, what to expect from various support services, and how to integrate these resources into their academic plans. By promoting academic support services, advisors contribute to students' overall success and help them develop strategies for addressing any challenges they may encounter.

Research Opportunities and Scholarships

Encouraging students to engage in research opportunities and apply for scholarships is an essential aspect of academic advising. Advisors can discuss the benefits of participating in research projects, including developing critical thinking skills, hands-on experience in their field, and potential career advantages. Creamer (2000) highlights that involvement in research can significantly enrich students' academic experiences and open doors to future opportunities. Advisors also guide students in identifying and applying for scholarships, which can provide financial support and recognition for their academic achievements.

By helping students navigate the process of finding and applying for research opportunities and scholarships, advisors contribute to their academic and professional development. This support ensures that students can access resources that can enhance their educational experiences and reduce financial burdens. Advisors play a crucial role in helping students make the most of these opportunities, supporting their overall success and growth.

Graduation and Post-Graduation Plans

As students advance in their academic journey, advisors should initiate discussions about graduation requirements and post-graduation plans. These conversations involve reviewing the student's progress toward meeting all graduation criteria, exploring career opportunities, and considering options for further education, such as graduate school. Grites (2015) emphasizes that advisors help students plan for a smooth transition from college to the professional world by discussing job search strategies, networking, and application processes. These discussions are crucial for ensuring students are well-prepared for life after graduation and can make informed decisions about their future.

Advisors also assist students in evaluating their post-graduation options, including potential career paths and additional educational opportunities. By providing guidance on preparing for job interviews, crafting effective resumes, and exploring graduate programs, advisors support students in making strategic decisions that align with their long-term goals. This comprehensive approach helps students transition successfully from their academic careers to their professional lives.

Global and Cultural Competence

Advisors can discuss the importance of global and cultural competence in today's interconnected world. Encouraging students to participate in study abroad programs, language courses, or cultural immersion experiences contributes significantly to their personal and academic growth. Habley, Bloom, and Robbins (2012) highlight that exposure to different cultures and global perspectives enhances students' understanding of the world, prepares them for diverse workplaces, and fosters a greater appreciation for cultural differences. Advisors play a crucial role in helping students recognize the value of these experiences and guiding them through incorporating global competence into their academic and professional plans.

By promoting global and cultural competence, advisors help students develop essential skills for navigating an increasingly globalized world. This includes fostering open-mindedness, adaptability, and intercultural communication skills. Advisors assist students in finding opportunities that align with their interests and career goals, enriching their educational experiences and preparing them for successful, culturally aware careers.

Health and Well-Being

Addressing students' health and well-being is a critical component of academic advising. Advisors can discuss the importance of maintaining a healthy lifestyle, managing stress, and seeking support when needed. According to Nutt (2003), a holistic approach to student success involves recognizing the impact of physical and mental health on academic performance and overall well-being. Advisors support students by providing information on health resources, counseling services, and strategies for managing stress and maintaining a balanced lifestyle.

In addition, advisors help students develop healthy habits and coping mechanisms to manage the pressures of college life. By proactively addressing health and well-being, advisors contribute to a more comprehensive approach to student success, ensuring that students have the support they need to thrive both academically and personally.

Discussions in academic advising should extend beyond course selection to encompass a holistic approach to student success. By addressing these key topics, advisors can guide students in their academic and personal development, ensuring a well-rounded and fulfilling college experience.

Interpreting Information Received: Navigating Guidance for Informed Decision-Making

Academic advising provides students with a wealth of information that is critical for making informed decisions about their educational journey. The interpretation of this information is a crucial step in ensuring students can effectively apply guidance received from advisors. Below are key aspects of interpreting information from academic advising.

Understanding Degree Requirements

Academic advisors play a crucial role in helping students understand their degree requirements, including core courses, major prerequisites, and elective options. This involves providing detailed information about the sequence and significance of each requirement concerning the student's academic and career goals. As Habley, Bloom, and Robbins (2012) note, a thorough understanding of these requirements is essential for students to effectively plan their academic journey. Advisors ensure that students are aware of the specific courses they need to complete, the prerequisites that must be met, and how elective options can enhance their educational experience. By clarifying these aspects, advisors help students create a structured academic plan that aligns with their personal and professional aspirations, ensuring they meet all necessary criteria for graduation.

Additionally, advisors assist students in interpreting how these requirements fit into their overall academic plan, including how to balance their coursework to avoid potential scheduling conflicts and manage their workload effectively. This guidance is vital for students to stay on track and make informed decisions about their academic trajectory, ultimately supporting their successful completion of the degree program.

Clarifying Academic Policies

Academic advisors are instrumental in communicating institutional policies and procedures to students, ensuring they understand grading systems, attendance policies, and academic standing regulations. According to Grites (2015), advisors help students grasp the implications of these policies on their academic journey, which is essential for maintaining good academic standing and making informed decisions. Advisors explain how these policies impact students' grades, financial aid eligibility, and overall academic progress. Clear communication of these policies helps students navigate their academic responsibilities effectively and avoid potential pitfalls.

Moreover, advisors assist students in understanding how institutional policies interact with their academic plans and goals. This includes providing guidance on how to handle academic appeals, adjust their study plans, and utilize available resources to address any policy-related concerns. By fostering a comprehensive understanding of academic policies, advisors support students in managing their academic experiences successfully.

Navigating Extracurricular Opportunities

Advisors are significant in presenting information about extracurricular and enrichment opportunities, such as internships and study abroad programs. According to Creamer (2000), interpreting these opportunities involves assessing how they align with students' personal and career goals and understanding their potential impact on academic and professional development. Advisors help students explore how participating in these activities can complement their academic experiences and contribute to their growth. By providing insights into the benefits and requirements of various extracurricular options, advisors support students in making informed decisions that enhance their educational journey.

In addition, advisors assist students in evaluating the relevance of these opportunities to their long-term aspirations and how they can leverage these experiences to build a strong resume and network. This guidance is crucial for helping students maximize the value of their extracurricular involvements and integrate them into their academic and career plans.

Incorporating Career Development Insights

Advisors are essential in providing students with career development resources and strategies, helping them align their academic choices with future career paths. Habley, Bloom, and Robbins (2012) highlight that interpreting career development information involves making informed decisions about internships, networking events, and other career-building activities. Advisors assist students in understanding how their academic experiences and extracurricular involvements can support their career goals, and they guide how to leverage these experiences for professional advancement.

Furthermore, advisors support students in exploring various career options and developing a strategic plan for their career development. This includes helping students identify relevant resources, such as career services and professional organizations, and advising on how to build a network and gain practical experience. By integrating career development insights into academic advising, advisors contribute to student's readiness for the workforce and their overall career success.

Utilizing Academic Support Services

Academic advisors guide students to utilize available academic support services, including tutoring, writing centers, and counseling resources. According to Nutt (2003) interpreting this information involves recognizing the importance of seeking assistance when faced with academic challenges and understanding how these services can contribute to academic success. Advisors help students identify the appropriate support services and explain how to access these resources effectively.

In addition to providing information on available services, advisors assist students in integrating these resources into their academic plans. This includes advising on when and how to seek help, setting up appointments, and using the services to address specific academic issues. By promoting academic support services, advisors help students enhance their learning experiences and overcome obstacles to achieve their academic goals.

Financial Aid Decision-Making

Advisors play a key role in informing students about financial aid options and scholarships, helping them navigate the complexities of funding their education. Grites (2015), emphasizes that interpreting financial aid information involves assessing the financial implications of academic choices, understanding eligibility criteria, and making informed decisions about funding opportunities. Advisors assist students in understanding the different types of financial aid available, such as grants, loans, and scholarships, and how to apply for them effectively.

Moreover, advisors guide how financial aid decisions can impact students' academic and career plans. This includes helping students budget effectively, manage their financial resources, and make choices that align with their financial situation. By offering comprehensive support in financial aid decision-making, advisors help students reduce financial stress and focus on their academic and career goals.

Planning for Graduation and Beyond

Academic advisors are instrumental in helping students plan for graduation and their post-graduation futures. According to Habley, Bloom, and Robbins (2012), this involves creating a clear timeline for meeting degree requirements, understanding the steps involved in graduation, and developing a strategic plan for a career or further education. Advisors guide students through completing all necessary coursework, filing graduation applications, and preparing for the transition from college to the professional world.

In addition, advisors assist students in exploring career opportunities, applying to graduate programs, and developing strategies for a smooth transition into their chosen fields. By providing detailed guidance and support in these areas, advisors help students achieve their academic goals and prepare for successful futures beyond graduation.

Evaluating Research Opportunities

Advisors inform students about research opportunities and potential funding sources, helping them assess how these experiences align with their academic and career goals. Creamer (2000) highlights that interpreting research opportunities involves understanding the relevance of these experiences to students' academic and professional development. Advisors assist students in evaluating the benefits of participating in research projects, including gaining hands-on experience, developing research skills, and enhancing their resumes.

In addition, advisors help students navigate the application processes for research opportunities and funding, guiding how to secure positions and manage research responsibilities. By supporting students in engaging with research activities, advisors contribute to their academic growth and readiness for future careers.

Embracing Global and Cultural Competence

Advisors encourage students to embrace global and cultural competence by participating in initiatives such as study abroad programs and language courses. According to Nutt (2003), interpreting this information involves recognizing the value of diverse experiences and understanding how these opportunities contribute to personal growth. Advisors provide students with information about various global and cultural programs, helping them understand the potential benefits for their academic and professional development.

Additionally, advisors support students in making informed decisions about participating in these programs, including how to integrate these experiences into their academic plans. By promoting global and cultural competence, advisors help students develop essential skills for navigating an interconnected world and enhance their educational experiences.

Prioritizing Health and Wellness

Advisors play a crucial role in helping students prioritize their health and wellness, which is essential for academic success. Grites (2015) emphasizes that interpreting health and wellness information involves recognizing the importance of maintaining physical and mental well-being and understanding the resources available on campus. Advisors provide students with information about health services, counseling options, and strategies for managing stress, ensuring they can access the support they need.

Additionally, advisors assist students in developing healthy habits and coping mechanisms to handle the pressures of college life. By proactively addressing health and wellness, advisors contribute to a holistic approach to student success, supporting students in achieving a balance that enhances their academic performance and overall quality of life.

Interpreting information from academic advising is a dynamic process that involves aligning guidance with individual goals and aspirations. By understanding and applying the insights advisors provide, students can make informed decisions that contribute to their overall academic and personal success.

Key Takeaways: A Roadmap

Academic advising is a crucial component of the college experience, providing students with guidance and support as they navigate their educational journey. The key takeaways from academic advising encompass a range of insights and actions that contribute to student success. Here are some critical considerations.

Individualized Educational Planning

Academic advising underscores the significance of individualized educational planning by recognizing and addressing each student's unique needs, goals, and aspirations. Advisors work closely with students to develop personalized academic plans that align with their individual interests, strengths, and long-term career objectives. According to Habley, Bloom, and Robbins (2012), this tailored approach ensures that students are not only meeting degree requirements but also pursuing a path that resonates with their personal and professional aspirations. By customizing academic plans, advisors help students navigate their educational journey more effectively, ensuring that each student receives the support and guidance necessary to achieve their unique goals.

Proactive Engagement in Career Development

Academic advising plays a crucial role in fostering proactive engagement in career development. Advisors encourage students to explore career options early in their academic journey, participate in internships, and utilize career development resources to enhance their employability. As Grites (2015) highlights, this proactive approach helps students gain clarity about their career goals and the steps needed to achieve them. By integrating career development into the advising process, advisors assist students in building practical experience and professional networks that are essential for successful career planning and job placement.

Holistic Approach to Student Success

Academic advising adopts a holistic approach to student success, addressing not only academic concerns but also personal and career development. Advisors recognize that a student's overall well-being is integral to academic performance and success. According to Nutt (2003), this comprehensive approach ensures that advisors support students in all facets of their college experience, from managing stress and balancing responsibilities to exploring career opportunities and personal growth. By considering the full spectrum of student needs, advisors contribute to a more balanced and enriching educational experience.

Strategic Use of Academic Resources

Advisors emphasize the strategic use of academic resources to help students enhance their learning and overcome academic challenges. This involves guiding students to utilize resources such as tutoring services, writing centers, and academic workshops effectively. Grites (2015) notes that by leveraging these resources, students can address specific academic difficulties, improve their skills, and achieve better outcomes in their coursework. Advisors play a critical role in directing students to the appropriate resources and encouraging them to take full advantage of their support.

Continuous Monitoring and Goal Setting

Continuous monitoring of academic progress and goal setting are integral components of effective academic advising. Regular check-ins with advisors help students stay on track with their academic goals, make necessary adjustments, and maintain a sense of accountability. As Habley, Bloom, and Robbins (2012) emphasize, this ongoing dialogue ensures that students are progressing toward their degree requirements and adapting their goals and strategies as needed. By keeping students engaged and focused, advisors support their success throughout their academic journey.

Integration of Experiential Learning

Advising encourages integrating experiential learning into students' academic experiences by promoting participation in internships, research opportunities, and study abroad programs. Creamer (2000) highlights that these hands-on experiences complement academic studies and provide valuable real-world insights. Advisors support students in exploring these opportunities, helping them understand how such experiences can enhance their education and career prospects. By integrating experiential learning, advisors help students apply classroom knowledge in practical settings, fostering personal and professional growth.

Informed Decision-Making for Financial Planning

Academic advising supports informed decision-making for financial planning by providing guidance on financial aid options, scholarships, and the financial implications of academic choices. Grites (2015) notes that advisors help students navigate the complexities of funding their education and make realistic financial decisions. This includes understanding eligibility criteria, managing financial resources, and planning for the cost of education. Advisors ensure that students are well-informed about their financial options, helping them develop sustainable strategies for funding their academic pursuits.

Emphasis on Health and Well-Being

Advisors place a strong emphasis on health and well-being, recognizing the critical link between physical and mental wellness and academic success. Nutt (2003) underscores that advisors guide students towards resources and strategies that support their overall well-being, including stress management, healthy lifestyle choices, and mental health services. By addressing these aspects, advisors help students maintain balance and resilience, essential for achieving academic and personal goals.

Lifelong Learning and Adaptability

Academic advising promotes a mindset of lifelong learning and adaptability, encouraging students to embrace new challenges and seek continuous improvement. Creamer (2000) emphasizes that advisors support students in developing skills for adapting to evolving academic and professional landscapes. This includes fostering curiosity and resilience and helping students navigate changes and opportunities throughout their careers. By instilling these values, advisors prepare students for ongoing personal and professional development beyond college.

Building Strong Advisor-Student Relationships

Building strong advisor-student relationships is fundamental to effective advising. Grites (2015) highlights that successful advising is built on open communication, trust, and collaboration. When advisors establish a supportive and trusting relationship with students, it fosters a positive advising environment where students feel valued and understood. This strong rapport is essential for providing meaningful guidance and support, ultimately contributing to student success and satisfaction throughout their academic journey.

Academic advising provides students valuable insights and actions that contribute to their success. These key takeaways underscore the importance of personalized planning, proactive engagement, a holistic approach to development, strategic resource utilization, continuous monitoring, and building advisor-student solid relationships.

Awareness of Learning Styles

The purpose of this information is to help teachers and students understand different learning styles so they can create and use effective teaching and learning strategies. Understanding these styles can benefit both teachers and students. Learning styles refer to how individuals prefer to learn and process information. According to Keefe (1991), learning occurs when a person's behavior changes as a result of their experiences. For instance, if someone touches a hot stove and feels pain, they learn to be more cautious in the future to avoid getting burned again.

This change in behavior demonstrates learning. Learning isn't just a collection of experiences; it involves underlying principles that influence how we learn uniquely. Throughout history, educators have employed various teaching methods that align with different learning styles. Modern scientific studies continue to confirm the effectiveness of these techniques (Instructional Strategies, 2001; Vincent & Ross, 2001).

Visual Learners

Visual learners learn best by seeing images rather than hearing verbal instructions. They have vivid imaginations and often think in pictures, like having a movie playing in their minds. When they want to remember something, they visualize the information they've learned. For example, they might say, "I see" or "I get the picture." (Learning, 2001).

In a classroom setting, visual learners excel because most assessments are presented in written formats, allowing them to create mental images to recall information. They benefit from reading text and converting it into mental pictures, aiding memory retention. Visual learners typically adapt well to classroom expectations, such as sitting quietly, writing neatly, and organizing materials efficiently. To support visual learners, teachers should incorporate plenty of visual aids and cues into their teaching strategies (Kanar, 1995).

To cater to visual learners, teachers can employ various strategies. They can utilize video equipment to visually present information, making it more engaging and more accessible for visual learners to comprehend. Providing written assignments allows visual learners to process information at their own pace and refer to it visually. Additionally, using charts and pictures in teaching materials can help reinforce concepts and make information more accessible. It's helpful for teachers to incorporate bright colors in visual aids, encourage students to take detailed notes, and even draw pictures in their notes to help them associate visuals with facts (Kanar, 1995; Learning, 2001).

For visual learners, there are several tips to enhance their learning experience. First, they can occasionally change the color of ink in their pens while taking notes to keep their attention engaged. It's also beneficial for them to thoroughly examine all the pictures, charts, and graphs in their textbooks, as these visual aids can help reinforce concepts. Additionally, visual learners should make sure to read all assignment directions carefully to understand what is expected of them. When encountering new ideas or information, it's helpful for them to visualize these concepts in their minds. Furthermore, they can prepare for class discussions by reading the assigned topic beforehand and visualizing the details of the material they've read (Kanar, 1995; Learning, 2001).

Auditory Learners

Auditory learners thrive on listening and talking, often displaying outgoing personalities. They may struggle with written instructions and find it easier to understand information when it's presented orally (Kanar, 1995). Unlike visual learners, who create mental images, auditory learners process incoming information through their listening and repeating skills.

These learners excel in storytelling and problem-solving through verbal communication. They often express their thoughts using phrases like "I hear you," "that clicks," or "that sounds right." In the classroom, auditory learners prefer learning through listening and can easily repeat information to the teacher. They enjoy participating in class discussions but may get easily distracted. Among the different learning styles, auditory learners tend to be the most talkative and may even engage in self-talk. They may also encounter challenges with writing tasks (Learning, 2001).

To effectively teach auditory learners, educators should incorporate various auditory stimuli into their teaching methods. This includes providing verbal reinforcement, engaging students in group activities, and fostering class discussions where students can verbally exchange ideas (Learning, 2001). Additionally, teachers can implement drills to reinforce auditory learning, encourage students to read aloud to enhance their comprehension and allow them to express information in rhythmic patterns such as poems, songs, or raps. These strategies cater to auditory learners' preference for learning through listening and verbal communication, helping them better understand and retain information (Kanar, 1995).

For auditory learners seeking guidance, several helpful strategies can enhance their learning experience. Firstly, they can record their class notes and listen to them later to reinforce learning through auditory repetition. Additionally, auditory learners can mentally "hear" the conversations in their minds to recall details from previous discussions. Actively participating in class discussions is beneficial for auditory learners, allowing them to engage with the material verbally and exchange ideas with peers. Asking questions and volunteering in class not only fosters active engagement but also encourages auditory learners to clarify concepts verbally. When studying, reading assignments out loud can aid auditory learners in comprehension and retention. Lastly, when alone, whispering new information can further reinforce auditory memory (Learning, 2001).

Kinesthetic Learner

Kinesthetic learners are those who prefer learning through touch and physical activity. They struggle with listening and are more inclined to learn by actively engaging in hands-on tasks (Kanar, 1995). For these learners, physically interacting with the subject matter is crucial for understanding and remembering it effectively. In a classroom setting, kinesthetic learners often exhibit restlessness and difficulty staying focused, as they may need to move around to learn effectively. They express their understanding of concepts through physical actions and may describe their learning experiences in terms of their emotions, saying phrases like "I feel" or expressing a desire to gain a better understanding of the material (Learning 2001).

Kinesthetic learners typically don't create mental images of neatness and organization like visual learners do, which can make it challenging for them to demonstrate their knowledge in traditional classroom settings. Their preference for hands-on learning may clash with the structured nature of conventional education. Additionally, they may struggle with time management due to a weaker sense of time (Learning, 2001).

To effectively teach kinesthetic learners, educators should incorporate various interactive activities into their lessons. This includes providing hands-on tasks that allow students to physically engage with the material, integrating opportunities for movement within the classroom environment, and encouraging notetaking to reinforce learning (Learning, (2001). Teachers can also enhance learning experiences by incorporating rich stories in action and movement. Additionally, students can benefit from summarizing daily activities in their notes, which serves as a helpful study aid for reinforcing concepts learned through physical engagement (Kanar, 1995).

For kinesthetic learners seeking advice, several strategies can enhance their learning experience. Firstly, they should focus on learning by actively engaging in hands-on activities, touching, or practicing tasks to reinforce understanding (Kanar, 1995). Taking detailed notes during lectures and discussions can aid in memory retention, and underlining important information in textbooks can help them stay focused and identify key concepts. Kinesthetic learners can also benefit from taking frequent breaks to stand up and stretch, as movement can help them refocus and maintain concentration. Additionally, drawing pictures or diagrams of their learning can provide a visual representation that reinforces understanding. Finally, building projects related to the subject matter can serve as a practical way to explain complex ideas and solidify learning (Learning, 2001).

In addition to specific strategies tailored to different learning styles, there are general guidelines that contribute to effective teaching for all types of learners while also helping students understand their classroom experiences. Firstly, educators must have a thorough understanding of the material they are teaching. They should establish clear objectives and ensure these objectives guide their planning and evaluation processes. Informing students about the learning objectives helps them understand their expectations. Teachers should also assess the learning styles of their students beforehand and educate them on their individual learning styles to facilitate effective learning. Adapting teaching styles to match the predominant learning style of the class while accommodating students with different styles is important.

Additionally, beginning lessons with attention-grabbing activities and illustrating the relevance of the subject matter to students' futures can enhance motivation. Providing organizational tools such as outlines or concept maps aids in structuring learning.

Teachers should review previous lessons, present new material, summarize information, and relate it to future learning to reinforce understanding. Using audiovisual aids and interactive activities makes instruction more engaging and memorable. Breaking down complex tasks into manageable units and varying activities sustains learners' attention.

Assessment through questions and answers and observing nonverbal cues help gauge learning progress. Allowing time for reflection and providing immediate feedback is essential for effective learning. Assigning tasks that promote self-learning, such as independent research or group projects, fosters autonomy and deeper understanding. Incorporating hands-on activities whenever possible and creating a positive, supportive learning environment contributes to overall learning success. When Learning, (2001).

Meeting with Professors

Clarification of Course Material

Meeting with professors to clarify course materials is a crucial aspect of academic success. According to Chickering and Gamson's seminal work on "Seven Principles for Good Practice in Undergraduate Education" (1987), engaging with faculty outside of the classroom is one of the critical principles for effective teaching and learning. Professors are a valuable resource for students seeking a deeper understanding of complex topics. They can provide additional explanations, real-world examples, and insights into the nuances of the subject matter (Chickering & Gamson, 1987).

Research by Kuh, Kinzie, Schuh, and Whitt (2005) also emphasizes the positive impact of student-faculty interaction on learning outcomes. Regular communication with professors allows students to actively participate in their education actively, fostering a deeper connection with the course content and promoting a more meaningful learning experience (Kuh et al., 2005).

Moreover, the concept of "teacher immediacy" suggests that the perceived approachability and availability of instructors positively influence student learning (Mehrabian, 1971). When students actively seek clarification through professor meetings, it contributes to a supportive learning environment. Professors appreciate students' efforts to understand the material and are often willing to invest time in addressing questions.

This aligns with the idea of a student-centered approach to teaching, emphasizing the importance of tailoring instruction to students' needs and promoting a collaborative learning environment (Weimer, 2002). Therefore, meeting with professors for clarification not only enhances individual understanding but also fosters a positive and interactive learning culture within the academic community.

Feedback on Assignments

Seeking feedback from professors on assignments is an integral part of the learning process, aligning with the principles of formative assessment and constructive feedback in education. According to Hattie and Timperley's feedback model, effective feedback should be timely, specific, and actionable to enhance learning outcomes (Hattie & Timperley, 2007). Meeting with professors allows students to receive personalized feedback, facilitating a deeper understanding of their strengths and areas for improvement.

Research by Shute (2008) underscores the importance of feedback in promoting metacognition and self-regulation, crucial elements in the development of higher order thinking skills. By engaging in one-on-one discussions with professors, students can gain valuable insights into their thought processes, decision-making, and overall academic performance (Shute, 2008).

Furthermore, the impact of feedback on student motivation and engagement cannot be overstated. As highlighted by Nicol and Macfarlane-Dick (2006), feedback should address the task at hand and contribute to students' overall development as independent learners. Meeting with professors allows for a more nuanced exchange of feedback, fostering a supportive relationship between educators and students. This aligns with the student engagement literature, emphasizing the positive correlation between constructive feedback and student engagement in the learning process (Fredricks, Blumenfeld, & Paris, 2004).

The practice of meeting with professors for feedback on assignments not only aligns with established educational theories but also contributes significantly to students' cognitive development, motivation, and overall academic success.

Discussion of Academic Goals

Meeting with professors to discuss academic goals is a strategic initiative that aligns with the broader context of student success and goal-setting theories. Locke and Latham's goal-setting theory (1990) posits that setting specific and challenging goals can lead to higher performance and motivation. By conversing with professors about academic goals, students can align their aspirations with the course content and broader educational objectives.

Moreover, Bandura's social cognitive theory emphasizes the role of social influences, such as mentorship, in shaping individuals' aspirations and achievements Bandura (1986). Meeting with professors allows for establishing mentor-mentee relationships, providing students with guidance and support as they navigate their academic journeys (Pascarella & Terenzini, 1991).

Furthermore, the significance of goal alignment between students and educators is highlighted in the literature on academic advising and student success. According to Crookston's developmental advising model (1972), academic advisors, including professors, play a pivotal role in helping students clarify their educational goals and providing guidance on how to achieve them. Regular meetings with professors can foster a sense of accountability and commitment to academic goals, contributing to improved retention rates and overall student satisfaction (Creamer, 2000).

In essence, discussing academic goals with professors draws from well-established theories of goal-setting and social cognitive learning and enhances the effectiveness of academic advising in promoting student success.

Building a Professional Relationship

Establishing and nurturing professional relationships with professors is a strategic practice for students, with its roots in theories of mentorship and interpersonal communication. The concept of mentorship is deeply ingrained in educational literature, emphasizing the positive impact of mentor-mentee relationships on academic and professional development (Zachary, 2000).

By meeting with professors outside of formal class settings, students can initiate and cultivate these mentorship bonds. Tinto's student integration model (1975) supports the idea that strong social integration, including meaningful interactions with faculty, contributes to increased student satisfaction and retention. Thus, building a professional relationship with professors can enhance students' sense of belonging and engagement within the academic community (Tinto, 1975).

Moreover, the importance of networking in academic and professional success is well-documented. Building on Granovetter's strength of weak ties theory (1973), interactions with professors represent valuable weak ties that can open doors to broader networks and opportunities. Meeting with professors provides students with the chance to seek advice on career paths, gain insights into industry trends, and potentially secure recommendation letters for internships or jobs (Granovetter, 1973).

These professional relationships can extend beyond the classroom, contributing to students' long-term success by providing access to valuable resources and guidance. Therefore, the act of meeting with professors for the purpose of building a professional relationship draws on both established theories of mentorship and networking, underscoring its significance in students' holistic development and future career endeavors.

Exploration of Research Opportunities

Engaging with professors to explore research opportunities is a strategic move that aligns with the transformative potential of undergraduate research experiences. According to the Boyer Commission on Educating Undergraduates in the Research University, involving students in research is a key aspect of fostering a vibrant intellectual community within universities (Boyer Commission, 1998).

Meeting with professors allows students to express their interest in research and learn about ongoing projects, creating pathways for involvement. Research has shown that active participation in research positively influences students' critical thinking skills, problem-solving abilities, and overall academic achievement (Lopatto, 2004). By initiating conversations with professors about potential research collaborations, students can tap into these benefits and contribute meaningfully to advancing knowledge within their academic disciplines.

Furthermore, the literature on undergraduate research underscores the role of mentorship in shaping students' research experiences (Linn et al., 2015) emphasize that effective mentorship from faculty members is crucial for maximizing the impact of research opportunities on student learning and development. Meeting with professors allows students to identify mentors who can guide them through the research process, providing support in formulating research questions, designing experiments, and presenting findings.

These mentor-mentee relationships extend beyond the immediate research project, offering students valuable insights into the culture of academia and potential career paths (Linn et al., 2015). Thus, meeting with professors to explore research opportunities aligns with national calls for increased undergraduate research and positions students to benefit from the mentorship that enhances the quality and depth of their research experiences.

Preparation for Exams and Assessments

Meeting with professors to prepare for exams and assignments is a proactive strategy rooted in active learning and cognitive psychology principles. The concept of active learning, as advocated by Prince (2004), emphasizes student engagement in the learning process through activities that encourage analysis, synthesis, and application of knowledge. Regular interactions with professors, especially in exam preparation, offer students the opportunity to clarify complex concepts, receive guidance on effective study strategies, and gain insights into the instructor's expectations (Prince, 2004).

The cognitive load theory, as proposed by Sweller (1988), further supports the idea that adequate exam preparation involves the reduction of extraneous cognitive load, which can be achieved through well-designed learning interactions such as those between students and professors (Sweller, 1988).

Moreover, the literature on student-faculty interaction underscores the positive impact of such interactions on academic outcomes. Studies by Pascarella and Terenzini (2005) emphasize that frequent and meaningful interactions with faculty contribute to higher levels of student engagement and retention. Meeting with professors for exam and assignment preparation aligns with these findings, providing students with a supportive learning environment and personalized guidance that enhances their academic performance (Pascarella & Terenzini, 2005).

The practice of meeting with professors for exam and assignment preparation is not only rooted in established theories of learning and cognition but also aligns with empirical evidence highlighting the positive effects of student-faculty interaction on academic success.

Understanding Course Expectations

Meeting with professors to gain a clear understanding of course expectations is an essential step toward academic success, drawing from the principles of transparent teaching and constructive alignment in educational design. Winkelmes et al. (2016) argue for the importance of transparent teaching practices, emphasizing the need for explicit communication of course expectations and learning objectives. By meeting with professors, students can seek clarification on syllabus details, assignment requirements, and the overall structure of the course, aligning with the principles of transparency advocated by Winkelmes and colleagues (2016).

This approach contributes to the constructive alignment framework proposed by Biggs and Tang (2011), where learning activities, assessment tasks, and intended learning outcomes are explicitly linked. Meeting with professors allows students to understand how each course component contributes to their overall learning and achievement (Biggs & Tang, 2011).

Meeting with professors to gain a deeper understanding of course expectations is a proactive step that aligns with best practices in higher education. The significance of clear communication about course expectations is highlighted by Chickering and Gamson's Seven Principles for Good Practice in Undergraduate Education (1987), where explicit expectations are fundamental to effective teaching. Regular interactions with professors allow students to seek clarification on assignments, assessments, and overall course requirements, ensuring they are well informed and better equipped to meet academic standards (Chickering & Gamson, 1987).

Furthermore, the role of transparent communication in the classroom, including discussions about expectations, is emphasized in the literature on student success Tinto (2000). By meeting with professors, students can actively participate in shaping their learning experiences and align their efforts with the intended outcomes of the course (Tinto, 2000).

The literature on student success and retention highlights the role of clear expectations in fostering student engagement and motivation. Tinto's (1975) student integration model underscores the importance of academic and social integration in promoting student success, with clarity in course expectations playing a pivotal role.

Regular communication with professors, as highlighted by Tinto (1975), helps students navigate the academic environment and understand the requirements for success. Therefore, meeting with professors to comprehend course expectations is aligned with best practices in transparent teaching and supports the broader goals of student integration and success as outlined in Tinto's model.

The impact of understanding course expectations on student motivation and engagement is evident in the research on self-determination theory Deci & Ryan (1985). According to this theory, when students clearly understand the relevance and expectations of their academic tasks, they are more likely to be intrinsically motivated and actively engaged in their learning process (Deci & Ryan, 1985).

Meeting with professors fosters an environment of open communication, empowering students to take ownership of their education and contributing to their sense of autonomy and competence, as outlined in self-determination theory. Therefore, meeting with professors to understand course expectations is not only rooted in foundational principles of effective teaching but also aligns with psychological theories that underscore the importance of clarity and autonomy in promoting student success.

Seeking Academic Advice

Actively seeking academic advice through meetings with professors is a strategic approach grounded in educational theories and the scholarship of teaching and learning. Astin's Theory of Student Involvement (1984) underscores the significance of student-faculty interaction in influencing students' academic and personal development. Meeting with professors allows students to seek guidance on course selection, career paths, and academic strategies, fostering a sense of connection and engagement that positively impacts their educational experience (Astin, 1984).

Moreover, the concept of academic advising, as articulated by Creamer (2000), emphasizes the importance of personalized guidance in helping students navigate their educational journeys. Regular meetings with professors provide students with a trusted source of advice, contributing to their academic success and helping them make informed decisions about their academic pathways (Creamer, 2000).

Furthermore, the literature on student support services in higher education emphasizes the role of academic advising in promoting student retention and success (Habley, Bloom, & Robbins, 2012). Seeking academic advice through meetings with professors aligns with these findings, as personalized guidance can address individual challenges, enhance goal setting, and provide students with the tools to overcome academic obstacles. Habley et al., (2012).

The positive correlation between academic advising and student success underscores the value of proactive interactions with professors. These meetings contribute not only to academic achievement but also to students' overall sense of well-being and satisfaction in their academic pursuits. Therefore, meeting with professors for academic advice is firmly grounded in established theories of student involvement and academic advising, highlighting its importance in fostering student success.

Addressing Personal Challenges

Meeting with professors to address personal challenges represents a proactive approach to holistic student support, rooted in theories of student development and well-being. Chickering's psychosocial theory of student development (1969) emphasizes that the college experience is a critical period for personal growth, and student's ability to address and overcome challenges contributes significantly to their overall development. By meeting with professors to discuss personal challenges, students can tap into a support network that extends beyond academic concerns, fostering a sense of belonging and connection with the university community (Chickering, 1969).

Moreover, the literature on student success highlights the interconnectedness of academic and personal factors, emphasizing the importance of a supportive campus environment that acknowledges and addresses students' challenges Tinto, (2000). Regular interactions with professors can contribute to the creation of such an environment, positively impacting students' well-being and resilience (Tinto, 2000).

The relationship between personal support and academic success is further emphasized in the work of Kuh et al. (2005), who stress the importance of student-faculty interactions in promoting engagement and persistence. Addressing personal challenges through meetings with professors can lead to identifying resources and support mechanisms, enhancing students' ability to navigate difficulties and remain focused on their academic goals (Kuh et al., 2005).

Therefore, meeting with professors to address personal challenges aligns with foundational theories of student development and success, emphasizing the integral role of personal well-being in the overall educational experience.

Enhancing Communication Skills

Meeting with professors to enhance communication skills is a strategic initiative aligned with the broader educational goals of developing practical interpersonal competencies. The importance of communication skills in education and beyond is underscored by the American Association of Colleges and Universities (AAC&U) in their Essential Learning Outcomes, which includes "communication" as a key skill for student success (AAC&U, 2007).

Regular interactions with professors allow students to practice articulating thoughts, asking questions, and engaging in meaningful dialogue, contributing to the development of both written and verbal communication skills. This aligns with the principles of active learning, where students actively participate in their education through discussions, presentations, and collaborative activities, fostering the refinement of their communication abilities (Prince, 2004).

Furthermore, the concept of teacher immediacy, as outlined by Mehrabian (1971), suggests that the perceived approachability and availability of instructors positively influence student learning experiences. Meeting with professors allows students to engage in face-to-face communication, providing a platform to receive constructive feedback on their communication skills in a supportive environment.

This aligns with the broader literature on effective teaching practices, emphasizing the importance of clear communication between educators and students for optimal learning outcomes (Chickering & Gamson, 1987). Therefore, meeting with professors to enhance communication skills is firmly grounded in educational principles and aligns with national frameworks promoting essential skills for college graduates.

Navigating the Academic Load

Handling the academic load in college can be challenging for the average student. While academic success is paramount, it must be pursued with ethical integrity. We explore effective strategies for managing the workload in college while upholding ethical principles.

Time Management and Prioritization

Effective time management is essential for handling the academic workload and maintaining a balanced approach to education. According to Macan, Shahani, Dipboye, and Phillips (1990), managing time efficiently involves setting clear priorities for assignments, exams, and deadlines and allocating time-based on the importance and urgency of each task. By establishing a structured schedule and adhering to deadlines, students can reduce stress and enhance their academic performance. Ethical integrity in time management is crucial; it includes avoiding procrastination and ensuring that all tasks are completed honestly and punctually to uphold academic honesty (Macan et al., 1990). Adhering to these principles helps foster a responsible and disciplined approach to academic endeavors.

Seek Support

Seeking support when the academic load becomes overwhelming is not only a practical approach but also an ethical one. According to Pascarella and Terenzini (2005), reaching out to professors, academic advisors, and support services is an important step in managing academic challenges. This action demonstrates a commitment to personal and academic growth and aligns with ethical practices in education. Seeking help when needed, rather than struggling in isolation, reflects a proactive attitude toward overcoming obstacles and maintaining academic integrity

(Pascarella & Terenzini, 2005). Utilizing available resources ensures that students can navigate their academic journey more effectively.

Balance Course Selection

When selecting courses, maintaining a balanced workload is crucial to academic success and integrity. Pavela (1979) emphasizes that students should consider course difficulty, prerequisites, and personal interests to avoid excessive stress and potential academic dishonesty. A balanced approach in course selection helps students manage their responsibilities effectively, ensuring that they do not become overwhelmed by an unmanageable academic load. By carefully planning their course schedule, students uphold academic integrity by preventing situations that might lead to ethical breaches due to stress or overload (Pavela, 1979).

Avoid Over commitment

Avoiding over commitment is crucial for maintaining a manageable academic load and upholding ethical integrity. Fisher and Nuss (2018) suggest that taking on too many extracurricular activities or part-time jobs can lead to academic stress and negatively impact performance. Recognizing personal limits and making sustainable commitments are essential for balancing academic responsibilities with other activities. Ethical integrity in this context involves acknowledging one's capacity and avoiding commitments that could compromise academic performance or lead to unethical practices (Fisher & Nuss, 2018). Properly managing commitments helps ensure that students remain focused and responsible in their academic pursuits.

Academic Honesty

Upholding academic honesty and integrity is fundamental to the educational process. Bretag (2019) underscores that practices such as plagiarism and cheating undermine the ethical foundation of education and compromise the value of academic achievements. By adhering to principles of academic honesty and seeking help from professors and tutors when needed, students can avoid unethical practices and maintain the credibility of their academic work (Bretag, 2019). Ensuring that all academic endeavors are conducted honestly fosters a culture of trust and integrity within the academic community.

Stress Management

Ethical stress management involves taking proactive steps to maintain mental and physical well-being. Hunt and Eisenberg (2010) highlight that managing stress through self-care practices such as regular exercise, balanced nutrition, adequate sleep, and seeking emotional support is crucial for overall health. Recognizing the value of personal well-being and implementing effective stress management strategies are essential for sustaining academic performance and personal integrity (Hunt & Eisenberg, 2010). Addressing stress in a healthy manner contributes to a more balanced and ethical approach to managing academic responsibilities.

Ethical Decision-Making

When confronted with academic dilemmas, applying ethical decision-making processes is essential for maintaining academic and personal integrity. Knefelkamp, Widick, and Parker (2011) emphasize the importance of evaluating the consequences of decisions and aligning choices with ethical standards. Making informed and principled decisions helps ensure that academic practices remain honest and that students uphold the values of integrity and fairness in their educational pursuits (Knefelkamp et al., 2011). Ethical decision-making supports the development of a responsible and principled approach to handling academic challenges.

Navigating the academic load in college is challenging for the average student. While academic success is a worthy goal, it should be pursued ethically, with a commitment to academic honesty, time management, stress management, and well-balanced course selection. By following these strategies, students can manage their workload effectively while maintaining ethical integrity.

Balance of Background Knowledge: Introductory vs. Extensive

The level of background knowledge a college student should possess when entering a course is a critical factor in academic success. Striking the right balance between introductory and extensive prior knowledge is essential for optimal learning outcomes. We explore the significance of background knowledge in college coursework and how students can effectively navigate this spectrum.

Importance of a Strong Foundation

Introductory background knowledge is crucial for students embarking on new academic courses as it establishes a solid foundation upon which further learning can be built. Bransford, Brown, and Cocking (2000) emphasize that a strong foundational understanding of basic concepts and terminology is essential for grasping more complex ideas later in the course. This initial knowledge serves as the scaffolding that supports deeper comprehension and facilitates the integration of new information. Without a robust foundation, students may struggle to connect advanced concepts, which can impede their overall learning and academic performance (Bransford et al., 2000).

Promoting Equity

Emphasizing introductory background knowledge is fundamental for promoting equity in education. Tobolowsky and Beach (2016) argue that providing all students with the necessary foundational knowledge ensures that those with varying prior experiences and educational backgrounds have equal opportunities to succeed. By offering a baseline of essential information, educators can level the playing field, enabling every student to access and engage with course material more effectively. This approach helps to minimize disparities and fosters a fair and inclusive educational environment (Tobolowsky & Beach, 2016).

Inclusivity

Introductory background knowledge plays a crucial role in creating an inclusive learning environment by accommodating students from diverse backgrounds, including first-generation college students and international students. Harper and Harris (2010) highlight that providing a foundational understanding of the subject matter helps bridge gaps in prior knowledge, making it easier for all students to engage with the material. This inclusivity not only supports students who may have limited exposure to a subject but also fosters a learning atmosphere where diverse perspectives are valued and integrated (Harper & Harris, 2010).

Balanced Assessment

Incorporating introductory background knowledge into course design facilitates balanced assessment practices that are fair and reflective of students' starting points. Huba and Freed (2000) assert that assessments should be aligned with the foundational knowledge provided at the beginning of the course, allowing students to demonstrate their understanding without undue stress. By designing assessments that consider students' initial knowledge and learning progress, educators can ensure a more equitable evaluation process that accurately measures comprehension and skill development (Huba & Freed, 2000).

Preparing for Advanced Courses

Extensive background knowledge is often essential for advanced coursework, as it allows students to engage effectively with complex concepts, theories, and research. Boyd et al. (2011) notes that disciplines such as mathematics, physics, and advanced sciences require a deep understanding of foundational principles to tackle higher-level material. This in-depth prior knowledge is crucial for students to successfully navigate and contribute to advanced studies, ensuring they are well-prepared for the demands of their field (Boyd et al., 2011).

Research Opportunities

Extensive background knowledge is essential for engaging in research-based coursework, as it equips students with the necessary skills and expertise to conduct thorough investigations. Labaree (2007) highlights that a solid foundation in the subject matter is critical for students to effectively contribute to academic research and make meaningful advancements in their fields. This prior knowledge enables students to understand existing research, formulate research questions, and apply appropriate methodologies, thereby enhancing their contributions to the academic community (Labaree, 2007).

Professional Preparation

Extensive background knowledge is not merely beneficial but mandatory in professions such as law, medicine, and engineering. Pfeiffer and Snell (2018) emphasize that these fields require a comprehensive understanding of the subject matter from the outset to ensure professional competence and public safety. A deep knowledge base allows professionals to make informed decisions, apply specialized skills, and adhere to industry standards, which is crucial for success and ethical practice in these disciplines (Pfeiffer & Snell, 2018).

Customized Curriculum

Institutions offering specialized tracks or majors often design coursework with extensive background knowledge to align with students' career aspirations. Kinzie and Wechsler (2008) discuss how customized curricula are tailored to meet the needs of students who have specific professional goals, ensuring that the coursework builds on prior knowledge and prepares students for their future careers. This approach supports students by providing relevant and targeted education that aligns with their chosen fields, enhancing their preparedness for professional success (Kinzie & Wechsler, 2008).

The level of background knowledge required for college coursework varies according to the subject, course level, and students' goals. Institutions and instructors should aim for a balanced approach, offering introductory courses that foster inclusivity and providing advanced courses for students with extensive background knowledge. A flexible curriculum and strategic advising can help students navigate this spectrum effectively.

Role of Reading

Reading is a fundamental aspect of college coursework, serving as a cornerstone for academic success. It plays a significant role in shaping students' understanding, critical thinking, and knowledge acquisition. Furthermore, the way students approach reading is closely tied to ethical integrity. We explore the importance of reading in college coursework, emphasizing the ethical implications of this practice.

Fundamental Skill

Reading is a fundamental skill integral to all academic activities, as it forms the basis for engaging with various course materials, textbooks, scholarly articles, and instructional content. According to Pritchard (2013), effective reading strategies are essential for students to successfully navigate and comprehend academic texts. Mastery of reading skills enables students to access and interpret complex information, which is crucial for their success in coursework and overall academic achievement. The ability to read critically and efficiently facilitates deeper understanding and application of knowledge across different subjects (Pritchard, 2013).

Knowledge Acquisition

Reading is the primary means of knowledge acquisition in higher education, exposing students to a diverse array of perspectives, theories, and ideas. Bean (2011) highlights that through extensive reading, students gain access to a wide spectrum of academic literature, which contributes to their comprehensive understanding of the subject matter. Engaging with various texts allows students to build a robust knowledge base, facilitating their ability to synthesize information and develop well-rounded insights into their field of study (Bean, 2011).

Critical Thinking

The process of engaging with academic texts fosters critical thinking skills, as students are required to evaluate, analyze, and synthesize information. Chaffee (2017) argues that critical reading encourages intellectual growth by prompting students to question assumptions, analyze arguments, and integrate diverse viewpoints. This analytical approach enhances students' ability to engage deeply with the material, promoting the development of sophisticated reasoning and problem-solving skills that are essential for academic and professional success (Chaffee, 2017).

Ethical Use of Information

The ethical use of information is a vital aspect of academic reading. Students must adhere to principles of proper citation, avoiding plagiarism, and giving appropriate credit to original sources. Pecorari (2017) emphasizes that understanding and applying ethical practices in reading and writing helps maintain academic integrity and respect the intellectual contributions of others. By following these guidelines, students uphold ethical standards and contribute to a culture of honesty and respect in academic environments (Pecorari, 2017).

Citation and Attribution

Ethical reading involves the practice of proper citation and attribution, which requires students to acknowledge the sources of information they utilize in their academic work. Howard (1999) discusses how effective citation practices ensure that intellectual property rights are respected and that original authors receive credit for their contributions. By adhering to citation standards, students demonstrate academic integrity and contribute to the credibility of their own work (Howard, 1999).

Plagiarism Avoidance

Avoiding plagiarism is a crucial aspect of ethical reading and writing. Bretag (2019) asserts that presenting the work of others as one's own undermines academic integrity and erodes trust within the educational community. Students must understand the importance of original work and the consequences of plagiarism, which include academic penalties and damage to one's reputation. Upholding ethical standards in reading and writing ensures that scholarly contributions are respected and valued (Bretag, 2019).

Respect for Copyright

Ethical reading extends to respecting copyright laws, which involves understanding and adhering to copyright regulations when using copyrighted materials for academic purposes. Gardner and Eng (2005) highlight the importance of seeking permissions when necessary and avoiding unauthorized use of copyrighted content. By respecting copyright, students ensure that they comply with legal standards and support the rights of content creators, which fosters a culture of respect and responsibility in academic settings (Gardner & Eng, 2005).

Critical Engagement

Ethical reading requires critical engagement with sources, where students assess the credibility and reliability of the material they encounter. Bailin (2002) emphasizes that students should avoid the uncritical acceptance of information and instead practice skepticism and evaluation. By critically engaging with texts, students enhance their analytical skills and ensure that their academic work is based on sound and credible evidence, thereby promoting intellectual rigor and integrity (Bailin, 2002).

Reading is an indispensable component of college coursework, serving as the foundation for academic success. Ethical reading practices encompass proper citation, plagiarism avoidance, respect for copyright, and critical engagement with sources. By integrating ethical integrity into their reading habits, students not only enhance their academic performance but also contribute to the integrity and credibility of the educational community.

Effective Management: Reviewing Material

The amount of time students spend reviewing course material is a crucial factor in achieving academic success at the college level. Effective time management is essential for ensuring that students have the right balance between studying, coursework, and personal life. We explore the importance of dedicating an appropriate amount of time to reviewing material for college courses and offer insights into strategies for efficient time management.

Consolidation of Knowledge

Reviewing course material is crucial for consolidating knowledge gained from lectures, readings, and assignments. According to Dunlosky et al. (2013), this process reinforces understanding and helps to solidify the information in long-term memory. By revisiting previously covered material, students are able to connect new information with existing knowledge, which enhances comprehension and retention. This repetitive engagement with the content not only strengthens memory but also enables students to apply their knowledge more effectively in different contexts (Dunlosky et al., 2013).

Enhancing Long-Term Retention

Regularly reviewing material significantly enhances the long-term retention of information. Cepeda et al. (2008) highlight the effectiveness of the spacing effect, a phenomenon where information is learned more effectively through distributed practice rather than cramming. By spacing out review sessions over time, students allow for better encoding and retrieval of information, leading to improved retention. This method ensures that material is revisited periodically, which helps to solidify knowledge and maintain it over extended periods (Cepeda et al., 2008).

Identification of Gaps

Reviewing material is an effective way to identify gaps in understanding. Pintrich et al. (2000) assert that this process allows students to pinpoint areas where their comprehension is lacking, thereby facilitating targeted further study. By recognizing these gaps, students can seek additional resources or clarification, which leads to a more thorough grasp of the subject matter. This self-assessment is critical for addressing misunderstandings and improving overall academic performance (Pintrich et al., 2000).

Improved Exam Performance

Effective review strategies can significantly enhance exam performance. Hartwig et al. (2012) suggest that a well-structured review schedule allows students to prepare thoroughly for assessments, thereby boosting their confidence and ability to perform well. Regular and systematic reviews ensure that students are familiar with the material and can recall information more easily during exams. This preparation not only improves accuracy but also helps manage exam-related stress and anxiety (Hartwig et al., 2012).

Use of Active Learning Techniques

Engaging actively with the material during review sessions can significantly improve retention and understanding. Dunlosky et al. (2013) emphasize the effectiveness of techniques such as summarizing key points, generating flashcards, and teaching the material to peers. These active learning strategies promote deeper information processing, which aids in better encoding and recall. By actively interacting with the content, students can enhance their grasp of the subject and improve their academic performance (Dunlosky et al., 2013).

Establish a Consistent Routine

Establishing a consistent review routine is essential for effective time management. Hartwig et al. (2012) recommend setting aside dedicated time each day or week for review to maintain a structured approach to learning. By adhering to a regular schedule, students can ensure that they cover all necessary material and avoid last-minute cramming. Consistency in review practices helps to reinforce learning and maintain steady academic progress (Hartwig et al., 2012).

Prioritization

Prioritizing review material based on importance and upcoming assessments is a key aspect of efficient time management. Zimmerman and Schunk (2011) suggest that focusing review efforts on high-priority topics and areas that are likely to be tested ensures that students use their time effectively. By identifying and concentrating on critical content, students can optimize their study sessions and enhance their preparedness for exams and assignments (Zimmerman & Schunk, 2011).

Adaptability

Flexibility in the review process is crucial for effective studying. Zimmerman and Schunk (2011) argue that students should adapt their review strategies and time allocation based on their own comprehension and retention levels. Some subjects may require more in-depth review than others, and being responsive to these needs allows for more efficient use of study time. This adaptability ensures that students can address their weaknesses and strengths appropriately, leading to more effective learning outcomes (Zimmerman & Schunk, 2011).

The appropriate amount of time spent reviewing material in college is vital for academic success. Effective time management, active learning techniques, and a well-structured routine contribute to efficient review practices. By recognizing the importance of reviewing and implementing these strategies, students can optimize their understanding and retention of course material, ultimately enhancing their performance in college courses.

Imperative on Completion of Coursework

Completing all coursework in college is not only an academic requirement but also an ethical obligation. Ethical integrity in education entails academic honesty and a commitment to fulfilling one's responsibilities and embracing opportunities for personal growth. We delve into the importance of completing all coursework in college, emphasizing its ethical dimension and providing insights into the benefits of upholding this commitment.

Academic Honesty

Academic honesty is a fundamental principle that underpins the integrity of educational institutions. When students complete coursework, they engage in a commitment to uphold honesty and authenticity, which involves producing original work and avoiding plagiarism or cheating. McCabe and Treviño (1993) emphasize that academic dishonesty undermines the educational process and devalues the efforts of those who adhere to ethical standards. By maintaining academic honesty, students not only adhere to institutional policies but also contribute to a culture of trust and fairness within the academic community (McCabe & Treviño, 1993).

Respect for the Learning Process

Ethical integrity in college involves a deep respect for the learning process and adherence to institutional policies. Rhode (2008) argues that valuing education means recognizing and honoring the resources invested in one's academic growth, including time, effort, and institutional support. This respect is reflected in a student's commitment to engaging genuinely with coursework, following academic guidelines, and appreciating the broader educational experience. Such respect not only enhances personal learning but also contributes to a positive academic environment (Rhode, 2008).

Accountability and Responsibility

Completing coursework with dedication is a key aspect of demonstrating accountability and responsibility in one's academic journey. Hrabowski (2009) highlights that meeting deadlines, producing high-quality work, and taking ownership of one's learning process are essential for personal and academic success. This sense of responsibility not only reflects a student's commitment to their education but also prepares them for future professional environments where accountability is crucial. By embracing these values, students build a foundation for their academic and professional growth (Hrabowski, 2009).

Personal and Professional Development

An ethical approach to college education underscores the importance of personal and professional development. Kuh et al. (2006) emphasize that a commitment to ethical standards fosters the growth of well-rounded, informed, and competent individuals. This development is not only crucial for academic success but also for preparing students to navigate their future careers with integrity and competence. By valuing personal growth and ethical behavior, students lay the groundwork for lifelong learning and professional excellence (Kuh et al., 2006).

Academic Success

Upholding ethical integrity in coursework is closely linked to academic success. Robbins et al. (2004) demonstrate that students who consistently complete assignments and assessments with honesty are better prepared for exams and tend to achieve higher grades. This commitment to ethical behavior ensures that students engage meaningfully with the material, which enhances their learning outcomes and academic performance. By valuing academic integrity, students not only achieve personal success but also contribute to a fair and equitable educational environment (Robbins et al., 2004).

Skill Development

Engaging with coursework actively is crucial for skill development. Bean (2011) asserts that through the process of completing assignments, students enhance their abilities in research, critical thinking, time management, and problem-solving. These skills are developed through direct interaction with academic content and are essential for academic and professional success. By immersing themselves in their coursework, students build a toolkit of competencies that will serve them well beyond their academic careers (Bean, 2011).

Ethical Professionalism

Adhering to ethical integrity in college education lays the groundwork for ethical professionalism in future careers. Pecorari (2017) highlights that the ethical habits developed during academic work, such as honesty and respect for intellectual property, directly translate into professional conduct. By cultivating these values in their academic lives, students prepare themselves to navigate their future careers with integrity and ethical responsibility. This preparation is essential for maintaining professionalism and trust in the workplace (Pecorari, 2017).

Lifelong Learning

Upholding ethical integrity in coursework fosters a commitment to lifelong learning. Merriam and Bierema (2014) argue that students who engage in their studies with integrity are likelier to develop a passion for continuous learning and personal growth. This ethical approach encourages students to seek knowledge throughout their lives, adapting to new challenges and opportunities. By valuing ethical behavior in education, students cultivate a mindset that supports ongoing learning and adaptability in an ever-evolving world (Merriam & Bierema, 2014).

Completing all coursework in college is not merely a requirement but an ethical obligation. Upholding ethical integrity in education involves academic honesty, responsibility, accountability, and a commitment to personal and professional development. By embracing this ethical imperative, students achieve academic success and cultivate skills, ethical professionalism, and a lifelong love for learning.

Igniting Passion for Learning: The Significance of Interest Level

A student's level of interest in their college courses is a critical factor that profoundly influences their academic success, engagement, and overall college experience. We explore the importance of interest level in college courses, highlighting the impact on motivation, learning outcomes, and personal growth.

Motivation and Engagement

Interest in a college course is a powerful motivator, significantly influencing student engagement. When students are passionate about a subject, they are more likely to actively participate in class, attend sessions regularly, and contribute meaningfully to discussions. Ainley (2006) asserts that such intrinsic enthusiasm enhances the learning experience and fosters a more dynamic and interactive classroom environment. This heightened engagement often translates into a deeper connection with the material and a more rewarding educational journey (Ainley, 2006).

Improved Learning Outcomes

Genuine interest in a college course can significantly improve learning outcomes. According to Hidi and Renninger (2006), when students are captivated by a topic, they are more likely to devote additional time and effort to their studies, leading to enhanced academic performance. This intrinsic motivation drives students to engage more deeply with course materials, resulting in a better understanding and retention of knowledge. Consequently, students who are passionate about their studies often achieve higher grades and a more comprehensive grasp of the subject matter (Hidi & Renninger, 2006).

Intrinsic Motivation

Interest in academic subjects fosters intrinsic motivation, which is characterized by a deep-seated drive to learn for the sake of learning itself. Ryan and Deci (2000) describe intrinsic motivation as the internal enthusiasm that propels students to engage with course material out of genuine curiosity and enjoyment. This form of motivation leads to a more enduring commitment to learning as students pursue knowledge beyond external rewards or grades. Intrinsically motivated students are often more dedicated and resilient in their educational pursuits, reflecting a profound engagement with their academic experiences (Ryan & Deci, 2000).

Intellectual Curiosity

Interest in college courses stimulates intellectual curiosity, driving students to explore topics beyond the standard curriculum. Linnenbrink-Garcia et al. (2008) emphasize that when students are genuinely interested, they are more likely to ask questions, seek additional resources, and engage in independent research. This curiosity enhances their learning experience and fosters a lifelong habit of inquiry and exploration. Intellectual curiosity nurtured during college contributes to continuous personal and professional development, encouraging graduates to remain engaged with their fields and contribute innovatively (Linnenbrink-Garcia et al., 2008).

Personal Development

Interest in college courses significantly contributes to personal growth. Pascarella and Terenzini (2005) highlight that when students engage with subjects they are passionate about, they develop critical thinking skills, problem-solving abilities, and a broader perspective on various issues. This engagement enhances their academic skills and prepares them to be more adaptable and open to diverse viewpoints. The personal development fostered by pursuing one's interests helps students navigate complex problems and embrace continuous learning throughout their lives (Pascarella & Terenzini, 2005).

Career Satisfaction

Pursuing courses aligned with personal interests can lead to greater career satisfaction. Robbins et al. (2004) suggest that individuals passionate about their academic fields are more likely to excel in their professional lives because their enthusiasm drives them to exceed expectations and perform at higher levels. This intrinsic motivation often results in greater fulfillment and achievement in their chosen careers, as they are more committed and engaged with their work, leading to higher job satisfaction and career success (Robbins et al., 2004).

Enhanced Well-Being

Interest in college courses positively impacts overall well-being by providing a fulfilling educational experience. Chen (2008) argues that students engaged in subjects they find meaningful experience increased self-esteem, self-efficacy, and overall life satisfaction. This sense of fulfillment stems from aligning academic pursuits with personal interests, which contributes to a more positive and rewarding educational experience. Consequently, students who are passionate about their studies often report higher levels of well-being and a more satisfying academic journey (Chen, 2008).

Future Impact

Interest in college courses lays the groundwork for lifelong learning and innovation. Bloom et al. (2014) highlight that students who are passionate about their fields are more likely to make significant contributions to society through their work. Their enthusiasm drives them to pursue continuous learning and professional development, often leading to advancements in their areas of expertise. This enduring passion benefits their personal growth and has a lasting impact on their fields and society as a whole (Bloom et al., 2014).

The level of interest students have in their college courses is a powerful determinant of their academic success, motivation, and personal growth. It goes beyond immediate learning outcomes, influencing students' engagement, intrinsic motivation, and lifelong learning habits. College educators and institutions should recognize the significance of interest level and strive to foster an environment that nurtures students' passions, thus igniting their love for learning.

Significance of Concentration: Understandings, Challenges, and Solutions

Concentration is a vital aspect of a college student's academic journey and is deeply intertwined with ethical integrity. Achieving and maintaining the right level of concentration is essential for effective learning and ethical academic practices. We delve into what concentration level means to college students, explore the challenges they face in staying focused, and provide examples of strategies to enhance concentration while upholding ethical integrity.

Active Engagement

Concentration for college students means actively engaging with the learning process by dedicating one's full attention and cognitive resources to the material at hand. Pekrun et al. (2019) emphasize that this deep involvement is essential for effective learning and comprehension. Active engagement involves focusing on lectures and readings and participating in discussions, asking questions, and applying concepts in practical scenarios. By immersing themselves wholly in their studies, students enhance their ability to understand, retain, and apply information, which is crucial for academic success (Pekrun et al., 2019).

Focused Learning

Concentration implies focused learning, where students direct their mental energy toward specific tasks or subjects. Pintrich (2000) describes focused learning as essential for grasping complex concepts and achieving academic excellence. When students concentrate on a single task, they can process information more effectively and develop a deeper understanding of the material. This focused approach not only improves comprehension but also enhances the ability to apply knowledge in various contexts, contributing significantly to academic performance (Pintrich, 2000).

Ethical Academic Integrity

Concentration also encompasses maintaining ethical academic integrity. This involves avoiding cheating, plagiarism, and other dishonest practices that compromise the educational process. Bretag (2019) highlights that ethical concentration requires a commitment to honesty and fairness, ensuring that one's work reflects genuine effort and understanding. Adhering to these principles not only upholds the integrity of one's academic achievements but also fosters a fair and credible learning environment for all students (Bretag, 2019).

Efficient Time Management

Effective concentration is closely related to efficient time management. College students must allocate dedicated time to studying and completing coursework to maximize their learning opportunities. According to Huba and Freed (2000), managing time effectively involves setting specific study periods, avoiding procrastination, and creating a structured schedule. By adhering to a well-organized time management plan, students can ensure that they maintain focus and make the most of their academic efforts, ultimately leading to improved learning outcomes (Huba & Freed, 2000).

Distractions

College students frequently encounter distractions such as smartphones, social media, and environmental interruptions, which can impede concentration. Mark (2019) discusses the importance of ethical strategies in managing these distractions, such as setting boundaries for technology use and employing productivity tools. Recognizing and addressing these interruptions allows students to maintain their focus on academic tasks and uphold their commitment to their educational goals. Effective strategies for managing distractions are crucial for sustaining concentration and achieving academic success (Mark, 2019).

Academic Pressure

The pressure to excel academically can lead some students to engage in unethical behaviors like cheating. Ethical concentration involves managing this pressure effectively by employing stress reduction techniques and seeking support when necessary. Hunt and Eisenberg (2010) emphasize the importance of recognizing academic stress and adopting strategies to maintain integrity, such as mindfulness practices and time management skills. By addressing stress ethically, students can preserve their commitment to academic honesty while achieving their educational objectives (Hunt & Eisenberg, 2010).

Examples of Ethical Strategies: Utilizing the Pomodoro Technique

The Pomodoro Technique is a time management method that involves working in focused intervals, typically 25 minutes, followed by a short break. This approach helps students maintain concentration and manage their time efficiently. By dividing study sessions into manageable segments, students can enhance their focus and productivity while adhering to ethical principles of academic integrity. The technique encourages regular breaks to prevent burnout and sustain long-term engagement with coursework.

Group Study Ethics

Collaborative learning is a valuable component of the educational experience, but it is crucial to maintain ethical integrity during group study sessions. Ethical group study involves discussing and sharing ideas while ensuring that all members contribute their own work and avoid plagiarism. This approach fosters a collaborative environment where students can learn from one another while respecting academic standards and individual contributions. Maintaining ethical practices in group settings ensures that collaborative efforts enhance learning without compromising academic integrity.

Concentration for college students goes beyond the act of focusing; it encompasses ethical integrity, active engagement, and focused learning. It also involves addressing common challenges, such as distractions and academic pressure, while employing ethical strategies for maintaining focus and ensuring academic honesty. Ethical concentration is a fundamental aspect of a college student's academic journey, contributing to their overall success and growth.

Preparing for Assessments: Expected & Unexpected Questions on Assessments

College assessments, including exams and assignments, often include a mix of expected and unexpected questions. Preparing for these assessments requires a strategic approach to ensure academic success. We explore the importance of preparing for both types of questions, strategies to tackle them effectively, and the significance of such preparation in college education.

Comprehensive Understanding

Preparing for expected and unexpected questions is essential for developing a comprehensive understanding of course material. Expected questions typically address fundamental concepts and key facts that form the foundation of the subject, while unexpected questions challenge students to apply their knowledge in novel and complex situations (Gagne & Smith, 1962). This dual approach ensures that students cannot only recall essential information but also adapt their understanding to solve new problems and think critically about the material. By preparing for a range of question types, students build a robust grasp of the subject, enhancing their overall learning experience and academic performance.

Critical Thinking

Preparing for expected and unexpected questions plays a crucial role in developing critical thinking skills. Expected questions often require students to recall and articulate specific information learned during the course. In contrast, unexpected questions demand higher-order thinking, including analysis, synthesis, and problem-solving (Paul & Elder, 2006). By anticipating both types of questions, students cultivate the ability to remember facts and to apply and evaluate them in various contexts. This preparation fosters essential cognitive skills that are valuable for academic success and intellectual growth.

Exam Readiness

Effective preparation for expected and unexpected questions ensures that students are well-equipped for any exam scenario. Preparing for expected questions guarantees familiarity with the core content of the assessment, enabling students to handle standard queries confidently. Meanwhile, readiness for unexpected questions demonstrates adaptability and resilience, showcasing the students' ability to tackle novel challenges (Bransford & Schwartz, 1999). This dual approach not only improves exam performance but also builds skills that are crucial for problem-solving and critical thinking beyond the classroom.

Ethical Academic Integrity

A thorough approach to preparing for expected and unexpected questions aligns with the principles of ethical academic integrity. This preparation encourages students to engage deeply with the material and develop a well-rounded understanding, fostering honesty and fairness in their academic work (McCabe & Treviño, 1993). By thoroughly studying and anticipating various question types, students commit to authentic learning and avoid relying on shortcuts or unethical practices. This comprehensive preparation supports a fair academic environment and upholds the values of integrity and diligence.

Active Learning

Engaging actively with course material through strategies like note-taking, summarizing, and questioning is critical for adequate preparation. For expected questions, focus on recalling and understanding key concepts; for unexpected questions, practice applying and analyzing information (Bonwell & Eison, 1991). Active learning techniques encourage deeper cognitive processing and better retention of material. By actively participating in the learning process, students enhance their ability to handle predictable and unpredictable questions, leading to a more thorough and adaptable understanding of the subject matter.

Practice with Diverse Resources

Utilizing various resources, such as textbooks, supplementary readings, and online materials, is crucial for preparing for both expected and unexpected questions. Exposure to diverse sources of information helps students anticipate different types of questions and gain a more comprehensive understanding of the subject (Kuhlthau, 1993). By engaging with multiple resources, students can address gaps in their knowledge and develop a well-rounded perspective that enhances their ability to handle both familiar and unfamiliar questions.

Self-Assessment

Regular self-assessment is an effective strategy for preparing for expected and unexpected questions. By evaluating their knowledge and skills, students can ensure they provide accurate and detailed responses to expected questions and assess their ability to apply knowledge in novel contexts for unexpected questions (Butler & Winne, 1995). This ongoing evaluation helps students identify areas for improvement, adjust their study strategies, and build confidence in their ability to tackle various question types.

Review and Rehearse

Regularly reviewing course materials and practicing with past assessments is a crucial strategy for preparing for expected and unexpected questions. This approach familiarizes students with various question formats and helps refine their preparation techniques (Ambrose et al., 2010). By revisiting and rehearsing content, students can identify patterns, strengthen their understanding, and improve their ability to respond to different types of questions. This thorough preparation enhances overall exam readiness and academic performance.

Preparation for college assessments should encompass both expected and unexpected questions. Such an approach fosters a comprehensive understanding of the subject matter, enhances critical thinking skills, and aligns with ethical academic integrity. By actively engaging with the material, utilizing diverse resources, self-assessing, and reviewing regularly, students can effectively prepare for various questions they may encounter in their college assessments, ultimately contributing to their academic success.

Navigating Worries of Failure: Interruption of Thoughts

Worries of failure and interruptions of thoughts can significantly impede college success inside and outside the classroom. These concerns can affect students' academic performance, mental well-being, and overall learning experience. We explore the various aspects of worries related to failure and interruptions of thoughts, their impact on college success, and strategies to mitigate these challenges.

Academic Anxiety

Worries of failure frequently manifest as academic anxiety, a pervasive issue among college students. This anxiety is characterized by a deep-seated fear of not meeting academic expectations, performing poorly on exams, or failing courses, which can be overwhelming and disruptive to a student's educational experience (Cassady & Johnson, 2002). Academic anxiety not only affects students' mental well-being but can also impair their ability to perform effectively in their studies. The constant worry and stress associated with potential failure can create a barrier to learning, reducing overall academic achievement and quality of life.

Impacts on Concentration

Concerns about failure can significantly impact students' concentration and engagement in their coursework. When students are preoccupied with fears of not succeeding, they can be in a state of constant distraction, hindering their ability to focus deeply on academic tasks (Owens et al., 2008). This distraction can result in lower learning outcomes and academic performance, as students are unable to fully immerse themselves in their studies. The inability to concentrate effectively disrupts the learning process and can lead to a cycle of academic difficulties and stress.

Negative Self-Talk

The fear of failure often leads to negative self-talk, where students internalize self-doubt and question their abilities. This negative mindset can be detrimental not only to their academic performance but also to their overall well-being (Hartley, 2012). When students constantly undermine their capabilities, it undermines their motivation and confidence, leading to poorer academic outcomes and increased stress. Addressing and transforming negative self-talk is crucial for improving students' self-esteem and academic success.

Relationship with Procrastination

Worries of failure are often closely linked to procrastination. Students may delay tasks due to a fear of not meeting expectations, which creates a vicious cycle of increased stress and further academic challenges (Steel, 2007). Procrastination becomes a coping mechanism for dealing with the anxiety of potential failure, but it only exacerbates the problem by leading to rushed work and diminished quality. Understanding and addressing this relationship is essential for developing effective time management strategies and improving academic performance.

Cognitive Interruptions

Interruptions of thoughts, which can arise from external distractions, personal concerns, and technological disruptions, significantly hinder cognitive processes. These interruptions make it difficult for students to focus and engage in deep learning, as their attention is frequently diverted (Risko et al., 2012). The constant fragmentation of thought impairs students' ability to maintain sustained attention, reducing cognitive efficiency and learning outcomes.

Impaired Memory Retrieval

Frequent interruptions can negatively affect memory retrieval, affecting students' ability to recall information during exams or assignments. When cognitive processes are disrupted, it becomes challenging to access stored knowledge, leading to lower academic performance and hindered long-term knowledge retention (Hembrooke & Gay, 2003). Ensuring minimal interruptions and fostering an environment conducive to focus is essential for effective memory performance and academic success.

Disrupted Learning Flow

Interruptions of thought disrupt the natural learning flow, preventing students from fully immersing themselves in the educational experience. When students are frequently interrupted, it leads to frustration and decreased motivation, creating a sense of detachment from the learning process (Salvucci & Taatgen, 2008). This disruption affects the continuity of cognitive processes and can lead to reduced engagement and lower overall satisfaction with the learning experience.

Impact on Decision-Making

Constant interruptions can impair students' decision-making abilities, making it difficult to prioritize tasks, manage time effectively, and plan for academic success. This disruption in cognitive processes leads to stress and poor decision-making as students struggle to maintain an organized approach to their responsibilities (Baumeister et al., 2008). Effective time management and focus strategies are necessary to mitigate these impacts and support better decision-making in academic contexts.

Stress Management

Implementing stress management techniques is vital for addressing worries of failure. Techniques such as mindfulness practices, deep breathing exercises, and effective time management strategies can help alleviate anxiety and foster a positive mindset

(Shapiro et al., 2006). By managing stress effectively, students can reduce the impact of failure-related worries and maintain better academic performance and well-being.

Goal Setting and Planning

Establishing clear goals and creating a realistic plan to achieve them is an effective strategy for mitigating failure-related worries. By breaking down larger tasks into smaller, manageable steps, students can enhance clarity and reduce the overwhelming nature of academic challenges (Locke & Latham, 2002). This structured approach helps students stay focused and organized, making tracking progress and achieving academic success easier.

Building a Support System

Developing a strong support system, including friends, family, and mentors, is crucial for managing worries and interruptions that may impact college success. Emotional support provides students with outlets for expressing concerns and seeking guidance, essential for coping with academic pressures (Seeman, 2000). A well-established support network helps students navigate challenges and promotes resilience, contributing to a more successful academic experience.

Mindfulness and Focus Training

Mindfulness practices and focus training exercises are effective in managing interruptions of thoughts. Meditation and cognitive-behavioral strategies enhance students' attention and concentration, fostering a conducive learning environment (Lutz et al., 2008). By integrating mindfulness into their routines, students can improve their ability to stay focused and engaged in their studies, leading to better academic performance and well-being.

College students' worry of failure and interruptions of thoughts are pervasive challenges, impacting their academic success and overall well-being. By understanding the implications of these concerns and implementing effective strategies such as stress management, goal setting, building a support system, and mindfulness practices, students can navigate these challenges and cultivate an environment conducive to academic success inside and outside the classroom.

Note-taking Skills: (From books and lectures, before & after class)

Effective note-taking is a fundamental skill for college students, crucial for retaining and comprehending the vast amount of information presented in lectures, textbooks, and other learning materials. Proper note-taking techniques can significantly enhance the learning experience, making studying and performing well academically easier. We discuss some of the best practices for notetaking, drawing from the wisdom of educators and researchers in the field.

Actively Engage During Lectures

Actively engaging during lectures is vital for maximizing learning and retention. Simply recording information without interaction can lead to superficial understanding. Research by Kiewra (2002) emphasizes that students who participate actively in lectures—through asking questions, engaging in discussions, and connecting new information to existing knowledge—tend to have better recall and comprehension of the material. Active engagement involves not just listening but also interacting with the content, which helps in consolidating learning and making it more meaningful. For instance, asking clarifying questions or contributing to discussions can deepen understanding and reinforce memory. By relating lecture content to what they already know, students can better integrate new information and enhance their learning experience.

Choose the Right Note-Taking Method

Choosing an effective note-taking method is crucial for organizing and retaining lecture material. Two widely used techniques are the Cornell Method and the Outline Method. The Cornell Method, developed by Pauk (1974), involves dividing the page into three sections: a narrow left column for key points, a wider right column for detailed notes, and a summary section at the bottom. This approach helps in organizing information and encourages review and self-testing. Alternatively, the Outline Method uses a hierarchical structure to categorize information, making it easier to see the relationships between main ideas and supporting details. Selecting the method that aligns with your learning style and the nature of the content can significantly enhance the effectiveness of your notes and your ability to study from them.

Be Selective

Effective note-taking requires being selective about what to record. Rather than attempting to transcribe every word, focus on capturing the most critical information. Lang (2016) highlights that summarizing and paraphrasing during note-taking significantly improves retention. By distilling lectures into key concepts, definitions, and examples, students can better understand and remember the material. Avoiding verbatim transcription helps synthesize information and prevents cognitive overload. This selective approach not only aids in comprehension but also makes the review process more efficient, allowing students to focus on understanding the essential elements of the content.

Utilize Technology Wisely

In the digital age, technology offers numerous tools for note-taking, which can enhance organization and accessibility. Apps such as Evernote, OneNote, and Notion provide features for efficiently organizing, searching, and retrieving notes. These digital tools can help students manage large volumes of information and access their notes from various devices. However, it is crucial to use these technologies wisely by staying focused and avoiding distractions that can arise from digital devices. Balancing the advantages of digital note-taking with mindfulness about potential interruptions can lead to a more effective learning experience.

Stay Organized

Maintaining organization in note-taking is essential for effective studying and retrieval. Whether using a physical notebook or a digital platform, structured notes help review and understand material. Employing headers, bullet points, and numbering creates a clear and logical format while color coding can enhance visual clarity and ease of reference. A well-organized set of notes facilitates quicker review and better comprehension of complex information, making locating and understanding key concepts easier during study sessions.

Review and Revise Regularly

Regular review and revision of notes are critical for long-term retention. Roediger and Karpicke (2006) demonstrate that frequent retrieval practice, such as self-quizzing and using flashcards, significantly enhances memory retention. Incorporating a routine for reviewing and consolidating notes shortly after lectures helps reinforce learning and solidify understanding. By revisiting and revising notes, students can address gaps in their knowledge, improve recall, and prepare more effectively for exams.

Collaborate with Peers

Collaborative note-taking can offer substantial benefits by providing diverse perspectives and filling gaps in individual understanding. Sharing and discussing notes with peers allows students to compare interpretations and insights, leading to a more comprehensive understanding of the material. Collaboration also fosters a supportive learning environment where students receive feedback and clarification on complex topics. Group study sessions and note-sharing helps consolidate learning and can improve overall academic performance.

Effective notetaking is a vital skill for college students, and implementing best practices can significantly improve your academic success. You can optimize your note-taking process by actively engaging during lectures, choosing the right note-taking method, being selective in what you record, using technology wisely, staying organized, regularly reviewing your notes, and collaborating with peers. These strategies will not only help you succeed academically but also enhance your overall learning experience.

Follow-Through and Outcomes: The Impact of Good and Poor Intentions

Intentions play a pivotal role in a college student's academic journey. They reflect a student's commitment, motivation, and ethical integrity, influencing their follow-through and outcomes. We explore the significance of intentions in college, examine the impact of good and poor intentions on academic performance, and provide insights into fostering ethical integrity through intention setting.

The Role of Intentions

Ethical Integrity

Intentions are crucial in reflecting a student's ethical integrity within the college environment. By setting high ethical standards, students demonstrate a commitment to honesty, accountability, and academic integrity. McCabe and Treviño (1997) highlight that students with clear, ethically grounded intentions are likelier to adhere to principles of fairness and truthfulness in their academic pursuits. Ethical integrity is not merely about following rules but involves a proactive stance toward maintaining a high standard of academic conduct. This approach fosters a trustworthy educational atmosphere and ensures students value and uphold ethical norms, contributing positively to the academic community.

Motivation and Commitment

Good intentions are deeply connected to students' motivation and commitment to their academic goals. Deci and Ryan (2000) argue that intentions rooted in intrinsic motivation lead to higher levels of persistence and focus. When students have clear, well-defined intentions, they are more likely to stay committed to their studies, overcome obstacles, and achieve their academic objectives. This intrinsic motivation drives students to engage deeply with their coursework, maintain resilience in the face of challenges, and ultimately enhance their educational experience through sustained effort and dedication.

Goal Setting

Intentions are foundational for practical goal setting, serving as a precursor to defining concrete and measurable objectives. Locke and Latham (2002) emphasize that clear intentions lead to specific goals that direct students' efforts and decision-making processes throughout their academic journey. By establishing intentions, students create a roadmap for their academic success, outlining actionable steps and benchmarks for achievement. This structured approach enables them to focus their efforts, prioritize tasks, and navigate their educational paths more effectively, ultimately facilitating better performance and progress.

The Impact of Good Intentions on Follow-Through and Outcomes

Enhanced Follow-Through

Good intentions significantly enhance follow-through in academic endeavors. Students who cultivate clear, positive intentions are more likely to persist in their studies, complete assignments on time, and actively engage in their learning processes. According to Lent et al. (2017), well-defined intentions and aligned with personal goals lead to increased motivation and commitment, resulting in better academic behaviors and outcomes. By maintaining a focus on their intentions, students can navigate challenges more effectively, manage their time efficiently, and remain dedicated to their academic responsibilities.

Improved Academic Performance

The correlation between good intentions and academic performance is well-documented. When students have a strong intention to excel, they are more likely to exhibit dedication, adopt effective study habits, and achieve higher grades. Hattie (2012) demonstrates that students who set high academic intentions and work diligently toward them are often more successful in their academic pursuits. This dedication translates into better preparation for exams, a more thorough understanding of course material, and overall improved academic performance, highlighting the importance of intentionality in achieving educational success.

Ethical Academic Integrity

Students with good intentions are more likely to uphold ethical academic integrity. Bretag (2019) asserts that a commitment to honesty and fairness is rooted in the quality of one's intentions. When students genuinely intend to maintain academic integrity, they are less likely to engage in dishonest practices such as cheating or plagiarism. This adherence to ethical standards not only fosters a fair academic environment but also ensures that students' achievements are based on their own efforts, reflecting true academic merit and integrity.

The Impact of Poor Intentions and Fostering Ethical Integrity

Negative Outcomes

Poor intentions, such as a lack of motivation or unclear goals, can lead to several adverse academic outcomes. Students with weak intentions may struggle with procrastination, miss classes, or engage in unethical behaviors that undermine their academic performance. Steel (2007) highlights that such intentions often result in procrastination, exacerbating stress and hampers academic achievement. Without clear goals or motivation, students are more likely to face difficulties in maintaining focus, leading to underperformance and a diminished academic experience.

Promoting Ethical Integrity

Fostering ethical integrity through intention setting is essential for cultivating a culture of academic honesty. Moss and DeSousa (2005) suggest that encouraging students to set intentions that align with academic integrity and personal growth helps build a strong ethical foundation. By emphasizing the importance of ethical behavior and supporting ethical decisions, educators can guide students in developing intentions that support honesty and fairness. This proactive approach helps prevent unethical conduct and promotes a positive academic environment where integrity is valued and upheld.

Strategies for Ethical Intentions

Educators can be pivotal in guiding students to set and maintain ethical intentions. Fishman et al. (2018) advocate teaching ethical decision-making skills and providing resources supporting students facing ethical dilemmas. By highlighting the importance of ethical academic integrity and offering practical strategies for making ethical choices, educators can help students navigate academic challenges while adhering to ethical standards. Such guidance fosters a culture of integrity and prepares students to handle ethical issues effectively throughout their academic and professional careers.

Intentions reflect a student's ethical integrity and commitment to their academic goals. Good intentions enhance follow-through, improve academic performance, and uphold ethical academic integrity. In contrast, poor intentions can lead to negative outcomes. Fostering ethical integrity through intention setting is a collective responsibility, involving students, educators, and institutions. Students can achieve their academic goals by prioritizing ethical intentions while maintaining honesty, accountability, and a commitment to academic integrity.

Assurance of Learning Processes

Assurance of learning is a fundamental component of the educational process in college, ensuring that students acquire the knowledge and skills necessary for their academic and professional development. From the student's perspective, having a surety of learning processes is essential for motivation, engagement, and overall success. We explore what it means for students to have assurance of learning processes, the factors contributing to this confidence, and the importance of student engagement in shaping their educational experiences.

Understanding Assurance of Learning Processes

Assurance of Learning (AOL)

Assurance of Learning (AOL) is a critical component in higher education that focuses on systematically assessing and verifying that students meet the intended learning outcomes of their programs. This process involves a continuous cycle of evaluation, feedback, and reflection to maintain and enhance the quality of education. According to the Association to Advance Collegiate Schools of Business (AACSB) (2021), AOL is essential for ensuring that educational programs effectively prepare students to achieve their academic and professional goals. By integrating regular assessments and feedback mechanisms, institutions can systematically verify that students acquire the necessary skills and knowledge, promoting educational excellence and accountability.

Student Perspective

From the student's viewpoint, assurance of learning translates to confidence in the educational process, knowing that their efforts are directed toward achieving meaningful and purposeful outcomes. Students perceive assurance of learning as an assurance that their educational experience is aligned with their personal and professional goals, providing them with the necessary skills and knowledge to succeed. This trust in the process is crucial for maintaining motivation and engagement, as students are more likely to be invested in their learning when they believe that the program is effectively supporting their growth and valuing their contributions.

Elements of AOL

Assurance of Learning (AOL) encompasses several key elements contributing to a robust educational framework. Pettit (2018) identifies these elements as clear program objectives, relevant and well-designed assessments, supportive faculty, and opportunities for reflection and improvement. Each component is crucial in ensuring that students understand what is expected of them, receive constructive feedback, and have access to the resources needed to enhance their learning. This comprehensive approach not only fosters students' trust in the educational process but also helps institutions continuously improve their programs to meet student needs better and achieve educational goals.

Factors Contributing to Assurance of Learning

Clear Program Objectives

Clear program objectives are fundamental to providing students with a structured roadmap for their educational journey. Maki (2010) emphasizes that well-defined objectives help students understand the goals and expectations of their program, making it easier for them to align their efforts with these targets. When students know what they need to achieve, they can more effectively focus their studies and measure their progress, leading to greater assurance in the learning process. Clearly articulated objectives also contribute to a more transparent educational experience, enhancing students' confidence that their program is designed to support their academic and career aspirations.

Ongoing Assessment

Ongoing assessment is crucial in reinforcing assurance of learning, as it provides students with regular feedback on their performance and progress. Suskie (2018) points out that both formative and summative assessments are essential for helping students gauge their understanding and identify areas for improvement. Continuous feedback allows students to adjust their learning strategies and focus on areas where they may need additional support, increasing their confidence in the learning process and enhancing their overall academic performance.

Supportive Faculty

The role of faculty in fostering assurance of learning cannot be overstated. Cuseo (2007) highlights that faculty members who provide support, guidance, and mentorship significantly enhance students' confidence in their educational experience. When students perceive that their instructors are genuinely invested in their success, they are more likely to feel supported and motivated to excel. Faculty support includes academic guidance and emotional encouragement, which collectively contributes to a positive learning environment and reinforces students' trust in the educational process.

The Importance of Student Engagement

Active Participation

Active participation is a cornerstone of effective learning and is integral to the assurance of learning. Kuh (2008) asserts that students who actively engage in classes, discussions, projects, and extracurricular activities are likelier to experience a richer educational experience. Engagement not only enhances students' understanding of course material but also reinforces their confidence in the learning process. By actively participating, students contribute to a dynamic learning environment and take ownership of their educational journey, further supporting their academic growth and success.

Reflection and Improvement

Engagement in reflection and improvement is a key aspect of the learning process that fosters continuous growth. Chickering and Gamson (1987) argue that when students actively reflect on their learning experiences, they become more aware of their strengths and areas for improvement. This reflective practice encourages students to actively participate in their education, making adjustments as needed to enhance their learning outcomes. By continuously evaluating their experiences and striving for improvement, students contribute to their personal development and maintain a high level of engagement in their academic pursuits.

Lifelong Learning

The assurance of learning experienced during college significantly influences students' perspectives on lifelong learning. Merriam and Bierema (2014) emphasize that when students feel confident in their educational processes and outcomes, they are more likely to view learning as a continuous journey rather than a finite experience. This positive perspective encourages students to seek out new knowledge and personal development opportunities throughout their lives, reinforcing the value of education beyond the college years and contributing to their ongoing growth and adaptability.

Assurance of learning from the student perspective is characterized by confidence in the educational process, clear program objectives, ongoing assessment, supportive faculty, and active engagement. It is a multifaceted concept that influences student motivation, engagement, and lifelong learning. Fostering assurance of learning is a shared responsibility between students, educators, and institutions, as it directly impacts the quality and effectiveness of higher education.

Test Preparations

Test preparation is a crucial aspect of the college experience, and ethical integrity should be at the core of these practices. Preparing for exams with honesty and fairness not only leads to better academic outcomes but also contributes to personal growth. We explore best practices for test preparation in college, emphasizing ethical practices.

Understanding the Importance of Ethical Test Preparation

Academic Integrity

Ethical test preparation is fundamentally tied to the principles of academic integrity, which are crucial for maintaining fairness and honesty in education. Upholding academic integrity ensures that students earn their grades based on their own efforts rather than through dishonest means. As Bretag (2019) highlights, maintaining these ethical standards is vital for preserving the value of academic qualifications and fostering a fair educational environment. Students who adhere to these principles contribute to a culture of trust and fairness and develop a solid personal and academic reputation that benefits their long-term academic and professional careers.

Long-Term Success

Ethical test preparation extends beyond merely passing exams; it is integral to acquiring knowledge and skills to serve students well into their future careers. Engaging in ethical practices during test preparation helps build a solid foundation of understanding and competence, which is crucial for long-term success. Gall (2018) argues that students who commit to ethical preparation practices not only perform better academically but also develop a more profound and lasting grasp of their field, which supports their future professional endeavors and lifelong learning.

Personal Development

Engaging in ethical test preparation fosters significant personal growth, including developing responsibility and self-discipline. According to Jennings (2018), adhering to ethical standards reinforces the value of hard work and cultivates effective study habits. This approach encourages students to take ownership of their learning process, promoting resilience and perseverance. Through ethical preparation, students improve their academic performance also enhance their personal development, leading to a more disciplined and responsible approach to their education and future challenges.

Respect for Peers

Ethical test preparation is crucial for showing respect toward peers and maintaining the integrity of the learning community. By avoiding dishonest practices, students ensure that everyone has an equal opportunity to succeed based on their abilities and efforts. McCabe and Treviño (1997) emphasize that adherence to ethical standards prevents unfair advantages and supports a fair testing environment, which is essential for fostering mutual respect among students and upholding the values of the academic community.

Best Practices for Ethical Test Preparation

Time Management

Effective time management is a cornerstone of ethical test preparation. Developing a structured study schedule allows students to allocate adequate time for review and breaks, avoiding the pitfalls of last-minute cramming. Macan et al. (1990) suggest that a well-organized study plan enhances comprehension and retention and reduces the likelihood of engaging in unethical behaviors associated with poor preparation. By managing their time effectively, students can approach their exams with confidence and integrity.

Active Learning

Active learning is essential for ethical test preparation and involves engaging deeply with course material throughout the semester. By attending classes regularly, taking comprehensive notes, and seeking clarification on difficult concepts, students can foster a deeper understanding of the subject matter. Bonwell and Eison (1991) argue that active learning techniques help reduce the need for unethical shortcuts, such as cheating or last-minute cramming, by promoting thorough and continuous engagement with the content. This approach not only improves academic performance but also reinforces ethical study habits.

Practice with Integrity

Maintaining ethical integrity when utilizing resources for exam preparation is crucial. Students should avoid seeking or sharing unauthorized exam content, as this compromises the fairness of the assessment process. Lang (2013) emphasizes that practicing ethical behavior when using previous exams or study aids ensures that students are prepared fairly and justly. By adhering to these principles, students contribute to a more equitable educational environment and uphold the standards of academic integrity.

Test Anxiety Management

Managing test anxiety through ethical means is essential for maintaining academic integrity. Students should seek support from counselors, faculty, or academic advisors when experiencing anxiety, rather than resorting to dishonest practices. Zeidner (1998) highlights that addressing anxiety ethically through techniques such as relaxation exercises or counseling helps students cope with stress in a constructive manner. This approach not only supports better academic performance but also aligns with the principles of honesty and fairness in education.

Tools and Resources for Ethical Test Preparation

Academic Integrity Workshops

Institutions can enhance students' understanding of ethical test preparation through academic integrity workshops. These workshops educate students about the importance of maintaining academic honesty and provide practical strategies for effective study and time management. McCabe and Pavela (2000) suggest that such workshops play a pivotal role in promoting a culture of integrity by equipping students with the knowledge and skills to approach their studies ethically and responsibly.

Online Resources

Online platforms offer valuable resources for ethical test preparation, including guidance on maintaining academic integrity and developing responsible study habits. Websites like Turnitin provide tools and information to help students understand and uphold ethical standards in their academic work. According to Turnitin (n.d.), these online resources help students avoid plagiarism and cheating by offering tools and advice for ethical behavior in academic settings.

Supportive Faculty

Faculty are critical in promoting ethical test preparation by providing clear guidelines and support. Driscoll (2014) notes that instructors who offer transparent expectations and are available to assist students facing challenges contribute significantly to fostering a culture of academic integrity. By supporting students through clear communication and guidance, faculty help ensure that ethical standards are maintained and that students have the resources they need to succeed honestly.

Ethical integrity should be at the heart of test preparation in college. It is essential for academic success, personal development, and a respectful and fair learning environment. Best practices for ethical test preparation involve time management, active learning, practice with integrity, and effective test anxiety management. Institutions and educators are vital in providing resources and support for ethical test preparation, ultimately contributing to a positive learning experience.

Role of Memory in Learning

Short-Term and Long-Term Memory

Memory is a fundamental cognitive process that plays a critical role in learning and academic success for college students. Understanding the intricacies of short-term and long-term memory is essential for educators and students alike. We delve into short-term and long-term memory use in the context of learning for college students, providing insights into their functioning, interplay, and practical implications.

Short-Term Memory (STM) in College Learning

Definition of Short-Term Memory

Short-term memory, or working memory, is a cognitive system responsible for temporarily holding and processing information. This type of memory has a limited capacity, typically allowing the retention of about seven items or chunks of information for a brief period, usually from a few seconds to a minute. According to Baddeley (2003), short-term memory is crucial for immediate tasks and cognitive operations, as it facilitates the temporary storage and manipulation of information necessary for ongoing activities and decision-making.

Role in College Learning

In college learning, short-term memory is essential for handling information that students need to process in real time. It temporarily stores data while students engage in activities such as taking notes, solving problems, or comprehending new concepts. Cowan (2008) highlights that effective use of short-term memory allows students to maintain focus on the task at hand, enabling them to manage and integrate new information effectively before it is either discarded or transferred to long-term memory.

Practical Implications

Maximizing the capacity and efficiency of short-term memory can significantly benefit college students. Strategies such as active listening, effective note-taking, and breaking complex information into smaller, manageable chunks can enhance short-term memory function. Mayer (2014) emphasizes that these practices help maintain focus and organization, which are essential for efficiently processing and recalling information during and after lectures, leading to improved academic performance.

Long-Term Memory (LTM) in College Learning

Definition of Long-Term Memory

Long-term memory is the system responsible for storing information over extended periods, ranging from hours to an entire lifetime. It has a vast capacity and encompasses two main types: explicit (declarative) memory, which includes episodic and semantic memory, and implicit (procedural) memory, which involves skills and habits. Schacter et al. (2015) describe long-term memory as fundamental for retaining and recalling information beyond immediate tasks, enabling accumulating knowledge and experiences over time.

Role in College Learning

In college learning, long-term memory plays a pivotal role in retaining and retrieving knowledge acquired through courses, readings, and academic experiences. Anderson et al. (2000) point out that long-term memory allows students to build upon prior knowledge, facilitating deeper understanding and integrating new information. Effective learning relies on the ability to store and access this knowledge, which supports academic success and the application of learned concepts in various contexts.

Practical Implications

To enhance long-term memory, college students should employ spaced repetition, which involves revisiting material at increasing intervals, and elaborative encoding, which connects new information to existing knowledge. Dunlosky et al. (2013) suggest that incorporating self-testing and active recall techniques can improve long-term retention and understanding of academic material. These strategies aid in memorization and facilitate a deeper grasp of content.

The Interplay between STM and LTM in College Learning

Encoding and Transfer

Effective encoding in short-term memory is essential for transferring information to long-term memory. Roediger and Karpicke (2006) emphasize that active engagement with material, such as making connections and rehearsing information, enhances the likelihood of retention in long-term memory. When students actively process and organize information during encoding, they facilitate its consolidation and retrieval in the future, making it more accessible for academic tasks and long-term learning.

Retrieval and Application

Retrieving information from long-term memory involves complex processes influenced by how information is encoded and organized. Bjork and Bjork (2011) highlight that effective retrieval is about accessing stored information and about how well it is integrated and organized within the memory system. The interplay between encoding and retrieval processes underscores the importance of employing effective study techniques to enhance both the storage and recall of academic material.

Implications for Learning

Understanding the interplay between short-term and long-term memory is crucial for effective college learning. By applying study techniques that improve encoding and retrieval, such as spaced repetition and self-testing, students can enhance the transfer of information from short-term to long-term memory. Pashler et al. (2007) argue that these techniques improve academic performance and deepen comprehension and retention of learned material, ultimately contributing to a more successful educational experience.

Memory, encompassing both short-term and long-term memory systems, plays a pivotal role in college learning. College students' capacity to actively engage with and manage information in their short-term memory while effectively encoding and retrieving it for long-term storage is essential for academic success. Educators and students alike can benefit from a deeper understanding of memory processes, enabling the development of effective learning strategies to optimize memory's role in education.

"Cramming" Pros and Cons: Memorization vs. Understanding

The debate over memorization versus understanding in the context of college learning, particularly when it comes to cramming, is ongoing. Memorization can be a valuable tool for short-term knowledge acquisition, but it may come at the cost of deep understanding. We explore the advantages and disadvantages of memorization, particularly cramming, and its impact on college students.

Advantages of Memorization (Cramming)

Immediate Recall

Memorization through cramming provides a rapid method for recalling information, which can be particularly advantageous during exams or assignments requiring immediate answers. This approach allows students to quickly access facts, definitions, and formulae, essential for performance in high-pressure situations. Kornell et al. (2009) emphasize that while cramming is not ideal for long-term learning, it can be effective for short-term recall, helping students retrieve necessary information under timed conditions.

Time Efficiency

Cramming is often used as a time-efficient strategy, especially when students face tight deadlines or have multiple exams approaching. This method allows for the quick review of a large volume of material, which can be critical in the demanding college environment. Roediger and Karpicke (2006) note that while cramming might not be the most effective for long-term learning, it enables students to cover extensive material in a condensed period, making it a practical approach when time is limited.

Performance Enhancement

For sure students, memorization through cramming can enhance performance, particularly in subjects requiring extensive rote learning. This approach can help students achieve short-term goals, such as passing exams, by focusing on immediate recall of key facts. Agarwal et al. (2008) suggest that although cramming may not support deep understanding, it can be effective for achieving high performance in exams where rote memorization is essential.

Disadvantages of Memorization (Cramming)

Limited Retention

One major drawback of cramming is its impact on long-term retention. The information learned through intense, short-term study is often quickly forgotten after the exam, limiting its utility for future courses or applications. Cepeda et al. (2006) found that cramming does not support retaining information over extended periods, making it less effective for building a foundation of knowledge that can be used in subsequent academic endeavors.

Shallow Understanding

Cramming often results in superficial learning, where students may remember facts but lack a deeper understanding of the material. This approach can hinder students' ability to apply concepts in complex problem-solving scenarios or real-world situations. Dunlosky et al. (2013) argue that without a deep engagement with the material, students may struggle to transfer knowledge effectively and apply it in diverse contexts.

Stress and Burnout

The pressure associated with cramming can increase stress and burnout among students. The intense focus required to absorb large amounts of information in a short period can be overwhelming, negatively affecting mental health and overall well-being. Ku (2016) highlights that the stress from cramming can contribute to burnout, reducing students' ability to engage in their studies effectively and maintain a healthy academic life.

Finding a Balance

Effective Learning Strategies

To balance memorization with deeper learning, students should employ strategies that enhance understanding and retention. Techniques such as spaced repetition, which involves reviewing material at increasing intervals, and retrieval practice, which focuses on actively recalling information, can improve long-term learning outcomes. Dunlosky et al. (2013) suggest that these strategies not only help with retention but also promote a deeper understanding of the material, making them more effective than cramming alone.

Contextual Relevance

While memorization is sometimes necessary for foundational knowledge, it is also essential for students to connect facts and concepts to real-world applications. Bransford et al. (2000) emphasize that understanding the relevance of information and relating it to practical scenarios can enhance learning and retention. Students should aim to integrate memorized information with deeper insights into how it applies beyond exams, fostering a more comprehensive grasp of their subjects.

Time Management

Effective time management is essential for optimizing learning outcomes. Relying solely on cramming can be detrimental, so students should use this technique sparingly and incorporate regular study sessions into their schedules. Macan et al. (1990) suggest that a well-structured study plan that includes periodic reviews and practice is more conducive to long-term retention and understanding, helping students manage their workload and academic responsibilities more effectively.

Memorization can be a double-edged sword in college education, especially through cramming. While it can be a quick fix for short-term knowledge acquisition, it often leads to limited retention and shallow understanding. To strike a balance, students should consider the context and relevance of memorization and employ effective learning strategies that emphasize understanding while retaining information. Ultimately, the key to successful college learning is finding the right equilibrium between memorization and comprehension.

CHAPTER 3

Institutional Detractors

Issues and Concerns

College students today face various challenges and concerns while pursuing higher education. We explore some of the critical issues and concerns vocalized by college students, and the impact of these challenges on their academic and personal experiences. The concerns presented are based on the student's voices and supported by relevant sources and research.

Financial Struggles and Student Debt

Rising Tuition Costs

The escalating cost of tuition is a primary concern for college students, contributing to significant financial stress and making higher education less accessible for many. Baum and Ma (2018) highlight that rising tuition fees have outpaced inflation and income growth, placing a considerable financial burden on students and their families. This trend has led to increased reliance on student loans and financial aid, exacerbating the financial strain experienced by students. The growing expense of college education affects students' ability to afford it and contributes to long-term financial insecurity and anxiety about future repayment.

Student Debt Burden

The burden of student loan debt has become a pressing issue, with many students expressing deep concerns about the long-term implications of their loans on financial stability. Dynarski (2015) reports that student debt has reached unprecedented levels, affecting graduates' ability to achieve financial independence, purchase homes, and save for retirement. This growing debt burden can lead to significant stress and anxiety as students worry about managing their finances in the years following graduation. The long-term financial impact of student loans can also affect career choices and overall life satisfaction.

Impact on Mental Health

Financial concerns, including rising tuition and student debt, can have severe effects on students' mental health, leading to increased stress, anxiety, and decreased academic performance. Hunt and Eisenberg (2010) emphasize that the pressure to manage educational expenses can overwhelm students, negatively impacting their emotional well-being and academic success. Financial stress can exacerbate mental health issues, leading to a cycle of anxiety and reduced academic performance. Addressing financial struggles is crucial to improving students' mental health and academic outcomes.

Mental Health and Well-Being

Stigma Around Mental Health

The stigma surrounding mental health issues often prevents college students from seeking the help they need. Eisenberg et al. (2009) note that many students avoid accessing mental health services due to fear of judgment or perceived weakness. This stigma can exacerbate mental health problems and delay necessary treatment, leading to worsening conditions and decreased academic performance. Efforts to reduce stigma and increase awareness about mental health are essential for encouraging students to seek support and improve their overall well-being.

Limited Access to Counseling

Limited access to counseling services is a common issue on many college campuses, with students often facing long waiting times for appointments. Lipson et al. (2018) highlight that inadequate availability of mental health resources can delay crucial support for students in need. The challenge of accessing timely counseling can lead to increased stress and unresolved mental health issues, impacting students' academic performance and overall well-being. Improving access to mental health services is critical for supporting student success and addressing mental health concerns effectively.

Academic Impact

Mental health concerns can significantly influence academic performance, with students often facing difficulties due to a lack of understanding or support from faculty and administration. Eisenberg et al. (2009) discuss how mental health issues can lead to decreased academic engagement, lower grades, and higher dropout rates. Students may feel frustrated when their mental health needs are not adequately addressed or understood by their institutions, underscoring the importance of integrating mental health support with academic resources.

Diversity, Inclusion, and Campus Climate

Campus Climate

Concerns about campus climate and inclusivity, particularly racial and ethnic diversity, are significant issues for many college students. Rankin and Reason (2008) highlight those experiences of discrimination, microaggressions, and exclusion can undermine students' sense of belonging and negatively affect their academic and social experiences. A positive and inclusive campus climate fosters a supportive environment where all students feel valued and respected. Institutions need to address these concerns proactively to enhance students' overall college experience.

Lack of Representation

Students frequently express concerns about the need for more representation of diverse voices within the curriculum, faculty, and administrative roles. Milem (2003) points out that increased diversity and inclusion initiatives are necessary to address these concerns and ensure that diverse perspectives are represented and valued. Representation in these areas is essential for creating an equitable learning environment that reflects and supports all students' diverse backgrounds and experiences.

Bias Incidents

Bias incidents and hate crimes on college campuses are critical concerns that affect student safety and institutional responses. Sue (2010) discusses how such incidents can create an unsafe and unwelcoming environment for affected students, impacting their academic and personal lives. Institutions must address these incidents promptly and effectively, supporting affected students and fostering a campus culture that actively combats bias and discrimination.

Educational institutions should actively listen to their students' voices and prioritize creating a supportive and inclusive environment. Policies and resources that address financial stress enhance mental health support, and promote diversity and inclusion can help alleviate these concerns and contribute to a positive and enriching college experience for all students.

Concerns Regarding Various Campus Environments

The physical infrastructure and learning environment on college campuses significantly shape students' educational experiences. We delve into the concerns and issues college students voiced about physical buildings and their locations, class size, class quality and locations, and the availability of adequate study facilities. Each section elaborates to provide an understanding of the challenges and their impact on students' academic journeys.

College campuses also serve as students' physical and social backdrop during their academic journeys. We also delve into the issues and concerns college students vocalize about other aspects of campus life, including campus size, housing, student demographics, campus safety and security, accessibility, and environmental considerations. Each section elaborates to provide an understanding of these challenges and their impact on students' overall college experience.

Physical Buildings and Locations

Aging Infrastructure

College campuses frequently face issues related to aging infrastructure, which can significantly impact students' learning experiences and overall comfort. Students often report problems such as leaky roofs, malfunctioning heating and cooling systems, and outdated classroom technology (Bresciani & Gardner, 2015). These issues disrupt the learning environment and can also detract from students' focus and engagement. For example, a malfunctioning HVAC system can create an uncomfortable learning atmosphere, affecting students' ability to concentrate and participate effectively in class.

Moreover, the maintenance of older buildings can often be neglected due to budget constraints, exacerbating the problem. Persistent infrastructure problems can lead to more severe consequences, such as safety hazards or further deterioration of facilities. Addressing these issues requires a proactive approach to campus maintenance and modernization to ensure students benefit from a safe and functional learning environment.

Accessibility Challenges

Accessibility challenges on college campuses are a significant concern, especially for students with disabilities. Many older buildings and facilities may not fully comply with the Americans with Disabilities Act (ADA), making it difficult for these students to navigate the campus effectively (Moore et al., 2018). The absence of essential features such as ramps, elevators, and appropriate signage can hinder students' mobility and ability to participate fully in campus life. This lack of accessibility not only affects students' physical mobility but can also impact their academic performance and overall college experience.

Efforts to improve accessibility should include regular assessments of campus facilities and updates to ensure compliance with ADA standards. Providing accessible learning spaces and accommodations is crucial for creating an inclusive environment that supports all students. Enhanced accessibility features can improve students' academic performance, participation, and overall satisfaction with their college experience.

Location Inconvenience

Students often need help with the location of certain academic buildings, particularly when these buildings are situated far from the central campus or other essential services. The inconvenience of traveling long distances between classes can lead to transportation issues and time constraints (Bresciani & Gardner,

2015). For example, a class held in a remote building might require students to navigate through poorly lit areas or crowded campus routes, which can be both physically and mentally taxing.

Furthermore, inconvenient building locations can disrupt students' schedules and impact their ability to participate in extracurricular activities or access campus resources. Effective campus planning and building placement are essential to minimizing these inconveniences and enhancing students' overall campus experience.

Class Size, Class Quality, and Locations

Overcrowded Classrooms

Overcrowded classrooms are prevalent on many college campuses, significantly impacting students' educational experiences. In large classes, students may have limited opportunities for meaningful engagement with professors and reduced interaction with peers, which can negatively impact their learning and satisfaction (Cuseo et al., 2016). The lack of personalized attention and the challenge of participating in discussions can diminish the overall quality of education and student outcomes.

Additionally, overcrowding can lead to logistical problems such as insufficient seating and inadequate space for group activities, further detracting from the learning environment. Institutions must address these challenges by considering class sizes when planning course offerings and ensuring that resources are allocated to maintain manageable student-to-faculty ratios.

Varied Quality

The quality of classrooms and educational technology can vary significantly across college campuses, impacting students' learning experiences. Some students report attending classes in outdated rooms with inadequate technological resources, making it challenging to engage with course material effectively (Chick et al., 2009). The inconsistency in classroom quality can create disparities in the learning environment, with some students benefiting from modern facilities while others face outdated and poorly equipped spaces.

This uneven quality can also influence students' perceptions of their education and the institution's commitment to providing a high-quality learning environment. Investing in modernizing classroom facilities and ensuring that all students have access to up-to-date technology is essential for maintaining equitable educational opportunities.

Remote Class Locations

Having classes located in distant or inconvenient areas of the campus can pose challenges for students, impacting their overall college experience. Students often spend considerable time traveling between classes, which can lead to increased stress and reduced efficiency in managing their schedules (Cuseo et al., 2016). This time-consuming commute can also detract from students' ability to participate in campus activities or utilize academic resources effectively.

Addressing remote class locations involves evaluating campus layout and considering strategies to improve accessibility and convenience for students. Efforts to streamline campus operations and ensure that academic buildings are centrally located can enhance students' overall experience and academic success.

Adequate Study Facilities

Limited Study Spaces

Adequate study spaces are crucial for student success, yet many students need more quiet and well-equipped areas for studying (Kuh et al., 2006). Overcrowded libraries and competition for study rooms can create frustration and hinder students' ability to focus and prepare effectively for exams and assignments. The lack of sufficient study facilities can also impact students' ability to collaborate with peers and engage in group work, which is essential for many academic programs.

Institutions should prioritize creating and maintaining study spaces that cater to different needs, including quiet individual study areas and collaborative workspaces. Expanding and improving study facilities can help alleviate these concerns and support students in achieving their academic goals.

Accessibility to Resources

Access to academic resources such as textbooks, library materials, and support services is a critical concern for many students (Houck et al., 2018). The high cost of textbooks and limited availability of required materials can pose significant barriers to academic success. Additionally, students may need help accessing academic support services due to long wait times or limited operating hours.

Improving access to academic resources involves addressing cost and availability issues, such as implementing textbook rental programs and expanding library hours. Ensuring that students have equitable access to the necessary resources is essential for supporting their academic achievement and overall success.

Campus Size

Overwhelming Campus Size

The size of a college campus can be overwhelming for students, especially during their initial transition to university life (Pike, 2011). Navigating a large campus can be time-consuming and confusing, leading to feeling overwhelmed and disconnected from the college community. New students may struggle to find their way around, impacting their comfort and sense of belonging on campus.

Institutions can mitigate these challenges by providing comprehensive orientation programs, clear campus maps, and navigational aids. Efforts to foster a sense of community and support students in acclimating to campus life can help ease the transition and enhance students' overall experience.

Limited Sense of Community

Large campus sizes can lead to a diminished sense of community, making it difficult for students to form close-knit relationships and feel a part of the university (Tinto, 1993). Students may experience a sense of anonymity, which can affect their engagement and satisfaction with their college experience. A strong sense of community is essential for fostering student involvement and overall well-being.

Colleges and universities should implement initiatives that promote community-building, such as smaller learning communities, student organizations, and social events. Creating opportunities for meaningful interactions can help students develop a sense of belonging and improve their overall college experience.

Housing

Housing Shortages

Housing shortages on or near college campuses are a significant concern for many students (Gardner & Holley, 2011). Limited affordable and adequate housing availability can make securing suitable accommodations challenging for students, leading to additional stress and logistical issues. This problem can be particularly acute in high-demand areas or institutions with limited on-campus housing options.

Institutions can address housing shortages by investing in new housing developments, expanding existing facilities, and offering support to students in securing off-campus accommodations. Ensuring all students have access to affordable and suitable housing is crucial for their overall college experience and success.

Housing Costs

The high cost of on-campus housing or rent in surrounding areas can be a significant financial burden for students (Houck et al., 2018). This financial strain can impact students' ability to focus on their academics and lead to additional stress. The cost of housing can also affect students' overall quality of life and academic performance.

To alleviate housing cost concerns, institutions should explore options for more affordable on-campus housing and offer financial support or resources to help students manage their housing expenses. Reducing the financial burden associated with housing can improve students' academic outcomes and overall satisfaction with their college experience.

Student Demographics

Lack of Diversity

The lack of diversity on college campuses can be a significant concern for students, as it may limit exposure to different perspectives and hinder cultural exchange (Hurtado et al., 2012). A homogeneous student body can stifle meaningful discussions on social and cultural topics and prevent the enrichment from a diverse academic community.

Colleges and universities should prioritize diversity and inclusion initiatives to create a more representative and inclusive campus environment. This includes recruiting a diverse student body, faculty, and staff and fostering an environment that supports cultural exchange and understanding.

Diversity Challenges

Students from underrepresented backgrounds, such as first-generation college students, often face specific challenges related to diversity and support (Strayhorn, 2012). These students may encounter difficulties accessing resources and support tailored to their unique needs, impacting their academic success and overall college experience.

To address these challenges, Institutions should develop targeted support services and programs for underrepresented students. Providing mentorship, academic advising, and other resources can help these students navigate their college experience and achieve their academic goals.

Campus Safety and Security

Safety Concerns

Campus safety and security are critical concerns for students, who often express worries about crime rates, lighting, and emergency response protocols (Fisher et al., 2016). Ensuring a safe campus environment is essential for student's well-being and overall satisfaction with their college experience. Safety concerns can affect students' comfort and willingness to engage in campus life, including extracurricular activities and late-night events.

Universities should invest in comprehensive safety measures, including improved lighting, regular safety audits, and effective emergency response protocols. Engaging students in safety initiatives and providing clear communication about campus safety can also enhance students' sense of security.

Mental Health Support

Many students feel that the mental health support services on campus are inadequate, especially given the increasing awareness of mental health challenges (Kadison & DiGeronimo, 2004). Insufficient mental health resources can lead to delays in receiving necessary care and contribute to students' overall stress and mental health issues.

Colleges and universities should prioritize investing in mental health services and support, including counseling, workshops, and crisis intervention. Providing accessible and effective mental health resources is crucial for supporting students' well-being and academic success.

Accessibility

Limited Accessibility

Accessibility issues extend beyond physical disabilities, affecting students with family responsibilities or off-campus jobs (Dolan, 2015). These students may struggle to access academic and support services during non-standard hours, impacting their ability to effectively balance academic and personal responsibilities.

Institutions can address these challenges by offering flexible service hours, online resources, and alternative access options. Improving accessibility for all students, including those with diverse needs and schedules, can enhance their college experience and success.

Digital Accessibility

The accessibility of digital resources and online learning platforms is an increasingly important concern, particularly for students from underserved communities (Gronseth et al., 2020). The digital divide can hinder educational experiences and limit opportunities for students who need access to reliable technology or high-speed internet.

To address digital accessibility, institutions should ensure that online resources and platforms are designed to be inclusive and accessible to all students. Supporting technology access and digital literacy can help bridge the digital divide and improve educational outcomes.

Environmental Considerations

Sustainability

Students are increasingly concerned about sustainability and environmental practices on their campuses, including efforts related to recycling, energy consumption, and transportation options (Lamb et al., 2016). Institutions are increasingly demanding to adopt more sustainable practices and reduce their environmental footprint.

Institutions can respond to these concerns by implementing comprehensive sustainability programs and engaging students in environmental initiatives. Promoting recycling, reducing energy consumption, and supporting sustainable transportation options are key strategies for addressing students' environmental concerns.

Climate Impact

The impact of climate change and environmental issues is a growing concern for students, who are actively involved in discussions and activism related to these topics (Leal Filho et al., 2021). Students are calling for more sustainable campus practices and advocating for actions to address climate change.

Colleges and universities should prioritize climate action and sustainability initiatives, incorporating students' perspectives and involvement in these efforts. Engaging students in sustainability practices and providing opportunities for environmental activism can enhance their college experience and contribute to broader climate action goals.

Impact on Students

Student's various concerns regarding physical buildings, class sizes, housing, and other aspects of campus life directly impact their academic performance, mental well-being, and overall satisfaction with their college experience. Problems such as inadequate infrastructure, inconvenient class locations, and limited study spaces can create stressful learning environments and hinder students' ability to focus on their studies (Kuh et al., 2006; Bresciani & Gardner, 2015). These challenges can lead to frustration and decreased academic success, emphasizing the need for institutional improvements.

Addressing these concerns requires a comprehensive approach that includes investing in campus infrastructure, improving accessibility, and ensuring adequate resources and support services. Addressing the challenges related to physical facilities, class quality, and student resources, colleges, and universities can enhance the overall college experience and support students' academic and personal development. Engaging with student feedback and implementing evidence-based solutions is essential for creating a supportive and enriching educational environment.

Student's additional concerns regarding campus size, housing, diversity, safety, and environmental considerations significantly shape their college experience. Addressing these issues requires a collaborative effort between students, institutions, and policymakers to create a more inclusive and supportive campus environment. By actively listening to student voices and implementing strategies to address these challenges, colleges and universities can enhance students' overall experience and promote a more equitable and successful educational journey.

Personal Detractors

Issues and Concerns

College life is a transformative period where students embark on academic, personal, and social growth. However, this phase is not without its challenges. Personal detractors, comprising a range of issues and concerns, can significantly impact college students' overall well-being and academic success. We will delve into prominent personal detractors faced by college students. College students may face various personal detractors, barriers, issues, and concerns that can impact their academic success and well-being. Here are examples of potential ways to overcome them:

Overcoming Financial Stress:

Financial stress is a pervasive issue for many college students, often stemming from high tuition costs, textbooks, and living expenses. Mitigating these challenges requires a multifaceted approach that combines proactive financial planning, seeking external financial support, and developing essential financial literacy skills.

Part-Time Employment

Taking on part-time employment during college can be a valuable way for students to generate a steady income stream to cover educational and living expenses. Many students find that working part-time provides financial relief, practical experience, and skills that can enhance their resumes. However, students must balance their work commitments with academic responsibilities to avoid compromising academic performance. Research conducted by the Institute for Research on Poverty (IRP, 2018) demonstrates that students who work moderate hours—typically up to 15-20 hours per week—tend to experience positive effects on their academic performance. This balance allows students to manage their time effectively, gain work experience, and maintain a focus on their studies.

Nevertheless, students must be mindful of the potential drawbacks of part-time employment, such as increased stress and potential impacts on academic engagement. Overworking can lead to burnout and negatively affect academic performance and overall well-being. It is essential for students to carefully assess their work schedules and academic workload to ensure they do not overextend themselves. Institutions can support students by providing flexible work opportunities and time management resources to help them successfully balance work and academics.

Budgeting and Financial Literacy

Developing a budget is a crucial component of effective financial management for college students. Creating a detailed budget helps students track their income and expenses, prioritize spending, and make informed financial decisions. Financial literacy education significantly equips students with the knowledge and skills necessary for responsible financial management. According to a study published in the *Journal of Financial Counseling and Planning* (JFCP, 2019), a positive correlation exists between financial literacy and improved financial behaviors among college students. This education empowers students to understand key financial concepts, such as saving, investing, and managing debt, which are essential for long-term financial stability.

Moreover, financial literacy education can help students develop habits that lead to better financial health and reduce the likelihood of accumulating excessive debt. By understanding how to create and maintain a budget, students can avoid common financial pitfalls and make more strategic financial decisions. Institutions offering financial literacy programs and workshops can significantly contribute to their students' ability to manage their finances effectively and achieve their academic and personal goals.

Negotiating Tuition and Fees

Exploring options to negotiate tuition payment plans or reduce fees can offer significant financial relief for students facing economic challenges. Engaging with the college's financial aid office to discuss potential accommodations or alternative payment arrangements is a proactive approach that can help alleviate financial stress. The Chronicle of Higher Education (CHE, 2021) reported that in response to the economic disruptions caused by the COVID-19 pandemic, many colleges began offering tuition discounts or fee waivers to support students. Such negotiations can provide crucial financial support and make higher education more accessible to students from diverse financial backgrounds.

Furthermore, students should know various financial aid options and work closely with financial aid advisors to explore all available resources. By actively seeking out and negotiating financial assistance, students can better manage their educational expenses and reduce the overall cost of their college education. Institutions should also consider implementing flexible financial policies to effectively support students in managing their tuition and fee obligations.

Financial Counseling Services

Many colleges offer financial counseling services designed to assist students in managing their finances effectively. These services can provide personalized advice, budget planning, and strategies for addressing financial challenges. A study by the National Endowment for Financial Education (NEFE, 2017) highlighted the positive impact of financial counseling on reducing financial stress among college students. Access to financial counselors allows students to receive tailored support and guidance, which can be instrumental in managing their financial obligations and developing sound financial practices.

Financial counseling services can also help students navigate complex financial situations, such as managing student loans, applying for financial aid, and planning future expenses. By taking advantage of these resources, students can better understand their financial situation and make informed decisions that support their academic success and overall well-being. Institutions should continue to invest in and promote financial counseling services to help students achieve financial stability and reduce stress related to their finances.

Scholarships and Grants

Actively pursuing scholarships and grants is a critical strategy for alleviating the financial burdens associated with higher education. Scholarships and grants provide financial assistance that does not require repayment, significantly reducing the overall cost of education. According to the National Center for Education Statistics (NCES, 2020), approximately 85% of undergraduate students in the United States received some form of financial aid during the 2018-2019 academic year, including scholarships and grants. This support can help cover tuition, fees, and other educational expenses, making higher education more accessible and affordable.

Scholarships and grants can ease financial strain and enhance students' academic and personal development. By reducing the need for student loans, these aid forms can decrease financial stress and allow students to focus more on their studies and extracurricular activities. Students should actively seek out and apply for various scholarship and grant opportunities to maximize their chances of receiving financial support and achieving their educational goals.

Scholarships for Higher Education: Investing in Future Leaders

Higher education has become increasingly important in today's competitive job market, but the rising costs of obtaining a degree can be a significant barrier for many students. Scholarships are crucial in making higher education accessible to individuals from diverse backgrounds and socioeconomic statuses. These financial awards provide students with the means to pursue their academic aspirations without the burden of excessive debt. We explore the importance of scholarships for higher education, the various types available, and strategies for securing them.

Importance of Scholarships for Higher Education

Financial Accessibility

Scholarships play a crucial role in making higher education financially accessible by bridging the gap between the cost of tuition and what students and their families can afford. For many students, especially those from low- and middle-income backgrounds, the financial burden of college tuition can be overwhelming. Scholarships provide essential financial support that alleviates some of these costs, making it possible for students to pursue a college education without the need for excessive financial strain. Without scholarships, many students might face the difficult decision of whether to attend college or forgo higher education altogether due to prohibitive costs.

The availability of scholarships can significantly impact a student's ability to attend college and achieve their academic goals. By reducing out-of-pocket tuition and other educational costs, scholarships ensure that financial limitations do not prevent deserving students from accessing higher education opportunities. This support helps students afford their education and contributes to greater equity in higher education by enabling students from diverse financial backgrounds to attend college (College Board. 2020).

Reducing Student Debt

In the context of rising student loan debt, scholarships provide a valuable alternative by reducing the amount of money students need to borrow. With student loan debt reaching record highs, the financial relief offered by scholarships helps students avoid accumulating excessive debt that could impact their financial well-being long after graduation. Scholarships that cover tuition, fees, and sometimes even living expenses enable students to concentrate on their studies rather than stressing over how they will manage loan repayments in the future.

By alleviating the need for student loans, scholarships help students graduate with less financial burden. This debt reduction can lead to better financial stability and greater career flexibility for graduates, allowing them to focus on their professional and personal goals without the constraint of significant student loan obligations. Ultimately, scholarships are critical in easing the financial pressures associated with higher education and supporting students in achieving their long-term career aspirations (Dynarski, S., 2015).

Promoting Diversity and Inclusion

Scholarships targeted toward underrepresented minority groups, first-generation college students, and those with financial need significantly promote diversity and inclusion within higher education. By providing financial support to students from diverse backgrounds, these scholarships help to level the playing field and ensure that a wide range of voices and perspectives are represented on college campuses. This financial assistance is crucial for fostering a more inclusive academic environment where students from various backgrounds can succeed.

In addition to supporting individual students, these scholarships contribute to the broader goal of creating a more diverse and equitable higher education system. They help address disparities and ensure that students who might otherwise be excluded due to financial constraints or lack of resources can pursue higher education. By enhancing diversity and inclusion, scholarships enrich the educational experience for all students and promote a more vibrant and comprehensive learning environment (Hurtado, Alvarez, Guillermo-Wann, Cuenca, & Arellano, 2012).

Rewarding Academic Excellence and Talent

Scholarships that reward academic excellence and talent are essential in incentivizing students to excel in their studies and pursue their passions. These merit-based awards are often based on academic performance, leadership abilities, and extracurricular involvement, providing recognition and support for students who demonstrate exceptional skills and achievements. By acknowledging and rewarding hard work and dedication, these scholarships motivate students to strive for excellence in their academic and personal endeavors.

Moreover, merit-based scholarships help to foster a culture of academic and extracurricular achievement by highlighting the importance of maintaining high standards and pursuing one's interests. This recognition benefits the recipients by providing financial support and sets a positive example for other students. By celebrating and supporting talented individuals, scholarships contribute to a more dynamic and motivated student body, enhancing the overall quality of the educational environment (Milem, J. F., 2003).

Types of Scholarships

Merit-Based Scholarships

These scholarships are awarded based on academic achievement, standardized test scores, and extracurricular activities. Colleges and universities often offer merit-based scholarships to attract top-performing students.

Need-Based Scholarships

These scholarships are awarded to students based on financial need, as determined by the Free Application for Federal Student Aid (FAFSA) or other financial aid applications. Government agencies, private organizations, and individual colleges and universities typically provide need-based scholarships.

Minority Scholarships

These scholarships are specifically targeted toward underrepresented minority groups, including African Americans, Hispanic/Latino Americans, Native Americans, and Asian Americans. Minority scholarships aim to increase diversity and representation in higher education.

Athletic Scholarships

These scholarships are awarded to student-athletes who demonstrate exceptional talent and skill in sports such as football, basketball, soccer, and track and field. Colleges and universities typically offer athletic scholarships to recruit talented athletes to their athletic programs.

Specialized Scholarships

These scholarships are awarded to students pursuing degrees in specific fields or disciplines, such as STEM (science, technology, engineering, and mathematics), business, education, healthcare, and the arts. Professional organizations, corporations, foundations, or individual donors may sponsor specialized scholarships.

Strategies for Securing Scholarships

Start Early

Starting the scholarship application process early is key to maximizing your financial aid chances. It is advisable to begin researching and applying for scholarships during junior high school or earlier. Many scholarship programs have early deadlines and require extensive documentation, making it essential to plan to avoid missing out on opportunities. By starting early, you can take the time to identify scholarships that align with your goals and qualifications, allowing for a more thorough and thoughtful application process. Additionally, early preparation gives you ample time to gather necessary materials, such as transcripts, recommendation letters, and personal statements, without the pressure of impending deadlines.

Early planning allows one to stay organized and meet all the application requirements. Creating a timeline for deadlines and organizing scholarship applications into a manageable schedule can help you avoid last-minute stress and ensure that your applications are submitted on time. As scholarship opportunities may arise throughout the year, having an early start allows you to remain informed and prepared to take advantage of new openings as they become available.

Research Thoroughly

Conducting thorough research is crucial when searching for scholarships, as it increases your chances of finding opportunities that best suit your qualifications and needs. Explore various sources, including colleges and universities, government agencies, private organizations, community foundations, and online scholarship databases. Many institutions and organizations offer scholarships with varying criteria and amounts, so casting a wide net can help you uncover opportunities you might otherwise overlook. Smaller, local scholarships, although less publicized, often have fewer applicants and can significantly contribute to your overall financial aid package.

Utilizing multiple resources in your scholarship search can lead to discovering unique opportunities that may not be listed on larger scholarship platforms. Community foundations and local businesses may offer scholarships specific to your area of interest. By broadening your search and applying to a diverse array of scholarships, you enhance your chances of receiving financial aid and potentially increase the total amount of funding available for your education.

Highlight Achievements

When applying for scholarships, it is essential to effectively highlight your achievements and experiences to stand out from other applicants. In your scholarship applications, emphasize your academic accomplishments, leadership roles, extracurricular activities, community service, and other relevant experiences. Each scholarship may have specific criteria, so tailor your application materials to align with the requirements and preferences of the scholarship provider. Showcasing your unique skills and contributions helps to demonstrate your suitability for the scholarship and makes your application more compelling.

In addition to presenting a solid academic record, provide concrete examples of how your experiences have shaped your goals and character. Use your statement or essay to illustrate your passion for your chosen field of study and your commitment to making a positive impact. By aligning your achievements with the scholarship's objectives, you create a more persuasive and tailored application that resonates with the selection committee.

Submit Quality Essays

Submitting high-quality essays is a critical component of a successful scholarship application. Craft essays that effectively communicate your passion, character, and aspirations, and ensure they are well-organized, clear, and free of grammatical errors. Take the time to brainstorm and outline your essay, focusing on how best to convey your unique story and experiences. Revising your essay multiple times can improve its clarity and coherence, helping to create a more polished final product.

Personalize each essay to reflect the specific criteria and values of the scholarship. Tailor your writing to address the prompts and highlight how your experiences and goals align with the scholarship's mission. By presenting a compelling narrative and demonstrating your genuine enthusiasm, you enhance your chances of making a solid impression on the selection committee.

Seek Letters of Recommendation

Requesting letters of recommendation from individuals who can speak to your character and accomplishments is an essential step in the scholarship application process. Choose recommenders such as teachers, counselors, coaches, or employers who know you well and can provide specific examples of your strengths and achievements. A strong letter of recommendation can provide valuable insights into your abilities and potential, making your application more persuasive.

Ensure you give your recommenders ample time to write and submit their letters by providing them with clear guidelines and deadlines. It is helpful to supply them with a resume or a summary of your accomplishments to assist them in crafting a detailed and supportive letter. By selecting recommenders who can offer meaningful and personalized endorsements, you enhance your scholarship application and increase your chances of receiving financial aid.

Scholarships are vital in making higher education accessible and affordable for students from all walks of life. By providing financial support, scholarships empower students to pursue their academic and career goals without the burden of excessive debt. Whether merit-based, need-based, minority-specific, athletic, or specialized, scholarships reward students for their achievements and invest in their future success. By employing strategic planning and proactive effort, students can increase their chances of securing scholarships and unlocking the doors to higher education opportunities.

Overcoming Time Management Challenges

Effective time management is a critical skill for college students, as the demands of coursework, extracurricular activities, and personal life can be overwhelming. Overcoming time management challenges involves adopting strategies that enhance productivity and prioritize tasks efficiently.

Utilize Time Management Tools

Implementing time management tools such as planners, calendars, or apps can aid students in organizing tasks and deadlines, enhancing their ability to visualize and structure their schedules effectively (Covey, 1994). These tools provide a tangible way to break down assignments into manageable steps and allocate time accordingly. By utilizing tools like these, students can track their progress, ensure they meet deadlines and balance their academic responsibilities with other commitments.

Prioritize Tasks

Prioritizing tasks based on urgency and importance is a fundamental strategy in effective time management (Eisenhower, 1954). This approach helps students focus on completing high-priority assignments first, reducing last-minute rushes and stress. By categorizing tasks into "urgent," "important but not urgent," and so forth, students can allocate their time and effort efficiently, ensuring that critical assignments are completed on time while allowing flexibility in their schedules.

Set Realistic Goals

Establishing realistic short-term and long-term goals is essential for students to maintain motivation and manage their workload effectively (Locke & Latham, 2002). By setting achievable objectives, students can create a roadmap for their academic journey, fostering a sense of accomplishment as they progress. Setting both challenging and attainable goals encourages students to stay focused and committed to their studies, reducing the likelihood of feeling overwhelmed by their academic responsibilities.

Learn to Say No

Recognizing personal limits and learning to decline additional commitments is crucial for students to avoid overloading their schedules (Covey, 1989). Saying no to non-essential tasks or activities helps students prioritize their academic responsibilities and maintain a healthy work-life balance. By understanding their capacity and setting boundaries, students can protect their time and energy for tasks that align with their academic and personal goals, ultimately enhancing their overall productivity and well-being.

Time Blocking

Allocating specific blocks of time to dedicated tasks is a practical technique to enhance focus and productivity (Newport, 2016). By scheduling uninterrupted periods for studying, students minimize distractions and reduce the temptation to multitask, which can lead to inefficiency. This method encourages students to immerse themselves in their work during designated time slots fully, improving their concentration and academic output quality.

Utilize Campus Resources

Many colleges offer workshops and resources designed to improve students' time management skills (refer to your college's academic support or counseling services). These resources provide tailored strategies and support to help students better organize their schedules and prioritize their academic commitments. By taking advantage of these campus resources, students can gain valuable insights and techniques to enhance their time management abilities, optimizing their academic success.

Regular Breaks and Self-Care

Incorporating regular breaks into study sessions is essential for maintaining cognitive function and preventing burnout (Trougakos et al., 2008). Breaks allow students to recharge mentally, improving focus and productivity when they return to their studies. Additionally, prioritizing self-care activities such as exercise, adequate sleep, and relaxation techniques contributes to overall well-being, enhancing students' ability to manage stress and maintain a balanced lifestyle amidst academic demands.

Evaluate and Adjust

Regularly evaluating and adjusting time management strategies based on effectiveness and changing priorities is key to continuous improvement (Drucker, 1967). By reflecting on their productivity and the outcomes of their time management efforts, students can identify areas for improvement and make necessary adjustments to their study habits. This adaptive approach ensures that students remain flexible and responsive to academic challenges, optimizing their efficiency and academic performance.

By integrating these strategies into their daily routines, students can enhance their time management skills, reduce stress, and improve their academic performance. Students to adapt these general recommendations to fit the specific demands and structure of their courses and programs, ensuring maximum effectiveness and personal success.

Overcoming Homesickness

Homesickness is a common challenge for many college students, particularly those transitioning to a new environment. Overcoming homesickness involves developing coping strategies, building a support network, and actively engaging in the college community.

Establish a Support System

Creating a support network with fellow students, roommates, or campus organizations is essential for alleviating loneliness and fostering a sense of belonging (Thurber & Walton, 2012). By building relationships and engaging with peers with similar interests or experiences, students can develop a reliable support system that offers emotional and social support. This network helps students navigate the challenges of college life and provides a foundation for personal growth and a sense of community, making the transition to college smoother and more enjoyable.

Stay Connected with Family and Friends

Regular communication with family and friends through phone calls, video chats, or social media can significantly contribute to emotional well-being and connection to familiar faces (Maltby, Day, & Barber, 2004). Maintaining these relationships helps students feel supported and grounded, reducing feelings of isolation and homesickness. By staying in touch with loved ones, students can share their experiences, seek advice, and receive encouragement, all of which can make adapting to college life more manageable and less overwhelming.

Engage in Campus Activities

Actively participating in campus clubs, events, and activities is an effective way for students to build a sense of community and make new friends with shared interests (Pascarella & Terenzini, 2005). Engaging in these activities enriches the college experience and provides opportunities for social interaction and personal development. By immersing themselves in campus life, students can discover new passions, develop skills, and form meaningful connections with others, which enhances their overall academic and social experience.

Explore the Local Community

Exploring the local community outside of the college campus can help students establish a sense of familiarity and make the new environment feel more like home (Ory & Mokel, 2003). Knowing local landmarks, shops, and recreational areas provides a broader perspective on the new surroundings and integrates students more deeply into their new environment. This exploration can also offer opportunities for relaxation and leisure, contributing to a balanced and fulfilling college experience.

Create a Home Away from Home

Personalizing living spaces with familiar items, such as photographs, decorations, or comforting belongings, can create a sense of home in the college environment (Trussell & Shaw, 2000). By incorporating elements from their home lives, students can establish a personal sanctuary that reflects their identity and provides comfort. This practice helps bridge the gap between home and the college setting, making the transition smoother and fostering a greater sense of stability and belonging.

Seek Campus Counseling Services

Campus counseling services are equipped to help students navigate homesickness and provide essential support for emotional well-being (American College Counseling Association, 2017). These services offer professional guidance, counseling, and resources to address mental health concerns and help students cope with the stresses of college life. By seeking these services, students can receive tailored support and strategies to manage homesickness and other emotional challenges effectively.

Establish Routines and Rituals

Creating daily routines or rituals can provide a sense of structure and familiarity, aiding students in adjusting to their new surroundings (Rubin & Kozin, 1984). Establishing consistent habits and routines helps students develop a stable environment, which can reduce feelings of uncertainty and stress. These routines can include regular study times, exercise, and social activities, all of which contribute to a balanced and organized lifestyle that supports academic and personal success.

Attend Homesickness Workshops

Many colleges offer workshops or seminars addressing homesickness and providing adjustment strategies. Attending such events can be highly beneficial for students struggling with the transition to college life (refer to your college's counseling or student support services for specific workshops). These workshops often provide practical tips, coping strategies, and opportunities to connect with others facing similar challenges, facilitating a smoother adaptation to the new academic environment.

By integrating these strategies, college students can effectively address homesickness and create a positive, enriching experience in their new academic setting. Students need to adapt these approaches to their personal needs and the unique demands of their college experience.

Overcoming Health-Related Challenges

Maintaining good health is essential for college students to succeed academically and enjoy a fulfilling campus life. Overcoming health-related challenges involves adopting preventive measures, accessing healthcare resources, and promoting overall well-being.

Access On-Campus Health Services

Utilizing on-campus health services offers students convenient and affordable access to medical professionals for routine check-ups, vaccinations, and prompt treatment of minor illnesses (American College Health Association, 2018). These services address common health issues and preventive care, ensuring students can maintain their health without the additional stress of off-campus appointments. By taking advantage of these resources, students can manage their health more effectively, contributing to their overall academic success and well-being. Did you know regular health check-ups can help detect potential health issues early, often before symptoms appear?

Understand and Utilize Health Insurance

Understanding the details of health insurance coverage is crucial for college students, as it empowers them to make informed decisions about seeking medical care and ensures they are aware of available resources (American College Health Association, 2019). Familiarity with what insurance policies cover, including emergency and routine care, helps students navigate healthcare options efficiently and avoid unexpected expenses. This knowledge is vital to maximizing the benefits of their insurance plan and receiving appropriate care when needed. Did you know that many students are eligible for additional health insurance options through their institution that can further reduce out-of-pocket costs?

Practice Preventive Health Measures

Adopting preventive health measures such as regular exercise, a balanced diet, adequate sleep, and immunizations plays a significant role in maintaining overall health and reducing the risk of illness (Sagner, Katz, & Egger, 2014). Engaging in these practices helps students stay physically healthy and supports mental well-being, enhancing their ability to cope with academic and social pressures. Preventive care is a proactive approach that can lead to long-term health benefits and fewer disruptions in academic performance. Did you know that preventive health measures can significantly reduce the likelihood of chronic diseases and improve longevity?

Manage Stress Effectively

Chronic stress can harm health, impacting both physical and mental well-being (Cohen, Janicki-Deverts, & Miller, 2007). Stress management techniques such as mindfulness, regular exercise, and effective time management can help students better cope with the demands of college life. By incorporating these strategies, students can improve their health and maintain a more balanced lifestyle. Effective stress management supports academic performance and contributes to long-term health and happiness. Did you know that chronic stress can impair memory and cognitive functions, making stress management even more crucial for academic success?

Stay Informed about Mental Health Resources

Mental health is a crucial aspect of overall well-being, and being aware of and utilizing on-campus counseling services, support groups, and hotlines is essential for students (American College Counseling Association, 2017). These resources provide valuable support for managing stress, anxiety, and other mental health challenges, ensuring students have access to professional help when needed. These services can improve students' mental health and contribute to a more successful and fulfilling college experience. Did you know that seeking mental health support early can significantly reduce the risk of developing more serious psychological issues later?

Establish Healthy Sleep Patterns

Adequate sleep is vital for physical and mental health, and establishing regular sleep patterns can enhance overall well-being (Walker, 2017). Creating a conducive sleep environment and adhering to a consistent sleep schedule helps regulate the body's internal clock, improving sleep quality and duration. Good sleep hygiene is essential for maintaining energy levels, cognitive function, and emotional stability, all of which are important for academic performance and daily functioning. Did you know that poor sleep habits can lead to impaired cognitive abilities and increased susceptibility to illness?

Practice Responsible Alcohol and Substance Use

Engaging in responsible alcohol and substance use is crucial for maintaining health and avoiding potential risks associated with misuse (White & Hingson, 2014). Understanding the effects of alcohol and substances and making informed decisions about their use helps students protect their health and well-being. Responsible use includes being aware of limits, recognizing the signs of substance misuse, and seeking help when necessary. Did you know that misuse of alcohol and substances can have long-term consequences on both physical health and academic performance?

Engage in Physical Activity

Regular physical activity benefits overall health, contributing to physical fitness and mental well-being (Warburton, Nicol, & Bredin, 2006). Participating in exercise, whether through sports, fitness classes, or other activities, helps students maintain a healthy weight, improve cardiovascular health, and reduce stress. Physical activity also plays a crucial role in enhancing mood and cognitive function, supporting both academic performance and general quality of life. Did you know that even short physical activity can boost mood and cognitive performance, making it a valuable addition to a busy college schedule?

By incorporating these strategies into their daily lives, college students can proactively manage health-related challenges, laying a solid foundation for academic success and a positive college experience.

Balancing Personal and Academic Responsibilities

Juggling academic demands and personal responsibilities can be a significant challenge for college students. Achieving a healthy balance between coursework and personal life requires effective time management, prioritization, and cultivating supportive habits.

Prioritize Tasks Effectively

Prioritizing tasks based on urgency and importance is crucial for managing academic and personal commitments effectively (Covey, 1994). By categorizing tasks into categories such as "urgent and important," "important but not urgent," "urgent but not important," and "neither urgent nor important," students can focus their efforts on high-priority assignments and responsibilities. This systematic approach helps prevent procrastination and ensures that critical deadlines are met allowing students to address personal needs and avoid last-minute stress. Prioritization enhances productivity and improves overall time management by aligning efforts with goals and deadlines.

Utilize Time Management Strategies

Effective time management techniques, such as creating detailed schedules, using productivity apps, and breaking tasks into smaller, manageable chunks, are essential for efficiently balancing academic and personal life (Allen, 2015). Creating a structured schedule helps students allocate specific time slots for studying, attending classes, and engaging in personal activities. Productivity apps can assist in tracking tasks and deadlines while breaking down larger projects into smaller tasks can make them less overwhelming and more accessible to complete. These strategies contribute to better organization, increased productivity, and reduced stress by ensuring time is used effectively.

Establish Boundaries

Setting clear boundaries between academic and personal time is crucial for maintaining a balanced and healthy lifestyle (Newport, 2016). students can prevent burnout and maintain overall well-being by designating specific periods for focused study and separate times for leisure and personal activities. Establishing these boundaries helps ensure that academic responsibilities are met without encroaching on personal time, essential for relaxation and social engagement. Clear boundaries contribute to a more structured and less stressful routine, promoting both academic success and personal satisfaction.

Learn to Say No

Recognizing personal limits and declining additional commitments is vital for maintaining a healthy balance between various aspects of life (McKeown, 2014). This involves saying no to extracurricular activities, social events, or additional responsibilities when they threaten to overwhelm one's schedule. By understanding and respecting one's capacity, students can avoid overextending themselves and ensure that they have adequate time and energy for their primary commitments. Learning to say no is a critical skill for managing stress and maintaining focus on what truly matters, thus supporting overall well-being and academic performance.

Engage in Self-Care Practices

Prioritizing self-care, including adequate sleep, regular exercise, and moments of relaxation, is essential for maintaining physical and mental health amidst the pressures of college life (Seligman, 2011). Engaging in self-care practices helps students manage stress, improve mood, and maintain overall well-being, which is crucial for academic success and personal happiness. Regular exercise boosts energy levels and cognitive function, while adequate sleep and relaxation contribute to better concentration and resilience. Self-care is not a luxury but a necessary component of a balanced and practical lifestyle.

Utilize Academic Support Services

Many colleges provide academic support services such as tutoring, writing centers, and study groups, which can significantly enhance academic performance and help manage workload (Tinto,

1993). Utilizing these resources allows students to receive additional help with coursework, improve their skills, and better understand challenging material. Academic support services provide valuable assistance and feedback, helping students overcome difficulties and achieve their educational goals more effectively. Engaging with these services can also reduce stress and enhance overall academic success.

Communicate with Professors

Building open and effective communication with professors is crucial for academic success (Grunert O'Brien, Millis, & Cohen, 2008). Discussing personal challenges, seeking clarification on academic expectations, and requesting accommodations when needed fosters a supportive educational environment. Professors aware of students' needs and concerns are better positioned to offer guidance and flexibility, which can lead to a more positive and productive academic experience. Open communication also helps build rapport and trust, contributing to a more supportive and understanding relationship with faculty.

Cultivate a Support System

Establishing a solid support system, including friends, family, or mentors, provides essential emotional support during challenging times (Seppälä, Rossomando, & Doty, 2013). A robust support network can help students navigate academic and personal difficulties by offering encouragement, advice, and a sense of connection. Having people to turn to for support can alleviate feelings of isolation and stress, making it easier for students to manage their responsibilities and maintain a positive outlook. Building and nurturing these relationships is key to a successful college experience.

By integrating these strategies into their daily routines, college students can effectively balance academic and personal responsibilities, promoting a more fulfilling and successful college experience.

Overcoming Motivational Challenges

Sustaining motivation is crucial for academic success, yet many college students face challenges maintaining high engagement and drive levels. Overcoming motivational issues involves implementing strategies that foster intrinsic motivation, goal setting, and a positive mindset.

Set Clear and Achievable Goals

Establishing clear, realistic goals gives students a sense of direction and purpose, which is essential for academic and personal success (Locke & Latham, 2002). By breaking down larger objectives into smaller, manageable tasks, students can create a structured plan that makes achieving their goals more approachable and less overwhelming. This process helps in tracking progress and maintains motivation as students experience a sense of accomplishment with each completed task. Clear goals and incremental steps contribute to a more focused and efficient approach, enhancing overall productivity and goal attainment.

Find Intrinsic Motivation

Identifying personal reasons for pursuing education and connecting coursework to individual interests is key to fostering intrinsic motivation, which is more enduring and influential than external pressures (Deci, Vallerand, Pelletier, & Ryan, 1991). When students link their academic pursuits to their personal passions and long-term aspirations, they develop a more profound sense of purpose and commitment. This internal drive enhances their engagement and persistence, making the learning experience more meaningful and enjoyable. Intrinsic motivation boosts academic performanceand encourages lifelong learning and personal growth.

Break Tasks into Manageable Steps

Dividing larger tasks into smaller, more manageable steps can significantly reduce the perceived difficulty of assignments, making them less daunting and increasing motivation to start and complete them (Steel & Konig, 2006). By breaking tasks down into achievable components, students can focus on one step at a time, simplifying the process and minimizing procrastination. This approach makes the workload seem more manageable and provides regular opportunities for accomplishment and progress, thereby enhancing overall motivation and productivity.

Develop a Routine

Establishing a daily routine provides structure and predictability, which are crucial for academic success (Clear, 2018). A consistent routine helps students build habits that support their academic and personal goals by creating a structured environment where specific times are allocated for studying, attending classes, and engaging in leisure activities. Over time, these habits become ingrained, making it easier for students to maintain focus and motivation. A well-developed routine also helps in balancing multiple responsibilities and managing time effectively.

Seek Support and Accountability

Sharing academic goals with friends, family, or mentors can provide valuable external support and accountability (Gollwitzer, 1999). By discussing their objectives and progress with others, students can receive encouragement, feedback, and practical advice that enhances their motivation and commitment. Regular check-ins with a study group or mentor help maintain focus and ensure that students stay on track with their goals. This external accountability complements intrinsic motivation and contributes to sustained engagement and success.

Celebrate Small Achievements

Recognizing and celebrating small victories along the academic journey can significantly boost morale and motivation (Pink, 2011). Acknowledging these incremental successes provides positive reinforcement, which reinforces the sense of progress and achievement. Celebrations of small milestones enhance self-esteem and maintain enthusiasm and drive towards achieving larger goals. This practice encourages students to continue their efforts and fosters a positive outlook on their academic endeavors.

Utilize Campus Resources

Colleges offer a variety of resources, including tutoring, career counseling, and academic advising, which can provide valuable support and motivation (Tinto, 1993). Taking advantage of these services helps students address academic challenges, gain additional insights, and develop strategies for success. By seeking assistance from campus resources, students can enhance their learning experience, receive guidance tailored to their needs, and stay motivated throughout their academic journey.

Reflect on Long-Term Goals

Regularly reflecting on long-term academic and personal goals can help reignite motivation and provide renewed commitment (Duckworth, Peterson, Matthews, & Kelly, 2007). Understanding the broader purpose of education and how it aligns with future aspirations helps students maintain perspective and stay focused on their objectives. This reflection allows students to reassess their progress, adjust their strategies, and reinforce their dedication to achieving their long-term goals.

By incorporating these strategies into their academic approach, students can effectively address motivational challenges, foster sustained engagement, and enhance their overall success throughout their college experience.

Navigating Relationship Challenges

Maintaining healthy relationships while navigating the demands of college can be a complex task. Overcoming relationship detractions involves effective communication, time management, and fostering mutual understanding. Implementing strategies to address relationship challenges contributes to emotional well-being and overall academic success.

Communication is Key

Open and honest communication is fundamental for resolving conflicts and understanding each other's needs in any relationship (Gottman & Silver, 2015). Regular check-ins and discussions about expectations can prevent misunderstandings and ensure that both partners are on the same page. Effective communication fosters trust and transparency, enabling partners to address issues before they escalate and to strengthen their connection. By prioritizing clear dialogue, students can build stronger, more supportive relationships that contribute positively to their overall well-being and academic success.

Establish Boundaries

Clearly, defining personal and academic boundaries is essential for maintaining a healthy balance between relationships and academic commitments (Cloud & Townsend, 1999). Setting boundaries helps prevent conflicts by respecting each partner's needs and responsibilities. Balancing time between academic obligations and relationship activities ensures that neither area is neglected, promoting a more harmonious and fulfilling life. Establishing these boundaries fosters mutual respect and helps partners navigate their commitments without feeling overwhelmed.

Prioritize Quality Time

Amidst busy academic schedules, dedicating quality time to relationships is crucial for maintaining strong connections (Doherty, 2002). Planning activities and moments of connection allow partners to nurture their bond and provide mutual support. Quality time strengthens relationships by reinforcing shared experiences and enhancing emotional intimacy. Even in a demanding college environment, making an effort to engage in meaningful interactions helps ensure that relationships remain a source of support and joy.

Seek Relationship Counseling

Professional guidance can be highly beneficial in addressing complex relationship issues (Markman, Stanley, & Blumberg, 2010). Campus counseling services often offer resources or referrals for couples seeking support, helping them navigate challenges and improve their relationship dynamics. Counseling provides a neutral space for partners to explore their concerns and develop effective communication and problem-solving skills. Seeking such support can enhance relationship satisfaction and resilience, contributing to a more balanced and fulfilling college experience.

Individual Growth and Independence

Encouraging personal growth and independence within a relationship allows each partner to pursue individual goals and aspirations (Schnarch, 2018). Supporting each other's personal development fosters a healthier connection by ensuring that both partners are fulfilled and self-reliant. This approach helps maintain a balanced relationship where both individuals can thrive academically and personally, contributing to a more supportive and resilient partnership.

Manage Stress Together

College life can be highly stressful, and managing stress as a team can significantly strengthen a relationship (Neff, 2011). Sharing challenges and supporting each other through difficult times fosters resilience and deepens the emotional connection between partners. By working together to handle stress, students can build a supportive network that enhances both their relationship and overall well-being, making it easier to cope with academic and personal pressures.

Set Relationship Goals

Establishing shared goals for the relationship provides direction and reinforces commitment (Stanley, Rhoades, & Whitton, 2010). Collaborating on short-term and long-term objectives helps partners align their efforts and strengthen their mutual understanding. Setting relationship goals encourages both partners to invest in their connection and work together towards common aspirations, enhancing the overall stability and satisfaction within the relationship.

Balance Social and Academic Life

Maintaining a balance between social life and academic commitments is crucial for overall well-being (Kuh, Cruce, Shoup, Kinzie, & Gonyea, 2008). Striking a healthy equilibrium ensures that social relationships complement rather than detract from academic responsibilities. By effectively managing their time and setting priorities, students can enjoy fulfilling social interactions while staying focused on their academic goals. This balance supports a more rounded college experience and helps students maintain both their personal and academic growth.

By integrating these strategies into their approach to relationships, college students can navigate challenges effectively and foster a supportive and fulfilling personal life alongside their academic endeavors.

Navigating Cultural Adjustment Challenges

Adjusting to a new cultural environment during college can be both exciting and challenging. Overcoming cultural adjustment detractions involves building cultural competence, seeking support, and fostering resilience. Strategies to address these challenges contribute to a more inclusive and enriching college experience.

Develop Cultural Competence

Understanding and appreciating cultural differences is essential for fostering a respectful and inclusive environment (Sue & Sue, 2016). Cultural competence training, workshops, or diversity courses enhance awareness and sensitivity toward various cultural backgrounds. This proactive approach helps students develop the skills necessary to interact effectively with individuals from diverse cultures. By increasing cultural competence, students are better equipped to contribute to a more inclusive campus community and navigate cross-cultural interactions with greater empathy and understanding.

Participate in Cultural Exchange Programs

Joining cultural exchange programs or clubs on campus offers valuable opportunities for interaction with peers from diverse backgrounds (Paige, Cohen, Kappler, Chi, & Lassegard, 2002). Engaging in these activities fosters cross-cultural friendships and broadens students' perspectives on global issues and different ways of life. Cultural exchange programs facilitate meaningful exchanges of ideas and experiences, enriching students' understanding of different cultures and enhancing their overall college experience through increased cultural exposure and interaction.

Connect with International Student Services

Utilizing services specifically designed for international students, such as cultural orientation sessions and mentorship programs, provides crucial support and guidance (Hoidn & Kim, 2014). These services help international students acclimate to their new environment by offering resources tailored to their unique needs. Cultural orientation sessions can ease the transition process by providing information on local customs, academic expectations, and support networks. Mentorship programs connect international students with experienced peers or staff who can offer personalized advice and support, helping them navigate cultural and academic challenges.

Build a Support Network

Establishing connections with fellow international students and forming relationships with local students creates a supportive network that enhances the college experience (Ward & Masgoret, 2004). By sharing experiences and challenges, students foster a sense of belonging and mutual support. A robust support network provides emotional reassurance, practical advice, and social interaction, all of which contribute to a smoother transition into the college environment. Building these relationships helps students feel more integrated and supported within the campus community.

Engage in Cross-Cultural Dialogue

Actively participating in cross-cultural dialogue through discussion groups, workshops, or forums promotes understanding and helps bridge cultural gaps (Bennett, 2009). Engaging in these dialogues allows students to explore different perspectives, address cultural misconceptions, and build mutual respect. Such interactions facilitate meaningful exchanges that enhance cultural awareness and create a more inclusive campus environment. By embracing cross-cultural dialogue, students can develop a deeper appreciation for diversity and improve their ability to communicate effectively across cultural boundaries.

Practice Self-Care

Prioritizing self-care is crucial for managing the stress associated with cultural adjustment (Pedersen, 2015). Taking time for personal reflection, relaxation, and engaging in activities that bring comfort helps maintain emotional well-being during transition periods. Self-care practices support mental and physical health, enabling students to better cope with the challenges of adjusting to a new cultural and academic environment. Students can enhance their resilience and overall well-being by incorporating self-care into their routine.

Utilize Counseling Services

Campus counseling services support navigating cultural adjustment challenges (Constantine & Sue, 2006). Seeking professional guidance provides a safe space for self-expression and helps students develop effective coping strategies. Counselors can offer tailored support to address specific issues related to cultural adjustment, such as managing stress, overcoming cultural barriers, and developing strategies for successful integration. Utilizing these services ensures that students can access to the resources needed to thrive in their new environment.

Embrace a Growth Mindset

Adopting a growth mindset involves viewing challenges as opportunities for learning and growth (Dweck, 2008). Embracing this perspective helps students develop resilience in the face of cultural adjustment difficulties. By focusing on the potential for personal development and improvement, students can approach challenges with a positive attitude and greater adaptability. A growth mindset fosters perseverance and a proactive approach to overcoming obstacles, enhancing the overall college experience and personal growth.

By integrating these strategies, college students can navigate cultural adjustment challenges with resilience and foster a positive and inclusive college experience.

Navigating Perfectionism Challenges

Perfectionism, while often associated with high standards, can become a significant detractor in a college setting, leading to stress, anxiety, and a fear of failure. Overcoming perfectionism involves adopting a balanced approach, fostering resilience, and cultivating a growth mindset.

Acknowledge and Understand Perfectionism

Recognizing the signs of perfectionism is crucial for addressing and overcoming it (Hewitt & Flett, 1991). Perfectionism often involves setting excessively high standards and experiencing intense fear of failure or mistakes. Understanding that such tendencies can hinder success rather than enhance, it helps shift perspectives towards more balanced and realistic expectations. By acknowledging these patterns, individuals can begin to challenge the unrealistic demands they place on themselves and take steps toward healthier, more constructive approaches to their goals and performance.

Set Realistic Goals

Establishing achievable and realistic goals is essential for countering the all-or-nothing mindset commonly associated with perfectionism (Locke & Latham, 2002). Breaking down larger tasks into smaller, manageable steps allows individuals to experience a sense of progress and accomplishment, reducing the pressure to achieve perfection in every aspect. By setting clear, attainable goals, individuals can create a more balanced and structured approach to their work, which helps diminish feelings of inadequacy and enhances motivation and satisfaction.

Embrace the Growth Mindset

Adopting a growth mindset involves viewing challenges and setbacks as opportunities for learning and development (Dweck, 2008). This perspective helps reduce the fear of making mistakes by emphasizing that abilities and intelligence can be developed over time. Embracing a growth mindset encourages individuals to approach tasks with curiosity and resilience, fostering an environment where mistakes are seen as valuable learning experiences rather than failures. This shift in mindset can significantly reduce the constraints of perfectionism and support personal and academic growth.

Practice Self-Compassion

Being kind to yourself in the face of setbacks is key to overcoming perfectionism (Neff, 2011). Practicing self-compassion involves treating yourself with the same understanding and support that you would offer a friend. This approach helps mitigate the harsh self-criticism accompanying perfectionistic tendencies and promotes emotional resilience. By cultivating a compassionate attitude towards oneself, individuals can better manage stress and setbacks, fostering a more positive and balanced outlook on their efforts and achievements.

Seek Feedback as a Tool for Growth

Viewing feedback as a valuable tool for improvement, rather than a judgment of inadequacy, is essential for overcoming perfectionism (Kluger & DeNisi, 1996). Constructive criticism provides insights into areas of growth and development, supporting a mindset of continuous learning and improvement. Embracing feedback helps individuals focus on the process of learning rather than the fear of making mistakes, reducing the impact of perfectionistic pressures and encouraging a more open and adaptive approach to personal and academic challenges.

Set Boundaries

Establishing boundaries on the time and effort invested in tasks helps prevent perfectionism from becoming overwhelming (Cloud & Townsend, 1999). Knowing when to step back and prioritize self-care is crucial for maintaining mental well-being and avoiding burnout. By setting clear limits on how much time and energy are dedicated to tasks, individuals can manage their workload more effectively and create space for relaxation and recovery. This approach helps maintain a healthier balance between achieving goals and caring for one's well-being.

Cultivate a Support System

Sharing struggles with perfectionism with friends, family, or mentors provides valuable emotional support and reassurance (Hewitt & Genest, 1990). Connecting with others who face similar challenges can reduce feelings of isolation and offer perspective on managing perfectionistic tendencies. A supportive network helps individuals feel understood and encourages open discussions about the pressures they experience. This support system plays a crucial role in navigating perfectionism and fostering a more balanced and resilient approach to personal and academic pursuits.

Utilize Counseling Services

Campus counseling services offer structured support for addressing perfectionism and its associated challenges (Stöber, 1998). Professional counselors can provide strategies and tools to help individuals manage perfectionistic tendencies, set realistic goals, and cope with stress. Seeking counseling provides a safe space for exploring underlying issues related to perfectionism and developing effective coping mechanisms. By utilizing these services, students can gain valuable insights and support in their journey toward a healthier and more balanced approach to their academic and personal lives.

By implementing these strategies, college students can effectively navigate and overcome perfectionism, fostering a healthier and more balanced approach to their academic and personal pursuits.

Addressing Test Anxiety

Test anxiety can significantly hinder academic performance and well-being. Overcoming test anxiety involves adopting effective coping strategies, developing a positive mindset, and implementing practical techniques to manage stress during exams.

Implement Stress-Reducing Techniques

Incorporating stress-reducing techniques such as deep breathing, progressive muscle relaxation, and mindfulness can significantly alleviate anxiety levels before exams (Hoge et al., 2013). These practices help activate the body's relaxation response, which counteracts the physiological effects of stress and fosters a calmer mental state. Deep breathing exercises, for instance, focus on slow, deliberate inhalations and exhalations, while progressive muscle relaxation involves tensing and then relaxing muscle groups to reduce physical tension. Mindfulness practices encourage present-moment awareness and acceptance, which can mitigate the overwhelming feelings of stress. Integrating these techniques into a pre-exam routine can improve focus and a more balanced emotional state.

Practice Time Management

Effective time management is crucial for reducing pre-exam anxiety. Creating a study schedule that allocates ample time for review and prevents last-minute cramming helps build confidence and reduces stress (Britton & Tesser, 1991). A well-structured schedule includes designated study periods, breaks, and time for relaxation, which helps ensure that all exam material is covered thoroughly. By breaking study sessions into manageable chunks and adhering to a plan, students can avoid the anxiety associated with inadequate preparation and feel more in control and prepared on exam day.

Adopt Positive Self-Talk

Cultivating positive self-talk is essential for managing exam anxiety. Negative self-talk can exacerbate feelings of inadequacy and increase stress (Hatzigeorgiadis et al., 2008). By focusing on strengths and capabilities rather than perceived weaknesses, students can foster a more encouraging and confident mindset. Positive affirmations and constructive self-dialogue help shift the focus from fear of failure to recognition of one's abilities and past successes. This approach enhances self-esteem and resilience, providing a mental boost that supports better performance during exams.

Break Down the Exam

Dividing an exam into smaller, more manageable sections can reduce feelings of overwhelm and anxiety (Cassady & Johnson, 2002). By focusing on one question at a time, students can approach the exam with a clearer and more organized strategy. This method prevents the task from seeming insurmountable and allows for a more methodical and focused approach to answering each question. Managing the exam in this way helps maintain a steady pace and reduces the stress associated with tackling a large, complex task simultaneously.

Prioritize Sleep and Physical Health

Adequate sleep and overall physical health are vital in cognitive function and stress management (Walker, 2017). Prioritizing a healthy lifestyle, including regular exercise, balanced nutrition, and sufficient sleep, enhances mental clarity and resilience. Good physical health supports optimal brain function, crucial for effective studying and exam performance. By maintaining these health practices, students can improve their overall well-being and readiness for exams, reducing the likelihood of stress-related impairments in cognitive and emotional functioning.

Utilize Test-Taking Strategies

Familiarizing oneself with various test-taking strategies can improve confidence and reduce anxiety during exams (Roediger III & Karpicke, 2006). This includes practicing with different types of test questions, managing time effectively during mock exams, and employing strategies such as skimming questions first or prioritizing easier ones. By developing and refining these strategies, students can approach the actual exam with greater assurance and efficiency. Effective test-taking techniques help streamline the process and reduce the uncertainty and stress associated with unfamiliar or high-stakes testing situations.

Seek Academic Support

Utilizing academic support resources, such as professors, tutoring services, and study groups, can provide valuable assistance and reduce exam-related anxiety (Tinto, 1993). Seeking clarification on difficult concepts and engaging in collaborative study sessions helps address uncertainties and reinforce understanding of the material. Academic support not only aids in grasping complex topics but also provides encouragement and a sense of community. This collective approach helps students feel more prepared and less isolated in their exam preparation.

Consider Professional Counseling

For persistent test anxiety, seeking professional counseling services can be highly beneficial (Cassady & Finch, 2014). Professional counselors offer personalized strategies and coping mechanisms tailored to individual needs. Counseling provides a safe space to explore underlying issues contributing to test anxiety and develop effective solutions. By addressing these concerns with a trained professional, students can gain valuable insights and support, ultimately improving their ability to manage stress and perform effectively in exam situations.

By integrating these strategies, students can effectively manage and overcome test anxiety, fostering a more positive and successful academic experience.

Addressing Unresolved Issues: Strategies for Resolution

Unresolved issues can significantly impact a college student's well-being, academic performance, and overall college experience. Whether from personal challenges, conflicts, or past traumas, addressing unresolved issues involves adopting coping mechanisms, seeking support, and implementing strategies to foster emotional healing.

Acknowledgment and Reflection

The first step in addressing unresolved issues is to acknowledge their presence and engage in self-reflection. Recognizing and naming these issues is crucial for understanding their root causes and impacts on one's life (Pennebaker, 2004).

Techniques such as journaling, where individuals write about their thoughts and feelings or seek guidance through counseling, can facilitate this reflective process. These practices help uncover underlying emotions and patterns, providing clarity on how unresolved issues affect daily life and well-being. Reflecting on these insights enables individuals to begin the process of addressing and resolving their challenges effectively.

Utilize Campus Counseling Services

Campus counseling services offer a valuable resource for students seeking support for unresolved issues. These services provide a confidential and supportive environment where students can explore personal challenges and work toward resolution with the help of trained professionals (American College Counseling Association, 2017). Professional counselors on campus are equipped to guide individuals through various therapeutic processes, offering tools and strategies to address emotional and psychological concerns. These services can facilitate healing and help students navigate their issues with expert support.

Engage in Supportive Networks

Building and engaging with supportive networks is essential for managing and overcoming unresolved issues. Connecting with friends, family, or campus groups provides a network of emotional support and understanding (Cohen & Wills, 1985). These relationships offer a space to share experiences and seek guidance, which can be crucial for personal growth and healing. Supportive networks help individuals feel less isolated in their struggles, offering both practical advice and emotional reassurance, which contributes to a more balanced and resilient approach to managing issues.

Practice Mindfulness and Meditation

Mindfulness and meditation are effective techniques for managing stress and enhancing emotional well-being. By incorporating these practices into a daily routine, individuals can develop a greater sense of presence and focus (Kabat-Zinn, 1994). Mindfulness involves paying attention to the present moment without judgment, while meditation provides a structured approach to calming the mind. These practices help reduce anxiety, improve emotional regulation, and foster a more balanced perspective on challenges. Regular engagement in mindfulness and meditation can significantly support overall mental health and resilience.

Set Boundaries

Establishing and maintaining clear boundaries in both personal and academic spheres is essential for managing stress and resolving unresolved issues. Setting boundaries involves recognizing one's limits and communicating them effectively to others (Cloud & Townsend, 1999). This practice helps prevent burnout and additional stress by ensuring that individuals do not overextend themselves. Clearly defined boundaries enable individuals to manage their time and energy more effectively, contributing to better emotional and mental health.

Seek Professional Help

For deeply rooted or traumatic unresolved issues, seeking professional help from a mental health professional is crucial. Therapists and psychologists provide specialized support and therapeutic interventions tailored to individual needs (American Psychological Association, 2017). Professional help can address complex emotional and psychological challenges, offering a structured approach to healing and growth. Engaging with a mental health professional provides access to expert guidance and strategies for managing and overcoming significant issues.

Participate in Supportive Workshops and Programs

Colleges often offer workshops and programs focused on mental health and personal development, which can benefit students dealing with unresolved issues. These activities provide valuable insights, practical tools, and a sense of community (Keyes, 2007). Such workshops allow students to gain new perspectives, learn coping strategies, and connect with others facing similar challenges. These experiences contribute to personal growth and a supportive environment that fosters well-being and resilience.

Cultivate Self-Compassion

Developing self-compassion is a key strategy for navigating challenges with resilience and acceptance. Self-compassion involves treating oneself with kindness and understanding, especially in the face of setbacks or difficulties (Neff, 2011). By embracing self-compassion, individuals can reduce self-criticism and foster a more positive and supportive inner dialogue. This approach helps build emotional resilience and provides a foundation for coping with unresolved issues in a more balanced and accepting manner.

By implementing these strategies, college students can more effectively address unresolved issues, promote emotional well-being, and create a more positive and fulfilling college experience.

Conquering Distraction Issues

In the digital age, distractions significantly challenge college students, affecting academic performance and overall well-being. Overcoming distraction issues involves implementing effective strategies, fostering discipline, and cultivating an environment conducive to focused learning.

Implement the Pomodoro Technique

The Pomodoro Technique is a time management method that involves breaking work into focused intervals, typically 25 minutes, known as "Pomodoros," followed by short breaks of about 5 minutes (Cirillo, 2007). This structured approach helps enhance concentration and productivity by maintaining a high level of focus during each Pomodoro and allowing for regular rest periods to prevent burnout. By adhering to this technique, students can manage their time more effectively, reduce procrastination, and maintain sustained attention to their tasks. The periodic breaks also help refresh the mind, making tackling complex or lengthy study sessions easier.

Create a Dedicated Study Environment

Designating a specific area solely for studying can significantly improve focus and productivity. A dedicated study environment signals to the brain that it is time to concentrate, which can enhance cognitive performance (Kuo & Sullivan, 2001). To create an effective study space, it is important to minimize external distractions, maintain a clutter-free workspace, and ensure that the area is well-lit and ergonomically designed. A personalized and organized study environment helps maintain focus and promotes a positive association with study sessions, making them more efficient and effective.

Utilize Focus Apps and Tools

Focus apps and tools are designed to help students manage digital distractions by blocking access to non-essential websites and limiting screen time. These tools can enhance productivity by ensuring that students remain focused during study sessions (Kostadinov, Read, & Riedel, 2018). Examples of such tools include website blockers that prevent access to social media and notification managers that control interruptions from various apps. By integrating these tools into their study routine, students can create a more controlled and distraction-free digital environment, which supports better concentration and task completion.

Practice Mindfulness Meditation

Mindfulness meditation is a practice that improves focus and attention by training individuals to maintain awareness and presence in the moment (Tang et al., 2007). Incorporating mindfulness exercises into a daily routine helps enhance overall concentration and resilience against distractions. Regular mindfulness practice, such as guided meditations or mindfulness breathing exercises, supports cognitive function and emotional regulation. This improved focus can lead to better academic performance and a more balanced approach to managing stress and distractions during study sessions.

Set Realistic Goals and Prioritize Tasks

Setting realistic goals and prioritizing tasks are essential strategies for maintaining organization and focus. Establishing clear, achievable objectives and breaking down larger tasks into manageable steps can help prevent feeling overwhelmed (Locke & Latham, 2002). Creating a to-do list and prioritizing tasks based on their importance and deadlines allows students to stay organized and clearly focus on their academic responsibilities. This structured approach helps manage workload effectively and supports consistent progress toward achieving academic goals.

Establish Digital Boundaries

Creating digital boundaries is crucial for minimizing distractions and enhancing focus during study sessions. Setting specific times for checking emails and social media and turning off non-essential notifications helps maintain a focused digital environment (Mark et al., 2014). By controlling digital interruptions, students can allocate uninterrupted time for study and reduce the cognitive load associated with frequent task-switching. Establishing these boundaries supports better concentration and productivity, contributing to a more effective learning experience.

Practice Active Learning Techniques

Active learning techniques, such as taking notes, asking questions, and participating in discussions, are effective for maintaining engagement and focus during study sessions (Freeman et al., 2014). Actively involving oneself in the learning process enhances understanding and retention of informatio reducing distractions' impact. By engaging in interactive and participatory learning methods, students can stay more focused on the material and improve their overall academic performance.

Prioritize Well-Being

Prioritizing well-being through adequate sleep, regular exercise, and a balanced diet is fundamental for maintaining cognitive function and focus (Walker, 2017). A healthy lifestyle supports the brain's ability to process information, manage stress, and maintain concentration. Ensuring that physical health needs are met contributes to improved mental clarity and resilience against distractions, making it easier for students to engage fully in their academic tasks and perform at their best.

By incorporating these strategies, college students can effectively manage distractions, enhance focus, and create a productive and supportive learning environment.

Building Confidence for Success

Confidence is a key determinant of academic success, yet many college students grapple with self-doubt. Overcoming confidence issues involves adopting a growth mindset, seeking support, and engaging in activities that foster self-assurance.

Adopting a Growth Mindset

Embracing a growth mindset involves believing that abilities and intelligence can be developed through dedication and hard work. This perspective, as outlined by Dweck (2008), transforms challenges into opportunities for learning and growth rather than viewing them as insurmountable obstacles. By focusing on effort and persistence, individuals with a growth mindset are more likely to embrace difficulties, view failures as valuable learning experiences, and continuously seek self-improvement. This mindset fosters resilience, boosts confidence, and encourages a belief in one's capacity to develop new skills over time, leading to greater academic and personal success.

Setting Realistic Goals

Setting realistic and achievable goals is crucial for building confidence and maintaining motivation. According to Locke and Latham (2002), breaking larger objectives into smaller, manageable tasks allows for incremental progress and a sense of accomplishment. This approach not only helps in organizing and prioritizing efforts but also provides a clear roadmap to success. By achieving these smaller goals, individuals experience continuous positive reinforcement, which contributes to increased confidence and motivation to tackle more significant challenges.

Celebrating Small Wins

Acknowledging and celebrating small achievements is essential for reinforcing a positive self-image and building confidence. Fredrickson (2004) highlights that recognizing even minor successes, whether academic or personal, fosters a sense of accomplishment and encourages further progress. Celebrating these incremental victories helps maintain motivation and creates a positive feedback loop, enhancing overall self-esteem and resilience. This practice of acknowledging progress contributes to a more optimistic outlook and sustained confidence in one's abilities.

Seeking Support from Peers and Mentors

Building a network of peers and mentors provides invaluable support and encouragement, significantly boosting confidence. Bandura (1997) emphasizes that interacting with individuals who share similar experiences and can offer constructive feedback creates a supportive environment that fosters a sense of belonging and validation. Such relationships provide practical advice and guidance and contribute to a stronger sense of self-efficacy, as individuals receive affirmation and encouragement from those who understand their challenges and goals.

Engaging in Skill-Building Activities

Participating in skill-building activities that align with personal interests or academic pursuits plays a crucial role in developing confidence. Csikszentmihalyi (1997) notes that engaging in activities that challenge and expand one's abilities leads to a greater sense of competence and self-assurance. By acquiring new skills and enhancing existing ones, individuals gain confidence in their ability to tackle various challenges. These activities provide opportunities for growth and accomplishment, reinforcing the belief in one's capacity to succeed.

Utilizing Campus Resources

College campuses often provide various resources, including writing centers, tutoring services, and career counseling, which are instrumental in building confidence. According to Tinto (1993), taking advantage of these resources offers targeted support that addresses specific academic or career needs. Accessing these services can enhance skills, clarify doubts, and provide personalized guidance, contributing to improved performance and greater confidence in one's academic and professional abilities.

Practicing Self-Compassion

Developing self-compassion involves treating oneself with kindness and understanding, especially in the face of setbacks or challenges. Neff (2011) argues that this mindset shift reduces harsh self-criticism and fosters a more supportive internal dialogue. By embracing self-compassion, individuals can navigate difficulties with greater resilience and maintain a positive self-image. This approach enhances overall confidence and emotional well-being, as individuals learn to accept imperfections and view challenges as opportunities for growth rather than failures.

Engaging in Public Speaking and Leadership Activities

Participation in public speaking and leadership activities is a powerful way to develop communication and leadership skills, which significantly contribute to increased confidence. Kouzes and Posner (2007) highlight that taking on roles that involve public speaking or leading groups helps individuals build competence and self-assurance. Success in these areas enhances one's ability to communicate effectively and boosts confidence in handling various situations, fostering a more assertive and capable self-image.

By integrating these strategies, college students can effectively address confidence issues, leading to a more positive self-image and overall success in their academic and personal endeavors.

Navigating Commitment Issues

Commitment issues, whether related to academic pursuits, extracurricular activities, or personal relationships, can impede a college student's overall success and satisfaction. Overcoming commitment issues involves fostering self-awareness, setting priorities, and adopting strategies to enhance dedication.

Reflect on Values and Goals

Reflecting on personal values and long-term goals is critical for aligning daily commitments with one's overarching aspirations. Emmons and McCullough (2003) emphasize that such reflection helps individuals understand the, more profound significance of their activities and choices, fostering a sense of purpose and direction. By regularly assessing how current commitments relate to their core values and long-term objectives, students can ensure that their efforts are meaningful and aligned with their vision, which enhances motivation and fulfillment in their academic and personal pursuits.

Prioritize Commitments

Prioritizing commitments based on their importance and impact is essential for, adequate time and energy management. Covey (1989) suggests that clear prioritization helps students focus on what truly matters, reducing overwhelming feelings and enabling a more structured approach to their responsibilities. By first identifying and addressing the most significant commitments, students can allocate their resources more efficiently, maintain a balanced workload, and achieve their goals with greater ease and effectiveness.

Break Down Large Tasks

Large tasks can often seem overwhelming and contribute to difficulties with commitment. According to Locke and Latham (2002), breaking these tasks into smaller, more manageable steps can make them less daunting and more approachable. This approach allows students to tackle one component at a time, providing a clearer path to completion and creating a sense of accomplishment with each milestone achieved. Gradually working through these steps can enhance motivation and make the overall task feel more manageable and achievable.

Establish Clear Goals

Setting clear, specific, and measurable goals is fundamental for maintaining commitment and motivation. Latham and Seijts (1999) highlight that well-defined goals provide a structured roadmap, offering clarity on what needs to be achieved and how to measure progress. By establishing clear objectives, students can maintain focus and direction, effectively track their achievements, and stay motivated throughout their academic and personal endeavors.

Develop a Routine

Creating a daily or weekly routine introduces structure and predictability into one's schedule, facilitating consistent commitment to tasks and responsibilities. Gardner and Rebar (2019) argue that routines help in forming positive habits and integrating tasks into one's regular schedule, making it easier to maintain commitment over time. A well-established routine reduces decision fatigue, streamlines daily activities, and supports a more disciplined approach to achieving goals and managing responsibilities.

Seek Accountability

Seeking accountability by sharing commitments with a friend, mentor, or study group can provide valuable external motivation and support. Gollwitzer and Sheeran (2006) explain that knowing others are aware of one's goals can enhance motivation and reinforce commitment. This external pressure and encouragement help students stay focused and diligent, as regular check-ins and shared progress updates can boost accountability and drive continued effort toward achieving their objectives.

Manage Time Effectively

Effective time management is crucial for balancing multiple commitments and responsibilities. Macan et al. (1990) emphasize that using calendars, planners, and productivity apps can help students organize their tasks, prioritize their workload, and allocate sufficient time for each commitment. By implementing these time management strategies, students can improve their organizational skills, reduce stress, and ensure that they meet deadlines and fulfill their responsibilities more efficiently.

Address Underlying Issues

Commitment issues can often be rooted in underlying concerns such as fear of failure or perfectionism. Flett et al. (1998) suggest that addressing these issues through self-reflection or professional counseling can lead to a healthier commitment approach. By exploring and resolving these underlying factors, students can overcome barriers to commitment, develop more realistic expectations, and adopt a more balanced and resilient mindset toward their goals and responsibilities.

By integrating these strategies into their approach, college students can effectively address and overcome commitment issues, leading to a more purposeful and successful academic experience.

Navigating Employment Issues

Balancing employment alongside academic responsibilities can be challenging for college students. Overcoming employment-related detractions involves effective time management, seeking flexible work arrangements, and utilizing campus resources to maintain a harmonious integration of work and academics.

Prioritize Time Management

Effective time management is essential for students balancing both work and academic commitments. According to Britton and Tesser (1991), creating a realistic schedule that allocates dedicated time for both work and study enables students to maintain a healthy balance between their responsibilities. By setting aside specific periods for each activity and using time management techniques, students can better organize their tasks, avoid procrastination, and ensure they meet their academic deadlines while fulfilling work obligations. This structured approach helps prevent the overlap of responsibilities and reduces the likelihood of stress and burnout.

Communicate with Employers

Open communication with employers regarding academic commitments is vital for achieving a harmonious balance between work and studies. Clark (2001) highlights that discussing workload expectations and the need for flexibility fosters mutual understanding and cooperation. By proactively informing employers about class schedules, exam periods, and other academic demands, students can negotiate adjustments to their work hours or responsibilities. This collaborative approach helps manage work expectations and demonstrates professionalism and commitment, benefiting both the student and the employer.

Explore Flexible Employment Options

Exploring part-time or flexible employment options can significantly alleviate the challenge of balancing work with academic commitments. Kossek, Lautsch, and Eaton (2006) suggest that seeking positions with adjustable hours or remote work possibilities provides greater flexibility to accommodate academic schedules. Such employment arrangements allow students to work around their class times and study needs, reducing the stress of rigid work schedules and enhancing their ability to effectively manage both work and academic responsibilities.

Utilize Campus Career Services

Campus career services are valuable resources for finding employment opportunities that align with academic schedules. Kanchier (2011) notes that career counselors offer guidance on balancing work and academic commitments, helping students find jobs that complement their study routines. By leveraging career services, students can access job listings tailored to their availability, receive assistance with job applications, and gain insights into managing work-study balance, thereby optimizing their academic and professional experiences.

Set Realistic Work Hours

Establishing realistic work hours is crucial for preventing burnout and ensuring ample time for academic responsibilities. According to Duxbury and Higgins (1991), setting work hours that do not overwhelm students and leave sufficient time for studying and relaxation contributes to overall well-being. By realistically assessing their capacity to handle work and academic tasks, students can avoid overextending themselves and maintain a sustainable balance, which is essential for long-term success and health.

Establish Boundaries

Setting clear boundaries between work and study time is essential for maintaining a healthy equilibrium. Cloud and Townsend (1999) emphasize the importance of avoiding overcommitment and learning to say no when necessary to prevent work or academic responsibilities from encroaching on each other. Establishing firm boundaries helps students manage their time effectively, ensuring that work and study commitments receive the attention they need without compromising personal well-being.

Practice Self-Care

Practicing self-care is crucial for students balancing demanding work and academic schedules. Walker (2017) highlights that prioritizing sleep, exercise, and relaxation contributes to overall well-being and resilience. By integrating self-care practices into their routines, students can better manage stress, maintain physical health, and enhance their ability to cope with the pressures of balancing work and studies. Self-care supports sustained academic performance and job efficiency while fostering a positive and balanced lifestyle.

Utilize Technology for Efficiency

Leveraging technology can enhance efficiency and help manage time more effectively. Rosen, Carrier, and Cheever (2013) suggest that productivity apps and tools can streamline tasks, reduce unnecessary stress, and facilitate better time management. By employing technology for scheduling, task management, and reminders, students can optimize their productivity, minimize distractions, and ensure they stay on track with academic and work responsibilities.

By incorporating these strategies, college students can effectively navigate the challenges of balancing employment with their academic commitments, fostering a balanced and successful college experience.

Navigating Family Issues

Family issues can pose significant detractions for college students, impacting academic performance and overall well-being. Overcoming challenges related to family issues involves communication, seeking support, and establishing boundaries to maintain a healthy balance between familial responsibilities and academic pursuits.

Open Communication with Family

Maintaining open and honest communication with family members is crucial for a supportive academic experience. Galvin and Brommel (2018) emphasize that clearly expressing one's academic commitments, expectations, and potential challenges to family members fosters understanding and support. When students share their schedules, academic pressures, and any difficulties they may face, family members can better appreciate their demands and offer more effective support. This transparency helps prevent misunderstandings and ensures family dynamics do not negatively impact academic performance.

Establish Boundaries

Setting clear boundaries between family responsibilities and academic commitments is essential for maintaining a healthy balance. Cloud and Townsend (1999) highlight that defining specific study times and communicating these boundaries to family members helps manage expectations and prevents conflicts. By establishing when they are available for family responsibilities and when they need uninterrupted study time, students can protect their academic focus and reduce stress caused by overlapping obligations. This structured approach allows for more efficient time management and helps maintain a productive study environment.

Utilize Campus Counseling Services

Campus counseling services offer valuable support for students facing family-related challenges. According to the American College Counseling Association (2017), these services provide a safe and confidential space where students can discuss their concerns and receive professional guidance. Counselors are equipped to help students navigate complex family dynamics, manage stress, and develop coping strategies, contributing to improved emotional well-being and academic performance.

Utilizing these resources can help students address family issues in a supportive and constructive manner.

Seek Peer Support

Connecting with peers who are experiencing similar family-related challenges can provide a sense of community and understanding. Cohen and Wills (1985) argue that peer support groups or student organizations offer valuable insights and encouragement, helping students feel less isolated in their struggles. Sharing experiences with others who understand the pressures of balancing family and academics fosters a supportive network, provides emotional relief, and enhances resilience. This communal support can be instrumental in managing both personal and academic challenges.

Establish a Support Network on Campus

Building a support network on campus is crucial for creating a sense of belonging and receiving guidance during difficult times. Tinto (1993) asserts that having a network of friends, professors, and advisors provides emotional and practical support, helping students navigate academic and personal challenges more effectively. These connections offer a range of assistance, from academic advice to emotional support, contributing to a more fulfilling college experience and helping students balance their familial and academic responsibilities.

Create a Flexible Study Schedule

A flexible study schedule is essential for accommodating academic and family commitments. Britton and Tesser (1991) suggest that creating a schedule that allows for adaptability in response to unexpected family events helps students fulfill their responsibilities more effectively. By incorporating flexibility into their study plans, students can better manage their time and reduce the stress associated with balancing academic work with family obligations. This approach enables them to stay on track with their studies while addressing any urgent family needs.

Practice Stress Management Techniques

Family issues can significantly contribute to stress, impacting academic performance. Kabat-Zinn (1994) emphasizes the importance of practicing stress management techniques, such as mindfulness, meditation, or exercise, to enhance resilience. These practices help students manage stress more effectively, maintain emotional balance, and improve overall well-being. Incorporating stress management strategies into daily routines can mitigate the negative effects of family-related stress and support better academic performance.

Consider Family Counseling

When family issues are complex, seeking the assistance of a family counselor can be highly beneficial. Nichols and Schwartz (2008) describe how family counseling provides a structured environment for addressing underlying challenges and improving family dynamics. Working with a professional counselor allows families to explore and resolve conflicts, enhance communication, and develop healthier relationships. This support can alleviate some of the pressures on students and contribute to a more balanced and positive academic experience.

By incorporating these strategies, college students can effectively manage family-related detractions, fostering a supportive environment that enhances both academic success and familial connections.

Navigating Burnout

Burnout, characterized by emotional exhaustion, cynicism, and reduced effectiveness, is a significant challenge for college students juggling academic demands, extracurricular activities, and personal responsibilities. Overcoming burnout involves proactive self-care, time management, and fostering a supportive environment to maintain well-being and academic success.

Prioritize Self-Care

Incorporating self-care practices such as adequate sleep, regular exercise, and healthy nutrition is essential for preventing burnout and maintaining overall well-being. Walker (2017) emphasizes that prioritizing physical and mental health directly impacts resilience and productivity. Adequate sleep helps with cognitive function and emotional regulation, exercise boosts mood and energy levels, and proper nutrition supports physical health and mental clarity. By committing to these self-care practices, students can enhance their ability to cope with stress and perform effectively academically and personally.

Establish Realistic Goals

Setting achievable and realistic goals is critical for managing expectations and avoiding burnout. Locke and Latham (2002) argue that breaking down larger tasks into smaller, manageable steps helps promote a sense of accomplishment and prevents feelings of being overwhelmed. By creating specific, measurable, attainable, relevant, and time-bound (SMART) goals, students can maintain focus and motivation. This structured approach allows for steady progress and reduces the risk of burnout by ensuring that goals are attainable within the available time and resources.

Practice Mindfulness and Stress Reduction

Engaging in mindfulness practices such as meditation and deep breathing exercises can significantly reduce stress levels and enhance emotional well-being. Kabat-Zinn (1994) highlights that mindfulness helps individuals stay present and manage academic pressures more effectively. Techniques like mindfulness meditation improve emotional regulation and cognitive flexibility, allowing students to cope better with stress and prevent burnout. Regular practice of these techniques fosters a calm and focused mindset, contributing to better overall academic performance and mental health.

Utilize Effective Time Management

Implementing effective time management techniques, such as prioritizing tasks and avoiding procrastination, is crucial for maintaining a balanced workload. Britton and Tesser (1991) emphasize that efficient time management helps prevent overwhelming workloads that can lead to burnout. By using tools like planners, to-do lists, and time-blocking strategies, students can organize their tasks, meet deadlines, and reduce stress. Effective time management ensures that academic responsibilities are met without excessive last-minute pressures, promoting a more sustainable and less stressful academic experience.

Seek Social Support

Building a strong social support network, including friends, family, and mentors, provides essential emotional assistance during challenging times. Cohen and Wills (1985) suggest that sharing concerns and seeking advice from supportive individuals fosters a sense of community and belonging. A robust support network can offer practical help, emotional comfort, and encouragement, which are crucial for managing stress and preventing burnout. Connecting with others who understand the pressures of academic life can enhance resilience and provide valuable perspectives and support.

Set Boundaries and Learn to Say No

Establishing clear boundaries and learning to say no when necessary is crucial for preventing burnout. Cloud and Townsend (1999) discuss that overcommitting to academic and extracurricular activities can lead to excessive stress and decreased productivity. By setting limits on how much time and energy is allocated to various commitments, students can manage their workload more effectively. Clear boundaries help maintain a healthy balance between responsibilities and personal time, reducing the risk of burnout and improving overall well-being.

Take Breaks and Schedule Downtime

Incorporating breaks into study sessions and scheduling regular downtime for leisure activities is essential for maintaining mental health and preventing burnout. Kuo and Sullivan (2001) find that taking breaks enhances focus and prevents mental fatigue. Regular intervals of rest and relaxation allow students to recharge and maintain productivity over longer periods. Students can manage stress more effectively and sustain their academic performance by scheduling time for hobbies, social activities, and relaxation.

Regularly Evaluate and Adjust Goals

Periodically assessing and adjusting academic and personal goals is important for staying aligned with current priorities and preventing burnout. Austin and Vancouver (1996) highlight that flexibility in goal-setting allows for adaptations based on changing circumstances and new information. By regularly reviewing goals, students can make necessary adjustments to ensure they remain realistic and attainable. This approach helps avoid the frustration and stress of unrealistic expectations and supports a more balanced and manageable academic journey.

By integrating these strategies, college students can proactively manage burnout and foster a healthy balance between academic responsibilities and personal well-being.

Navigating Uncertainty: Career and Personal Goals

Uncertainty regarding career paths and personal goals is a common challenge for college students. Overcoming these detractions involves self-exploration, goal setting, seeking guidance, and fostering adaptability to thrive in an ever-evolving landscape.

Engage in Self-Exploration

College is an ideal period for self-discovery and personal growth. Engaging in self-reflection allows students to explore their interests, values, and skills, which is crucial for setting meaningful career and personal goals. According to Super (1990), self-exploration during college helps individuals understand their unique attributes and preferences, which can guide their career choices and personal development. By reflecting on their experiences and aspirations, students can make informed decisions about their future paths, leading to a more fulfilling and aligned career and personal life.

Set Short-Term and Long-Term Goals

Establishing short-term and long-term goals is essential for creating a structured approach to achieving career and personal aspirations. Short-term goals provide immediate direction and actionable steps, while long-term goals offer a broader vision and sense of purpose. Locke and Latham (2002) emphasize that having a clear roadmap, with both types of goals, helps individuals stay motivated and focused. Short-term goals act as milestones on the way to long-term objectives, enabling students to track their progress and adjust their plans as needed, thus maintaining a sense of direction and achievement.

Seek Guidance from Career Services

College career services are valuable resources that offer career counseling, aptitude assessments, and job placement assistance. Brown and Ryan Krane (2000) highlight the importance of utilizing these services to clarify potential career paths. Career professionals can provide personalized advice and support, helping students explore various options and make informed decisions about their futures. By engaging with career services, students can better understand their strengths and interests, leading to more strategic and effective career planning.

Embrace Adaptability and Flexibility

In the ever-evolving job market, adaptability and flexibility are crucial traits for career success. Hargrove (2008) asserts that being open to change and willing to adjust goals in response to new opportunities allows individuals to navigate uncertainties more effectively. Embracing adaptability helps students respond to shifting career trends and emerging opportunities, enabling them to make the most of their evolving interests and circumstances. This flexible approach fosters resilience and enhances the ability to thrive in a dynamic and unpredictable work environment.

Network and Seek Mentors

Networking with professionals and seeking mentors can provide valuable insights into various career paths and industries. Kram (1985) underscores the importance of building relationships with experienced individuals who can offer guidance, share their experiences, and provide valuable perspectives. Mentors can help students navigate their career choices, provide support and encouragement, and open doors to new opportunities. By actively engaging with mentors and expanding their professional networks, students can gain a deeper understanding of their chosen fields and enhance their career prospects.

Participate in Internships and Experiential Learning

Participating in internships and other experiential learning opportunities is crucial for gaining practical experience and clarifying career goals. Andriotis (2015) notes that real-world exposure allows students to apply theoretical knowledge professionally, helping them refine their aspirations and make informed career decisions. Internships provide hands-on experience, build skills, and offer insights into industry practices, all contributing to a clearer understanding of career interests and readiness for the job market.

Develop a Growth Mindset

Cultivating a growth mindset involves viewing challenges and setbacks as opportunities for learning and personal development. Dweck (2008) emphasizes that adopting this mindset enhances resilience and fosters a positive attitude toward overcoming obstacles. Students with a growth mindset are more likely to embrace challenges, persist in the face of difficulties, and view failures as learning experiences. This approach improves their ability to handle uncertainties and supports continuous growth and adaptation in their career and personal lives.

Balance Realism with Optimism

Balancing realistic assessments of career options with an optimistic outlook is essential for a healthy approach to uncertainty. Carver and Scheier (2014) suggest that acknowledging potential challenges while maintaining a positive mindset enhances coping mechanisms and overall well-being. Students who balance realism with optimism are better equipped to navigate the complexities of career planning and personal development. This balanced perspective helps them stay motivated, adapt to changes, and remain resilient despite setbacks.

By integrating these strategies, college students can effectively manage uncertainties related to career and personal goals, fostering a proactive and adaptable approach to their future.

CHAPTER 4

Agreements

Strategic Agreements

Setting clear and strategic goals is paramount for college success. College students can enhance their academic performance and personal development by establishing well-defined agreements and following a structured approach. The following are key types of agreements and steps that students can undertake for effective goal setting.

Academic Agreements

Academic agreements involve setting clear and actionable goals for one's educational journey. These agreements should specify targets such as maintaining a particular GPA, completing required courses, and achieving milestones for major projects. Establishing such goals with oneself, including commitments to study habits, attendance, and active participation, lays a solid foundation for academic success. According to Locke and Latham (2002), setting specific and measurable goals enhances motivation and performance. By formalizing these academic agreements, students can create a structured plan that guides their efforts and helps them focus on achieving their educational objectives.

Personal Development Agreements

Personal development agreements extend beyond academic achievements to include goals related to leadership skills, communication abilities, and emotional intelligence. These agreements focus on nurturing qualities that contribute to overall personal growth and success. Covey (1989) emphasizes the importance of setting clear personal development goals as part of a holistic approach to self-improvement. By outlining specific objectives in these areas, students can systematically work on enhancing their interpersonal skills and emotional resilience, which are crucial for both professional and personal success.

Time Management Agreements

Time management agreements are essential for balancing academic responsibilities with other aspects of college life. These agreements involve creating a structured plan for allocating study hours, incorporating breaks, and managing extracurricular activities. Effective time management helps students maintain productivity and prevent burnout. Britton and Tesser (1991) highlight that structured time management practices contribute to a more organized and less stressful college experience. By setting clear agreements on managing their time, students can improve their efficiency and ensure they meet their academic and personal commitments.

Collaborative Agreements with Peers

Collaborative agreements with peers are crucial for enhancing group work and project efficiency. These agreements should clearly define roles, responsibilities, and expectations within study groups or project teams. Johnson and Johnson (2009) stress that well-defined collaborative agreements improve group dynamics and productivity. By setting these agreements, students can foster effective teamwork, streamline their collaborative efforts, and achieve more tremendous success in group assignments and projects. Clear communication and mutual understanding are key components of successful peer collaboration.

Mental Health and Well-being Agreements

Mental health and well-being agreements focus on prioritizing self-care practices and managing stress. These agreements should include commitments to regular self-care routines, stress management techniques, and seeking support when needed. Keyes (2002) underscores the importance of mental health in maintaining overall well-being and resilience. By establishing agreements to prioritize mental health, students can create a supportive framework that promotes a positive mindset and helps them navigate the challenges of college life more effectively.

Networking and Career Development Agreements

Networking and career development agreements involve setting clear objectives related to professional connections, internships, and career planning. These agreements should outline specific steps for enhancing networking efforts, gaining relevant work experience, and aligning academic coursework with future career goals. Brown and Ryan Krane (2000) emphasize the importance of structured career development plans for achieving professional success. By formulating these agreements, students can proactively work on building their professional networks and preparing for their future careers, leading to more effective career development and job placement outcomes.

Implementing Agreements

Self-Reflection

Self-reflection involves deeply examining personal values, strengths, and areas for growth. This introspective process helps individuals understand how their academic and personal goals align with their long-term aspirations. By evaluating one's core values and identifying key strengths and weaknesses, students can make more informed decisions about their educational and career paths. Understanding this alignment ensures that goals are meaningful and resonate with one's broader life objectives. As noted by Emmons and McCullough (2003), self-reflection is critical for setting goals that are authentic and relevant, thereby enhancing personal fulfillment and long-term success.

S.M.A.R.T. Goal Setting

The S.M.A.R.T. framework is a strategic approach to goal setting that enhances clarity and feasibility. Goals should be Specific, Measurable, Achievable, Relevant, and Time-bound. This method ensures that objectives are well-defined and realistic, providing a clear path to achievement. Specificity helps focus efforts, measurability allows for tracking progress, achievability ensures the goal is attainable, relevance aligns the goal with broader ambitions, and a time-bound element creates a sense of urgency. According to Locke and Latham (2002), employing the S.M.A.R.T. criteria can significantly improve goal-setting effectiveness and overall performance.

Prioritize Goals

Prioritizing goals involves assessing their relative importance and impact on overall success. By evaluating which goals contribute most significantly to personal or academic objectives, students can focus their efforts on what matters most.

This process helps in managing time and resources effectively, ensuring that high-impact goals receive adequate attention. Covey (1989) emphasizes the importance of prioritization in achieving long-term success and managing complex responsibilities. Effective prioritization not only improves goal achievement but also helps in maintaining motivation and avoiding burnout.

Create Action Plans

Creating detailed action plans is essential for translating goals into actionable steps. Each plan should outline specific actions required, resources needed, and potential obstacles. By breaking down goals into manageable tasks, students can create a clear roadmap for achieving their objectives. Action plans enhance accountability and provide a structured approach to overcoming challenges. According to Britton and Tesser (1991), well-developed action plans are crucial for maintaining focus and ensuring systematic progress towards goal attainment.

Seek Feedback

Seeking feedback from mentors, advisors, or peers is a valuable strategy for refining goals and plans. Sharing one's goals and action plans with others provides an opportunity to receive constructive criticism and additional insights. This external perspective can highlight potential improvements, uncover blind spots, and enhance effectiveness. As noted by Johnson and Johnson (2009), feedback from experienced individuals helps in adjusting strategies and increasing the likelihood of achieving desired outcomes. Engaging with others also fosters a supportive network and encourages collaborative growth.

Regular Review and Adjustment

Regularly reviewing progress and making necessary adjustments is key to effective goal management. Periodic evaluations help in assessing whether goals are being met and whether action plans need modifications. Flexibility allows students to adapt to changing circumstances and new information, ensuring continued relevance and effectiveness of goals. Austin and Vancouver (1996) highlight that ongoing review and adjustment are essential for aligning with evolving priorities and achieving long-term success.

Celebrate Achievements

Celebrating achievements and milestones is crucial for maintaining motivation and a positive mindset. Acknowledging progress, regardless of scale, reinforces a sense of accomplishment and encourages continued effort. Recognizing successes along the way boosts confidence and fosters a positive attitude toward future challenges. Fredrickson (2004) emphasizes that celebrating achievements contributes to overall well-being and motivation, which is vital in sustaining momentum and ensuring a fulfilling journey towards goal completion.

Implementing these strategies provides a structured framework for college students to navigate goal setting effectively, leading to a more successful and fulfilling college experience.

Action Steps

Taking effective action steps is crucial for college students to achieve success academically and personally. By establishing clear agreements and following strategic steps, students can navigate challenges and stay on the path to success. The following outlines key types of agreements and steps supported by relevant citations.

Types of Agreements for Action Steps

Commitment to Proactive Learning

Adopting a proactive approach to learning involves more than simply attending classes; it requires active engagement and a willingness to delve deeply into course material. This commitment includes participating actively in class discussions, asking questions, and seeking clarification on complex topics. Proactive learners take responsibility for their education by preparing for classes in advance, setting personal learning goals, and using available resources effectively. Research by Pintrich and De Groot (1990) highlights that students who actively engage with their learning environment and adopt a proactive stance tend to achieve better academic outcomes. This approach not only enhances understanding but also builds a more meaningful connection with the material, leading to increased motivation and academic success.

Effective Communication Agreements

Establishing effective communication agreements with professors, peers, and support services is crucial for academic success. These agreements involve clearly articulating concerns, seeking regular feedback, and participating actively in collaborative activities. Effective communication ensures that students can address any issues promptly and make the most of available support. Galvin and Brommel (2018) emphasize that transparent and open communication channels foster a supportive learning environment, which is essential for resolving misunderstandings and enhancing the overall learning experience. By actively engaging in dialogue and seeking constructive feedback, students can improve their academic performance and build strong professional relationships.

Time Management Commitments

Committing to effective time management is fundamental for academic achievement. This includes creating detailed schedules, prioritizing tasks based on urgency and importance, and implementing strategies to minimize procrastination. Effective time management practices help students balance their academic responsibilities with other commitments, reducing stress and improving productivity. According to Britton and Tesser (1991), managing time efficiently allows students to meet deadlines, engage more fully in their coursework, and maintain a balanced lifestyle. By adopting structured time management techniques, students can enhance their academic performance and achieve a more organized and fulfilling college experience.

Collaborative Learning Agreements

Engaging in collaborative learning involves agreeing to actively participate in study groups, peer discussions, and group projects. This approach not only helps in sharing knowledge but also in gaining diverse perspectives on the course material. Collaborative learning fosters a deeper understanding of the subject matter by allowing students to work together to solve problems and explore concepts more thoroughly. Johnson and Johnson (2009) demonstrate that collaborative learning environments can enhance critical thinking skills, improve retention of information, and build teamwork abilities. By committing to collaborative learning, students can enrich their educational experience and achieve better academic outcomes through mutual support and shared learning.

Implementing Action Steps

Set Clear Goals

Establishing clear and well-defined goals is crucial for academic success and personal development. Short-term goals might include completing assignments by their deadlines or improving grades in specific courses. In contrast, long-term goals could encompass achieving a certain GPA or preparing for a future career. Setting these goals provides direction and a sense of purpose, which can motivate students to stay focused and organized. According to Locke and Latham (2002), clearly defined goals are essential for directing effort and improving performance. Creating a roadmap with specific, measurable, and attainable goals allows students to track their progress, make necessary adjustments, and remain committed to their educational and personal objectives.

Break Down Goals into Actionable Steps

Breaking down larger goals into smaller, actionable steps makes them more manageable and less overwhelming. This process involves decomposing a significant goal into incremental tasks that are easier to accomplish and monitor. For instance, if the goal is to write a research paper, smaller steps might include selecting a topic, conducting research, drafting an outline, and writing individual sections. Zimmerman (1989) emphasizes that this approach enhances clarity and facilitates steady progress by providing a clear pathway to achieve larger objectives. By focusing on these manageable steps, students can maintain momentum, build confidence through incremental achievements, and ultimately achieve their larger goals more effectively.

Utilize Effective Study Techniques

Employing evidence-based study techniques is fundamental for improving learning outcomes and academic performance. Techniques such as active reading, which involves engaging with the text through questioning and summarizing, note-taking strategies like the Cornell method, and concept mapping, which visually organizes information, have enhanced comprehension and retention. Dunlosky, Rawson, Marsh, Nathan, and Willingham (2013) provide a comprehensive review of various study strategies, highlighting their effectiveness in promoting deeper learning. By adopting these proven methods, students can optimize their study sessions, improve their understanding of course material, and achieve better academic results.

Regularly Evaluate Progress

Regular evaluation of progress towards goals is essential for maintaining alignment with overall objectives and making necessary adjustments. Establishing a routine for self-assessment allows students to monitor their advancement, identify potential obstacles, and adjust their strategies as needed. Zimmerman (2008) underscores the importance of periodic evaluations in the self-regulation process, as they help students stay on track and refine their approaches to meet their goals. By consistently reviewing their progress, students can make informed decisions about their academic and personal development, ensuring that their efforts remain focused and effective.

Seek Support and Resources

Utilizing available support services, such as tutoring, counseling, and academic advising, plays a critical role in overcoming challenges and enhancing academic performance. These resources offer valuable assistance, guidance, and encouragement, helping students address difficulties and stay on track with their goals. Robbins et al. (2004) highlight that seeking support and leveraging resources can significantly improve resilience and academic outcomes. By actively engaging with support services, students can gain insights, receive personalized help, and build a network of support that contributes to their overall success and well-being.

Reflect and Adapt

Regular self-reflection is crucial for assessing strengths, weaknesses, and areas for improvement. Through self-reflection, students can evaluate their learning strategies, identify effective methods, and recognize areas where changes are needed. Boud, Keogh, and Walker (1985) emphasize that reflective practices enable students to adapt their approaches based on insights gained from their experiences. By incorporating feedback and adjusting to their study strategies, students can continuously improve their performance, enhance their learning experiences, and develop skills essential for lifelong learning.

Empowering Student Achievement

Achieving success in college involves more than just setting goals—it requires a series of intentional and well-thought-out action steps. By incorporating evidence-based strategies, college students can maximize their potential and navigate the complexities of academic and personal development. The following outlines key types of actions and steps, supported by relevant citations, that contribute to student success:

Effective Time Management

Implementing effective time management strategies is essential for academic success and personal efficiency. Creating a structured schedule that allocates specific time blocks for studying, attending classes, and engaging in extracurricular activities helps ensure that all responsibilities are met. Prioritizing tasks based on their urgency and importance allows students to focus on high-impact activities and avoid procrastination, which can lead to unnecessary stress and last-minute cramming. Britton and Tesser (1991) emphasize that effective time management not only enhances productivity but also reduces anxiety by providing a clear plan for balancing various demands. By mastering time management, students can create a more organized approach to their workload, resulting in improved performance and well-being.

Active Learning Techniques

Active learning techniques are crucial for deepening understanding and improving retention of course material. Methods such as note-taking during lectures, participating in group discussions, and teaching concepts to peers engage students more actively in the learning process. Prince (2004) highlights that these strategies promote a more profound grasp of content by encouraging students to process and apply information rather than passively receiving it. Active learning techniques also facilitate better long-term retention and comprehension, as they require students to interact with and manipulate the material actively. By incorporating these practices, students can enhance their learning outcomes and academic performance.

Utilizing Campus Resources

Taking full advantage of campus resources can significantly enhance academic performance and support overall student success. Resources such as tutoring services, academic advising, and writing centers provide valuable assistance with coursework, offer guidance on academic planning, and help improve writing skills. Kramer and Michel (2005) note that these resources are designed to supplement classroom learning and address individual challenges, making them an essential part of a student's academic support network. By actively seeking out and utilizing these resources, students can gain additional insights, receive personalized help, and better manage their academic responsibilities.

Networking and Building Relationships

Actively networking with professors, peers, and professionals within one's field of study can lead to significant career and academic benefits. Building relationships with these individuals provides opportunities for mentorship, professional advice, and potential career connections. Kram (1985) underscores the importance of networking as it helps students access valuable resources and guidance that can enhance their academic and professional development. Engaging in networking activities such as attending academic conferences, participating in workshops, and joining relevant student organizations can facilitate meaningful connections and open doors to future opportunities.

Effective Study Techniques

Employing evidence-based study techniques is essential for optimizing learning and retention. Techniques such as spaced repetition, retrieval practice, and self-testing enhance memory and understanding. Dunlosky et al. (2013) explain that spaced repetition involves reviewing material at increasing intervals, which helps reinforce long-term retention. Retrieval practice entails actively recalling information rather than passively reviewing it, strengthening memory recall. By incorporating these study methods into their routines, students can improve their ability to retain and apply knowledge effectively.

Balancing Commitments

Maintaining a balance between academic and personal commitments is crucial for overall well-being and success. Setting realistic priorities and learning to avoid non-essential activities helps manage time and reduce stress. Clark (2001) emphasizes the importance of practicing self-care and ensuring that personal needs, such as relaxation and social activities, are not neglected in the pursuit of academic goals. By establishing clear boundaries and prioritizing tasks, students can achieve a healthier equilibrium between their responsibilities and personal lives, leading to greater satisfaction and reduced risk of burnout.

Goal Progress Monitoring

Regularly monitoring progress toward academic and personal goals ensures continued alignment with overall objectives. Establishing a routine for assessing progress allows students to track their achievements, identify challenges, and make necessary adjustments. Locke and Latham (2002) highlight that goal-setting and progress monitoring are key components of successful performance, as they help maintain focus and motivation. By regularly reviewing their goals and making updates based on their experiences and outcomes, students can stay on track and achieve their desired results more effectively.

Seeking and Accepting Feedback

Actively seeking and accepting feedback from professors, peers, and mentors is essential for continuous improvement and development. Feedback provides valuable insights into performance and areas that need enhancement. Hattie and Timperley (2007) emphasize that constructive feedback helps students refine their approaches and better understand expectations. By being open to receiving feedback and incorporating it into their strategies, students can make informed adjustments, improve their skills, and achieve better academic and personal outcomes.

Personal Interest Areas

Role of Student Clubs: Definition, Purpose, and Relevance

Definition

Student clubs, also known as organizations, groups, or societies, are formal associations formed by students with shared interests, goals, or activities. These clubs exist on college campuses to provide a platform for students to connect, engage, and collaborate outside of the academic setting.

Purpose

The primary purpose of student clubs is to foster a sense of community and provide opportunities for students to explore their interests, develop skills, and build meaningful connections with peers who share similar passions. These clubs often focus on various activities, including academic, cultural, recreational, and community service initiatives.

Relevance

Participation in student clubs is highly relevant to the overall college experience and individual success. Clubs offer a space for students to extend their learning beyond the classroom, apply theoretical knowledge, and develop practical skills in a supportive environment. Additionally, involvement in clubs contributes to personal and professional growth, building a well- rounded skill set that goes beyond academic achievements.

Connectiveness

Student clubs act as a bridge, connecting students with similar interests, values, or career aspirations. This connectiveness facilitates networking, collaboration, and the exchange of ideas. By joining a club, students become part of a community that shares a common purpose, creating a sense of belonging that enhances the college experience.

Why Students Should Be Part of Clubs for Success

Skill Development

Student clubs serve as valuable platforms for honing a wide range of skills essential for personal and professional growth. Participation in clubs often involves activities such as organizing events, leading projects, and collaborating with others, which enhance leadership, communication, teamwork, and problem-solving abilities. Astin and Astin (2000) emphasize that involvement in extracurricular activities provides practical experiences that help students develop these competencies, which are highly transferable to the workplace. This experiential learning complements academic studies by fostering skills that are crucial for career success and personal development.

Networking Opportunities

Engaging in student clubs offers unique networking opportunities that can significantly benefit students' future careers. By participating in club activities, students interact with peers, faculty, and professionals, building a network of contacts that can provide mentorship, job referrals, and career advice. Pascarella and Terenzini (2005) highlight that these connections can be instrumental in securing internships, job placements, and professional growth, making student clubs a valuable resource for career development. Networking through clubs not only enhances professional relationships but also enriches the overall college experience.

Enhanced Well-being

Membership in student clubs contributes to improved mental well-being and overall satisfaction with the college experience. Being part of a club provides a sense of belonging and community, which can alleviate feelings of isolation and stress. According to Hurtado and Carter (1997), social support from club involvement plays a crucial role in enhancing students' emotional health and fostering a positive college environment. The social interactions and support networks developed through clubs contribute to a more balanced and fulfilling college life.

Application of Classroom Learning

Student clubs offer practical avenues for applying academic knowledge to real-world scenarios, bridging the gap between theory and practice. By participating in club projects and activities, students can use concepts learned in the classroom in a practical setting, reinforcing their understanding and gaining hands-on experience. The National Association of Colleges and Employers (2018) underscores that such practical experiences help solidify academic learning and prepare students for future professional challenges. Clubs provide a platform for students to test and apply their skills in a supportive environment, enhancing their educational journey.

Leadership Opportunities

Many student clubs provide valuable opportunities for students to take on leadership roles, such as club president, event coordinator, or committee chair. These roles allow students to develop and demonstrate their leadership potential, a quality that is highly valued by employers. Komives, Lucas, and McMahon (1998) assert that involvement in leadership positions within clubs helps students cultivate essential leadership skills, including decision-making, strategic planning, and team management. Such experiences are beneficial for personal growth and can significantly enhance students' resumes and career prospects.

Diversity and Cultural Understanding

Joining student clubs that focus on diverse interests or cultural backgrounds enhances students' understanding of different perspectives and promotes cultural competence. Clubs dedicated to various cultures or social issues expose students to a broad range of viewpoints, fostering greater empathy and appreciation for diversity. Chang, Astin, and Kim (2004) note that this engagement with diverse groups helps students develop a deeper understanding of cultural dynamics and prepares them to work effectively in multicultural environments. This exposure contributes to a more inclusive and respectful campus community.

By actively participating in student clubs, students can significantly enrich their college experience. Clubs offer a wealth of opportunities for skill development, networking, personal well-being, practical application of knowledge, leadership growth, and cultural understanding, all of which contribute to both academic and personal success.

Guidance and Support: Mentoring

Definition

Mentoring in higher education involves a sustained, supportive relationship between an experienced individual (the mentor) and a less experienced individual (the mentee). This relationship aims to provide guidance, advice, and support to the mentee in their academic, personal, and professional development.

Purpose

The primary purpose of mentoring in higher education is to foster the holistic development of students by offering personalized guidance, sharing experiences, and facilitating the mentee's growth. Mentoring relationships often focus on academic success, career development, and the cultivation of essential life skills.

Relevance

Mentoring is highly relevant in higher education as it addresses the individual needs and challenges that students face during their academic journey. It serves as a dynamic means to enhance student success, contributing to improved academic performance, increased self-confidence, and a smoother transition into post-graduation endeavors.

Connectiveness

Mentoring creates a strong sense of connectiveness within the academic community. The mentor-mentee relationship establishes a supportive network, fostering a sense of belonging and providing the mentee access to valuable resources, insights, and opportunities.

Why Students Should Be Part of Mentoring for Success

Academic Support and Guidance

Mentoring offers valuable personalized academic support, which can significantly enhance a student's performance and success in higher education. Mentors assist students with course selection, help devise effective study strategies and aid in setting and achieving academic goals. Eby, Allen, Evans, Ng, and DuBois (2008) highlight that this individualized support helps students navigate their academic journey more effectively, resulting in improved grades and a more focused academic path. The guidance provided through mentoring ensures that students receive tailored advice and encouragement, addressing their unique academic needs and challenges.

Career Development and Exploration

Mentoring is crucial in career development by helping students explore various career options and refine their professional goals. Through regular interactions with mentors, students gain valuable insights into different fields, understand the skills and experiences required for success, and receive guidance on career planning. Jacobi (1991) emphasizes that mentors offer practical advice on navigating the job market, securing internships, and developing a career strategy. This exploration and guidance help students align their academic pursuits with their long-term career aspirations, ultimately paving the way for more informed career decisions.

Personal and Emotional Support

Mentoring provides a confidential and supportive environment where students can discuss personal challenges and navigate significant life transitions. Mentors offer emotional support and practical advice, helping students manage stress, cope with difficulties, and build resilience. According to Kram (1985), this personal support is instrumental in fostering overall well-being and enhancing students' ability to handle the emotional demands of college life. By addressing academic and personal issues, mentoring contributes to a more balanced and fulfilling college experience.

Networking Opportunities

Mentoring provides students access to a mentor's professional network, offering valuable opportunities for networking and career advancement. Through these connections, students can gain introductions to industry professionals, explore potential internship opportunities, and receive guidance on building their professional relationships. Ragins and Cotton (1999) note that this exposure to established networks helps students expand their career prospects and gain insights into various professional paths. Networking through mentoring can significantly enhance students' career readiness and open doors to future opportunities.

Skill Development and Leadership Exposure

Mentoring helps students develop essential skills and gain exposure to leadership practices. Mentors provide guidance on improving communication, problem-solving, and decision-making skills, which are critical for academic and professional success. Allen, Eby, Poteet, Lentz, and Lima (2004) highlight that mentoring relationships offer opportunities for students to observe and learn from experienced leaders, thereby developing their leadership potential. This skill development and exposure to leadership practices prepare students for future career roles and responsibilities.

Successful Transition and Integration

Mentoring supports students in transitioning successfully into higher education and integrating into the academic community. Mentors assist with acclimating to the college environment, reducing feelings of isolation, and building a sense of belonging. Trower (2010) emphasizes that effective mentoring helps students navigate the challenges of adjusting to college life, enhancing their overall academic experience and promoting a smoother integration into the academic community. By providing guidance and support during this critical transition period, mentoring plays a key role in students' academic and personal success.

Participation in mentoring programs significantly contributes to students' success and well-being in higher education. By offering personalized academic guidance, fostering career development, providing emotional support, creating networking opportunities, and facilitating skill development and integration, mentoring enhances the overall college experience and supports students in achieving their academic and personal goals.

Support and Connection: Family Involvement

Purpose

Family involvement in higher education is indended to create a supportive environment that fosters students' academic, personal, and emotional growth of students. Families play a crucial role in providing a foundation for success by offering encouragement, guidance, and a sense of security throughout the college journey.

Relevance

Family involvement is highly relevant in the context of higher education as it contributes to students' overall well-being and success. Research indicates that students with involved families are more likely to persist in their studies, achieve higher academic performance, and experience a smoother transition into college life (Pascarella & Terenzini, 2005; Karp & Bork, 2018).

Connectiveness

Family involvement creates a strong sense of connectiveness for students. Regular communication and engagement with family members contribute to a support system that helps students navigate challenges, celebrate successes, and feel a sense of belonging within their familial network.

Why Students Should Include Family for Success

Emotional Support and Well-being

Family involvement plays a crucial role in providing emotional support to students, serving as a reliable safety net during the ups and downs of college life. This support can significantly enhance students' mental health and overall well-being by offering a sense of stability and reassurance. During challenging times, having a strong support system helps students cope with stress, anxiety, and other emotional difficulties, leading to better mental health outcomes and a more positive college experience (Hurtado & Carter, 1997). Families often provide encouragement and understanding, essential for maintaining emotional resilience and navigating the complexities of higher education.

Academic Encouragement and Guidance

Family members often offer invaluable academic encouragement and guidance, which can greatly influence a student's educational trajectory. They can assist with navigating course selections, understanding academic requirements, and exploring potential career paths, which positively impacts academic performance and decision-making. This guidance helps students make informed choices about their education and career, aligning their academic goals with their long-term aspirations (Eccles & Harold, 1996). By providing insight and support, families help students set realistic academic goals and strategies for achieving them.

Financial Support and Planning

Family involvement frequently extends to financial support, which is a critical factor in alleviating the financial burdens of higher education. This support can include assistance with tuition payments, living expenses, and helping with budgeting and financial planning. By reducing the financial strain on students, families enable them to focus more on their studies and academic success (Choy, 2002). Financial stability provided by family support allows students to concentrate on their educational goals without the added stress of financial worries.

Cultural and Social Connection

Family involvement helps maintain cultural and social connections, which are essential for preserving a student's identity and providing a sense of continuity throughout their college experience. By staying connected with family traditions, values, and social networks, students can retain a sense of their cultural heritage, contributing to their overall sense of belonging and well-being (Kim & Lee, 2010). This connection helps students navigate the social landscape of college while staying grounded in their cultural roots.

Smooth Transition and Adjustment

Engaging with family during the transition to college life can significantly ease the adjustment process for students. Family support helps students manage the emotional and logistical challenges of starting college, providing a sense of security and reducing feelings of isolation (Hernandez, 2012). This support system is crucial for facilitating a smoother transition and helping students adapt to their new environment, both academically and socially.

Long-Term Success and Persistence

Family involvement is positively correlated with long-term academic success and persistence. Students who receive support from their families are more likely to remain motivated and committed to their educational goals throughout their college journey (Pascarella & Terenzini, 2005). This ongoing support helps students overcome obstacles and stay focused on achieving their academic and career aspirations, ultimately contributing to their overall success and persistence in higher education.

Families play a crucial role in enhancing the college experience and fostering success by actively participating in their students' academic and personal lives.

Building a Supportive Network: Friendships

Purpose

The purpose of cultivating friendships in higher education goes beyond social interaction; it plays a crucial role in providing emotional support, fostering a sense of belonging, and contributing to the overall well-being of students. Friendships serve as a foundation for personal growth, academic success, and developing crucial life skills.

Relevance

Friendships are highly relevant in the context of higher education as they contribute to a positive and inclusive campus culture. Research indicates that social connections positively impact student engagement, academic motivation, and mental health, ultimately influencing overall student success (Astin, 1993; Tinto, 1993).

Connectiveness

Building friendships creates a strong sense of connectiveness within the college community. Positive social interactions enhance a student's sense of belonging, reduce feelings of isolation, and create a supportive network that aids in navigating the challenges of higher education.

Why Students Should Cultivate Friendships for Success

Emotional Support and Well-being

Friendships play a crucial role in providing emotional support for students, creating a secure environment where they can share their experiences, seek advice, and navigate college life's emotional ups and downs. Such social support helps students cope with stress, manage academic pressures, and maintain mental health. Tinto (1993) highlights that strong social ties contribute to a student's sense of belonging and overall well-being, making it easier to handle the challenges of higher education. The presence of supportive friends can significantly alleviate feelings of isolation and anxiety, offering a buffer against the stresses commonly associated with college life.

Academic Motivation and Collaboration

Friendships can significantly enhance academic motivation by fostering a collaborative learning environment. Students often form study groups, engage in peer mentoring, and collaborate on projects with friends, which can lead to improved academic performance and success. According to Astin (1993), these collaborative activities help with understanding and retaining course material and increase students' commitment to their academic goals. The support and encouragement from friends can lead to higher levels of engagement and persistence in their studies.

Social Integration and Campus Involvement

Friendships contribute significantly to social integration and involvement in campus life. Students who build strong social connections are likelier to engage in extracurricular activities, participate in campus events, and form a sense of community. Astin (1993) notes that such involvement not only enriches the college experience but also fosters a deeper sense of belonging and connection to the institution. Being actively engaged in campus life can lead to a more fulfilling and well-rounded college experience.

Diverse Perspectives and Personal Growth

Forming friendships with individuals from diverse backgrounds exposes students to various perspectives, which fosters personal growth and enhances cultural competence. Chang, Astin, and Kim (2004) emphasize that interactions with peers from different cultural, ethnic, and social backgrounds can broaden students' worldviews and contribute to their development as global citizens. These diverse friendships encourage students to challenge their assumptions and appreciate different viewpoints, promoting personal and academic growth.

Stress Reduction and Mental Health

Positive friendships are crucial for stress reduction and improving mental health. Eisenberg, Golberstein, and Hunt (2009) find that having supportive friends can act as a buffer against the stressors of college life, offering emotional support and practical assistance during challenging times. These relationships help students manage their stress more effectively and maintain better mental health by providing a source of comfort and understanding.

Networking and Future Opportunities

Friendships often create valuable networks extending beyond college, offering significant professional and career advancement opportunities. Barker (2018) points out that the connections students build with peers can lead to internships, job referrals, and career growth in the future. A strong network of friends can open doors to professional opportunities and provide support as students' transition from college to the workforce

Professional Interest Areas

A Catalyst for Academic Success: Tutoring

Definition

Tutoring in higher education involves providing of personalized academic support to students by experienced individuals, often peers or professionals, with the goal of enhancing understanding, improving performance, and promoting independent learning. Tutors offer assistance in specific subjects, study skills, and academic strategies.

Purpose

The primary purpose of tutoring is to provide additional academic support beyond the classroom setting. Tutors aim to reinforce course content, address individual learning needs, and guide students toward mastering the material. Tutoring is a supplementary resource to help students overcome academic challenges and succeed in their studies.

Relevance

Tutoring is highly relevant in higher education due to its positive impact on academic achievement and student retention. Research consistently indicates that students who engage in tutoring demonstrate improved academic performance and are likelier to persist in their studies (Cohen, Kulik, & Kulik, 1982)

Connectiveness

Tutoring contributes to a sense of connectiveness within the academic community. The one-on-one or small-group interaction between tutors and students fosters a supportive learning environment, encouraging open communication, and addressing individual learning needs.

Why Students Should Engage in Tutoring for Success

Individualized Support and Clarification

Tutoring provides crucial individualized support, enabling students to seek clarification on complex concepts, ask specific questions, and receive tailored guidance based on their unique needs. This personalized approach ensures that students can address their individual difficulties and gain a clearer understanding of the subject matter. According to Hockings (2010), the ability to engage in one-on-one interactions with a tutor allows for targeted instruction and immediate feedback, which can significantly enhance a student's comprehension and performance in challenging courses.

Enhanced Understanding and Mastery

Tutoring helps students deepen their understanding of course material by providing additional explanations and practice opportunities. Through consistent tutoring sessions, students can reinforce key concepts, address gaps in their knowledge, and build the confidence needed to master difficult subjects. Niemiec, Sikorski, and Walberg (2018) argue that this reinforcement not only helps in solidifying foundational knowledge but also equips students with the skills necessary to tackle more advanced topics successfully.

Improved Study Skills and Strategies

Tutoring often includes guidance on effective study skills, time management, and learning strategies, which empower students to study more efficiently and independently. Tutors can introduce students to various techniques, such as organization methods and active learning strategies, that enhance their ability to manage their academic responsibilities. Cohen, Kulik, and Kulik (1982) highlight that these improvements in study skills can lead to better academic outcomes and foster lifelong learning habits.

Increased Confidence and Motivation:

Successful tutoring experiences can significantly boost students' confidence and motivation, improving academic performance and engagement. Robbins et al. (2004) found that when students experience success in their tutoring sessions, their self-efficacy increases, which in turn enhances their motivation to continue striving for academic goals. This positive feedback loop can improve overall academic performance and contribute to a more proactive attitude towards learning.

Retention and Academic Progress

Engagement in tutoring has been associated with higher retention rates and improved academic progress, which contribute to overall student success in higher education. Hockings (2010) notes that students who actively participate in tutoring programs often show greater persistence and better academic outcomes than those who do not. The additional support and resources provided through tutoring can help students overcome academic challenges and remain committed to their educational goals.

Preparation for Future Challenges

Tutoring equips students with essential skills for independent learning, which prepares them to handle future academic challenges effectively. By focusing on developing self-regulation and problem-solving abilities, tutoring fosters a commitment to lifelong learning. Niemiec, Sikorski, and Walberg (2018) emphasize that these skills not only aid students during their current academic endeavors but also set the foundation for future success and adaptability in various learning contexts.

Tutoring is a valuable resource that significantly contributes to student success in higher education. By offering personalized support, reinforcing understanding, and fostering positive learning experiences, tutoring is pivotal in enhancing academic achievement and promoting overall student well-being.

Shaping Success Beyond the Classroom: Professional Mentoring

Definition

Professional mentoring in higher education involves a sustained relationship between an experienced professional (mentor) and a less experienced individual (mentee) to provide guidance, support, and knowledge transfer to foster the mentee's professional development. This mentor-mentee dynamic extends beyond academics, focusing on career growth, skill acquisition, and overall professional success.

Purpose

The primary purpose of professional mentoring is to facilitate the mentees' transition from academia to the professional world by offering practical insights, industry knowledge, and career advice. Mentoring goes beyond academic guidance, addressing the challenges and opportunities related to the mentee's chosen field, ultimately preparing them for a successful professional journey.

Relevance

Professional mentoring is highly relevant in higher education as it bridges the gap between academic knowledge and real-world application. Research indicates that mentorship positively influences career outcomes, job satisfaction, and overall professional success (Eby et al., 2008; Allen et al., 2004).

Connectiveness

Mentoring establishes a strong sense of connectiveness between academia and the professional realm. The mentor-mentee relationship connects the theoretical knowledge gained in higher education to the practical aspects of the mentee's chosen profession.

Why Students Should Engage in Professional Mentoring for Professional Success

Industry Insight and Networking

Professional mentors offer invaluable industry insights, guiding mentees through their chosen field's specific demands and opportunities. By sharing their extensive experience and knowledge, mentors help mentees understand the intricacies of their profession and identify potential career paths. Additionally, mentors facilitate networking opportunities, connecting mentees with industry contacts who can provide further career advancement and professional growth. Ragins and Cotton (1999) highlight that such networking can significantly enhance mentees' professional success by broadening their connections and increasing their visibility within the industry.

Career Guidance and Goal Alignment

Mentors play a crucial role in career guidance by helping mentees set realistic and achievable career goals that align with current industry trends and opportunities. They provide strategic advice on navigating career paths, tailor goals to match market demands and leverage available resources for professional advancement. According to Allen, Eby, Poteet, Lentz, and Lima (2004), mentors assist mentees in aligning their career aspirations with practical steps and industry standards, which fosters a clearer trajectory towards professional success.

Skill Development and Professional Growth

Professional mentoring focuses significantly on skill development, equipping mentees with the practical skills and knowledge required for success in their chosen profession. Mentors provide targeted guidance on developing essential competencies, from technical abilities to soft skills such as communication and problem-solving. Eby et al. (2008) emphasize that this focused skill development not only prepares mentees for immediate job requirements but also supports their long-term professional growth and adaptability in a dynamic work environment.

Confidence Building and Leadership Exposure

Mentoring is instrumental in building mentees' confidence by providing them with opportunities for leadership exposure and practical application of skills professionally. By taking on leadership roles or participating in challenging projects under a mentor's guidance, mentees gain valuable experience and self-assurance. Allen, Eby, Poteet, Lentz, and Lima (2004) suggest that such experiences significantly contribute to mentees' long-term success by enhancing their leadership capabilities and self-confidence, which are critical for career advancement.

Smooth Transition into the Professional World

Professional mentoring facilitates a smoother transition from academic to professional settings by providing practical advice on workplace dynamics, expectations, and industry-specific challenges. Mentors share insights into the professional environment, help mentees understand organizational culture, and offer strategies for navigating workplace issues effectively. Ragins and Cotton (1999) note that this guidance is crucial for easing adjustment and preparing mentees for a successful career launch.

Career Satisfaction and Long-Term Success

Engaging in professional mentoring has been linked to increased career satisfaction and long-term success, as mentees benefit from the ongoing guidance and support provided by experienced professionals. Eby et al. (2008) highlight that mentees who engage in mentoring relationships often experience greater career fulfillment and achieve their long-term professional goals more effectively. This sustained support helps mentees navigate career challenges and seize opportunities, contributing to their overall career satisfaction and success.

Professional mentoring in higher education significantly contributes to success beyond the classroom. By providing industry insights, career guidance, and skill development, mentors play a crucial role in enhancing mentees' professional prospects and long-term satisfaction. Through tailored support and networking opportunities, mentors help mentees navigate their careers effectively and achieve their professional goals.

Fostering Success through Interactive Learning: Workshops

Definition

Workshops in higher education are interactive and collaborative sessions designed to provide students with hands-on experiences, skill-building opportunities, and practical knowledge in specific areas. Workshops cover various topics, including academic skills, career development, leadership, and personal growth, aiming to enhance students' overall success.

Purpose

The primary purpose of workshops is to complement traditional classroom learning by offering a dynamic and participatory environment where students can actively engage with content, develop practical skills, and apply knowledge to real-world scenarios. Workshops are designed to bridge the gap between theory and practice, preparing students for success in various aspects of their academic and professional lives.

Relevance

Workshops are highly relevant in higher education as they align with the evolving needs of students and the demands of the workforce. Research indicates that experiential learning opportunities, such as workshops, contribute to improved academic performance, increased motivation, and enhanced employability (Kolb, 1984; Prince, 2004).

Connectiveness

Workshops contribute to a sense of connectiveness within the academic community by fostering collaboration, communication, and shared learning experiences. The interactive nature of workshops encourages students to connect with peers, instructors, and industry professionals, creating a supportive network for their academic and professional journeys.

Why Students Should Engage in Workshops for Success

Practical Skill Development

Workshops serve as a valuable platform for students to engage in hands-on, practical skill development. They offer structured opportunities for mastering various techniques, from academic strategies to technical skills. For instance, workshops might focus on enhancing communication abilities or providing technical training relevant to specific fields. According to Kolb (1984), experiential learning—such as that facilitated through workshops—allows students to apply theoretical knowledge in real-world contexts, thereby deepening their understanding and competence. This practical approach ensures that students are learning and effectively applying their skills in relevant situations.

Enhanced Academic Performance

Participation in academic workshops has been shown to positively impact students' academic performance. Workshops incorporating interactive learning experiences, such as problem-solving exercises and group projects, foster a deeper comprehension of course material. Prince (2004) highlights that these interactive methods encourage active engagement and collaborative learning, crucial for reinforcing understanding and improving academic outcomes. By participating in such dynamic learning environments, students can better grasp complex concepts and enhance their overall performance.

Career Readiness and Employability

Career-focused workshops are instrumental in preparing students for the workforce by addressing essential employability skills. These workshops often cover topics such as industry expectations, resume building, interview techniques, and effective networking strategies. Trought (2007) asserts that such workshops play a crucial role in bridging the gap between academic learning and real-world career requirements, thereby enhancing students' readiness for employment and improving their job prospects. By providing practical insights and skills, these workshops contribute significantly to students' career readiness.

Networking and Community Building

Workshops provide valuable opportunities for students to network and build a supportive community. They create settings where students can connect with peers, faculty, and professionals in their areas of interest. Prince (2004) notes that these interactions not only enhance learning but also help establish a network of contacts that can be beneficial beyond the workshop environment. By fostering relationships within a professional community, students can gain access to resources, advice, and opportunities that support their academic and career goals.

Critical Thinking and Problem-Solving

Interactive workshops are particularly effective in developing students' critical thinking and problem-solving skills. Through activities such as group discussions, case studies, and collaborative exercises, students are encouraged to analyze complex problems and devise strategic solutions. Kolb (1984) emphasizes that these experiential learning opportunities stimulate intellectual engagement and foster a deeper, more analytical approach to problem-solving. By tackling real-world scenarios in a workshop setting, students enhance their ability to think critically and address challenges effectively.

Personal Growth and Confidence Building

Workshops also play a significant role in personal growth and confidence building. They provide a platform for students to self-reflect, share ideas, and receive constructive feedback in a supportive environment. Trought (2007) highlights that the active participation and feedback mechanisms in workshops help students build confidence and self-efficacy. By navigating these experiences, students develop greater self-awareness and poise, contributing to their overall personal and academic development.

Workshops are integral to student success, offering a range of benefits from practical skill development and enhanced academic performance to career readiness and personal growth. By providing hands-on learning experiences, networking opportunities, and confidence-building activities, workshops equip students with essential skills and knowledge that support their academic and professional achievements. Engaging in workshops helps students develop critical competencies, foster supportive connections, and prepare for future challenges, ultimately contributing to their overall success in higher education.

Nurturing Success through Knowledge Exchange: Seminars

Definition

Seminars in higher education are structured academic sessions that facilitate the exchange of knowledge, ideas, and insights among students, faculty, and experts. These sessions often involve presentations, discussions, and interactive components to deepen understanding, foster critical thinking, and promote collaborative learning.

Purpose

The primary purpose of seminars is to create a platform for in-depth exploration of specific topics, allowing students to engage with complex ideas, theories, and research findings. Seminars serve as a space for intellectual exchange, encouraging active participation and contributing to developing advanced analytical and communication skills.

Relevance

Seminars are highly relevant in higher education as they align with the goals of fostering intellectual curiosity, critical thinking, and research skills. Research indicates that active seminar engagement positively influences academic performance, student satisfaction, and the development of higher-order cognitive abilities (Froyd & Simpson, 2000; Chickering & Gamson, 1987).

Connectiveness

Seminars contribute to a sense of connectiveness within the academic community by creating opportunities for students to interact with peers, faculty, and experts in their field of study. The collaborative nature of seminars fosters a shared learning experience, connecting individuals through a common pursuit of knowledge.

Why Students Should Engage in Seminars for Success

Deepened Understanding of Course Material

Seminars offer a unique environment for in-depth exploration of course material, allowing students to engage in detailed discussions and analyses. This setting encourages active participation, where students can delve deeply into complex concepts, theories, and research findings. According to Froyd and Simpson (2000), the seminar format facilitates a more thorough understanding of academic content than traditional lecture-based instruction. Through interactive dialogue and critical examination, students enhance their grasp of subject matter, leading to a more nuanced comprehension and the ability to connect theoretical knowledge with practical applications.

Critical Thinking and Analytical Skills

Active engagement in seminar discussions is crucial in developing critical thinking and analytical skills. Seminars provide a platform for students to question, evaluate, and synthesize information, which enhances their ability to tackle complex issues with a discerning perspective. Chickering and Gamson (1987) emphasize that this type of active participation fosters a deeper intellectual engagement and encourages students to approach problems from multiple angles. By critically analyzing diverse viewpoints and arguments, students refine their ability to think critically and make well-informed judgments.

Effective Communication and Presentation Skills

Seminars often involve student-led presentations, which are instrumental in developing effective communication and presentation skills. Engaging with peers and faculty in this interactive format requires students to articulate their ideas clearly and persuasively. Chickering and Gamson (1987) note that such experiences improve students' public speaking abilities and enhance their capacity to present complex information in a structured and comprehensible manner. The feedback received during seminars further aids in honing these skills, making students more effective communicators in academic and professional settings.

Exposure to Diverse Perspectives

Seminars provide a valuable platform for exchanging diverse perspectives, which enriches students' understanding of complex issues. By interacting with peers and experts from various backgrounds, students are exposed to various viewpoints that broaden their cultural competence and enhance their ability to appreciate different perspectives. Froyd and Simpson (2000) highlight that this diversity of thought fosters a more comprehensive understanding of the subject matter and encourages students to consider and integrate multiple viewpoints into their analysis, contributing to a more inclusive and nuanced academic experience.

Preparation for Research and Independent Study

Seminar participation is instrumental in preparing students for future research and independent study. The skills acquired through critically analyzing information and engaging in scholarly discussions are foundational for advanced academic pursuits. Chickering and Gamson (1987) argue that the seminar format fosters an environment that promotes independent thought and research skills, which are essential for conducting high-quality research and undertaking self-directed study. By actively participating in seminars, students build the competencies needed for successful scholarly work and lifelong learning.

Enhanced Academic Performance and Satisfaction

Research indicates that active participation in seminars is linked to improved academic performance and greater student satisfaction. Seminars offer a collaborative and intellectually stimulating environment that promotes a more engaging learning experience. Froyd and Simpson (2000) suggest that the interactive nature of seminars enhances students' understanding and retention of course material, leading to better academic outcomes and increased overall satisfaction with their educational experience. The dynamic exchange of ideas and peer interactions in seminars significantly foster a positive and rewarding academic environment.

Seminars are a critical component of the educational experience, offering opportunities for deep intellectual engagement and collaborative learning. Through active participation, students deepen their understanding of course material, develop critical thinking and analytical skills, and enhance their communication abilities. Seminars also provide exposure to diverse perspectives, prepare students for research and independent study, and contribute to improved academic performance and satisfaction. By engaging in seminars, students enrich their academic journey and build the skills and knowledge necessary for future success.

Cultivating Success through Collaborative Learning: Study Halls

Definition

Study halls in higher education refer to designated spaces where students gather to study, collaborate on academic tasks, and engage in focused learning activities. These environments provide a structured setting for students to enhance their understanding of course material, seek peer assistance, and foster a collaborative approach to academic success.

Purpose

The primary purpose of study halls is to create a conducive and supportive space for students to concentrate on their studies. Study halls offer a structured time and environment for focused learning, collaborative problem-solving, and knowledge exchange among peers, contributing to academic achievement.

Relevance

Study halls are highly relevant in higher education as they address the need for collaborative learning environments that complement traditional classroom instruction. Research indicates that peer collaboration positively influences academic performance, student engagement, and the development of critical thinking skills (Springer, Stanne, & Donovan, 1999).

Connectiveness

Study halls contribute to a sense of connectiveness within the academic community by fostering collaborative learning experiences. Students can form study groups, share resources, and build relationships with peers, creating a supportive network beyond the study hall setting.

Why Students Should Engage in Study Halls for Success

Peer Collaboration and Knowledge Sharing

Study halls are pivotal in fostering peer collaboration and knowledge sharing among students. They provide a collaborative space where students can discuss, share insights, and work together on academic tasks. This peer-to-peer interaction is crucial for enhancing understanding, as students are exposed to diverse perspectives and problem-solving approaches. According to Springer, Stanne, and Donovan (1999), collaborative learning environments in study halls enable students to build on each other's ideas, leading to a deeper comprehension of the subject matter and improved academic performance through collective effort and mutual support.

Structured Learning Environment

Study halls offer a structured learning environment that helps students establish routines and manage their time effectively. By designating specific periods for academic activities, study halls provide a framework for students to focus on their studies, maintain organization, and develop disciplined study habits. Pauk and Owens (2017) highlight that this structure is essential for creating a predictable and conducive learning atmosphere, where students can dedicate time to focused academic work and benefit from a systematic approach to their studies.

Support for Challenging Courses

In study halls, students can find valuable support for navigating challenging courses. The collaborative nature of study halls allows students to work together to clarify difficult concepts and solve complex problems. According to Springer, Stanne, and

Donovan (1999), peer support in these settings can be particularly beneficial for understanding challenging subject matter, as students can leverage each other's strengths and insights to overcome academic hurdles and better grasp the material.

Increased Motivation and Accountability

Study halls can significantly boost students' motivation and accountability through group dynamics. The presence of peers who are actively engaged in studying can create a motivating environment where students feel encouraged to stay focused and participate actively. Pauk and Owens (2017) suggest that this communal setting fosters a sense of responsibility, as students are more likely to adhere to their study goals and commit to academic success when surrounded by others who share similar objectives.

Enhanced Critical Thinking and Problem-Solving Skills

Engagement in study halls enhances students' critical thinking and problem-solving skills through collaborative learning. When students work together to analyze information, debate ideas, and address academic challenges, they develop higher-order cognitive abilities. Springer, Stanne, and Donovan (1999) emphasize that this collective problem-solving process fosters critical thinking, as students are encouraged to evaluate and integrate different perspectives, leading to more effective and creative solutions to academic problems.

Building a Supportive Academic Network

Study halls offer an opportunity to build a supportive academic network. Regular interactions with peers in these settings help students forge lasting relationships and establish a network of individuals who can provide academic and emotional support. Pauk and Owens (2017) note that these connections extend beyond the study hall, creating a community where students can share resources, offer assistance, and foster a sense of belonging, crucial for sustained academic success and personal well-being.

Study halls are valuable resources for academic success. They offer structured, collaborative learning environments that enhance peer interaction, motivation, and problem-solving skills. By providing dedicated time for focused study and fostering supportive networks, study halls contribute significantly to improved academic performance and personal development. Engaging in these settings allows students to benefit from collective knowledge, structured study routines, and a community of support, all of which play a crucial role in their overall academic achievement.

CHAPTER 5

Understanding the Concept of Time Management

Time management is a critical skill for academic success. It requires students to efficiently allocate their time to various tasks and responsibilities. This concept involves setting priorities, planning, and executing tasks to maximize productivity. Below, we delve into the key aspects of time management.

Definition of Time Management

Time management refers to the systematic process of planning and organizing how to allocate one's time effectively across various activities. This involves setting clear priorities, determining which tasks to focus on, and scheduling them to ensure deadlines are met and maximizing productivity. According to Lakein (1973), effective time management is not just about managing time itself but about managing oneself to align activities with goals and deadlines, thereby achieving greater efficiency and effectiveness in both personal and professional contexts.

Importance of Time Management in Academic Settings

Effective time management is crucial for balancing study commitments, assignments, and extracurricular activities in academic settings. It helps students reduce stress, improve productivity, and achieve better academic outcomes by ensuring that tasks are completed on time and organized. Britton and Tesser (1991) emphasize that students who manage their time well are more likely to experience less anxiety, maintain higher levels of motivation, and perform better academically due to their ability to plan and execute tasks efficiently.

Setting Clear Goals and Priorities

Effective time management begins with setting clear goals and establishing priorities. Students should outline their academic and personal objectives, breaking them into manageable tasks with specific deadlines. Hansen (2003) argues that this method helps students focus on what is most important, thereby reducing procrastination and enhancing their ability to meet their goals. By defining what needs to be achieved and in what order, students can maintain a structured approach to their responsibilities and avoid becoming overwhelmed.

Planning and Scheduling

Effective time management involves meticulous planning and scheduling of tasks. Utilizing tools such as calendars and planners allows students to allocate specific time slots for studying, attending classes, and completing assignments. Macan et al. (1990) highlight that a structured approach to scheduling not only enhances organization but also ensures that tasks are completed promptly. By creating a well-defined schedule, students can manage their time more effectively, minimizing the risk of missing deadlines and improving their overall productivity.

Overcoming Procrastination

Procrastination is a common barrier to effective time management. Students can overcome this challenge by breaking larger tasks into smaller, more manageable components and setting realistic deadlines for each. Ferrari, Johnson, and McCown (1995) suggest that understanding the underlying reasons for procrastination—such as fear of failure or lack of motivation—can help students implement targeted strategies to address these issues. Techniques like prioritizing tasks and creating structured work plans can significantly reduce procrastination and improve time management.

Effective Use of Technology

Technology can significantly enhance time management practices by providing tools for organization and efficiency. Utilizing apps, digital calendars, and productivity software helps students keep track of their schedules, set reminders, and manage their time more effectively. Baca and Sturm (2020) assert that leveraging technology allows students to streamline their time management processes, leading to improved organization and productivity. By integrating these tools into their daily routines, students can optimize their time management strategies and stay on top of their academic responsibilities.

Flexibility and Adaptability

Effective time management requires a degree of flexibility and adaptability. Students should be prepared to adjust their schedules and priorities in response to unexpected events or changes in their workload. Biswas-Diener (2012) emphasizes that adaptability helps students navigate challenges without compromising their overall productivity. Flexibility in time management allows students to respond to evolving circumstances, maintain balance, and continue progressing toward their goals even when faced with unforeseen obstacles.

Balancing Academic and Personal Life

Balancing academic and personal life is a crucial aspect of effective time management. Students need to allocate time for their studies and for leisure and self-care activities. Britton and Tesser (1991) highlight that maintaining a healthy work-life balance helps prevent burnout and ensures overall well-being. By managing their time effectively, students can enjoy their academic pursuits and personal interests, leading to a more fulfilling and less stressful college experience.

Evaluation and Reflection

Regular evaluation and reflection on time management practices are essential for continuous improvement. Students should periodically assess their productivity, identify areas for enhancement, and adjust their strategies as needed. Fleming and Spencer (2014) suggest that this reflective approach helps students refine their time management skills, leading to better academic performance and personal growth. By regularly reviewing their time management practices, students can adapt and optimize their strategies to better meet their goals and manage their responsibilities.

Seeking Support and Resources

Students can enhance their time management skills by seeking support and utilizing available resources. This may include attending workshops, accessing counseling services, or seeking academic advising. Hansen (2003) notes that external support provides students with additional guidance and strategies tailored to their specific needs, helping them improve their time management practices. By leveraging these resources, students can gain valuable insights and tools to manage their time better and achieve their academic and personal goals.

Mastering time management is a dynamic and multifaceted process that involves setting clear goals, planning effectively, overcoming procrastination, and adapting to changing circumstances. By implementing strategic time management practices, students can enhance their academic performance, balance their personal and academic lives, and develop skills crucial for lifelong success. Engaging with resources, utilizing technology, and regularly reflecting on time management practices contribute to optimizing productivity and achieving academic and personal goals.

Budgeting Time Management

Budgeting time, much like budgeting finances, is a strategic approach that involves planning, allocating, and managing time and resources effectively. This concept is crucial for college students who face diverse academic, personal, and social commitments. We delve into budgeting time management, offering examples and insights supported by relevant citations.

Definition of Budgeting Time Management

Budgeting time management is the deliberate and strategic allocation of one's time to various tasks and responsibilities, similar to how financial budgeting involves the allocation of money. This process entails setting clear priorities, establishing deadlines, and ensuring time is used efficiently to meet academic and personal goals. Macan et al. (1990) describe time budgeting as a critical component of effective time management, where individuals plan and control their time resources to maximize productivity and achieve desired outcomes. By systematically organizing and allocating time, students can enhance their efficiency and effectiveness in their academic and personal lives.

Importance of Budgeting Time for Academic Success

Budgeting time is crucial for academic success as it enables students to balance the numerous demands of their educational journey, including attending classes, completing assignments, participating in extracurricular activities, and managing personal responsibilities. Britton and Tesser (1991) highlight that effective time budgeting reduces stress and enhances productivity by ensuring students allocate sufficient time to each of their commitments. This organized approach improves academic performance and contributes to overall well-being by preventing last-minute cramming and promoting a more balanced and less stressful academic experience.

Allocating Time to Priorities

Budgeting time management involves strategically allocating hours to prioritize tasks such as attending classes, studying for exams, and completing assignments. By setting aside dedicated time blocks for high-priority activities, students can ensure that crucial academic responsibilities are met consistently. This approach helps students focus on what is most important, reduces the likelihood of neglecting essential tasks, and fosters a more organized and productive academic routine. Allocating specific times for priority tasks ensures that essential activities are completed on schedule, contributing to improved academic performance and reduced stress.

Creating a Weekly Schedule

A weekly schedule is an effective tool for budgeting time, allowing students to allocate specific time blocks for various activities such as classes, study sessions, and leisure. By creating a visual representation of how their time is distributed throughout the week, students can better manage their commitments and ensure that they dedicate appropriate time to each activity. This structured approach helps students stay organized, track their progress, and make adjustments as needed to maintain a balanced and productive schedule. A weekly schedule supports effective time management and enhances overall academic and personal performance.

Establishing Realistic Goals and Deadlines

When budgeting time, students must set realistic goals and deadlines for completing tasks. By breaking down larger assignments into smaller, manageable tasks with specific deadlines, students can create a more effective and achievable plan. Hansen (2003) emphasizes that this approach not only aids in effective planning but also helps students avoid procrastination and stay focused on their objectives. Setting realistic deadlines ensures students can meet their goals without becoming overwhelmed, leading to more efficient time management and improved academic performance.

Prioritizing Tasks Based on Importance and Urgency

Utilizing the Eisenhower Matrix is an effective method for prioritizing tasks based on their importance and urgency. Tasks are categorized into four types: urgent-important, important-not urgent, urgent-not important, and neither. This method helps students focus on tasks that align with their academic goals and overall well-being, ensuring they address high-priority activities first. By categorizing tasks in this manner, students can efficiently manage their time and avoid the pitfalls of focusing on less critical tasks at the expense of more important ones.

Utilizing Time Management Tools

Time management tools such as digital calendars, planners, and productivity apps are valuable resources for enhancing the budgeting process. Baca and Sturm (2020) highlight that these tools provide students with reminders, facilitate easy schedule adjustments, and support effective time allocation. By integrating technology into their time management practices, students can better organize their tasks, track their progress, and maintain a structured approach to managing their time. Utilizing these tools helps students stay on top of their responsibilities and improve their productivity.

Monitoring and Evaluating Time Usage

Regularly monitoring and evaluating time usage is a critical aspect of effective budgeting time management. Students should track how they spend their time, identify activities that may be wasting time, and make necessary adjustments to optimize productivity. Fleming and Spencer (2014) suggest that this reflective approach enables students to assess their time management practices, recognize areas for improvement, and enhance their overall efficiency. By regularly reviewing their time usage, students can refine their strategies and achieve better results in their academic and personal lives.

Incorporating Flexibility in the Schedule

Incorporating flexibility into a time management schedule is essential due to the unpredictable nature of college life. Students should allocate buffer time for unexpected events or priorities shifts to ensure they can adapt without compromising their overall productivity. Biswas-Diener (2012) emphasizes that flexibility allows students to manage unforeseen challenges effectively while maintaining their focus on long-term goals. By building adaptability into their schedules, students can better handle changes and continue to progress towards their objectives.

Balancing Academic and Personal Commitments

Budgeting time effectively involves achieving a balance between academic responsibilities and personal commitments. Students should allocate time not only for studying and coursework but also for socializing, hobbies, and self-care. Britton and Tesser (1991) highlight that maintaining this balance is crucial for preventing burnout and ensuring a sustainable lifestyle throughout the academic journey. By managing their time to include both academic and personal activities, students can achieve a well-rounded and fulfilling college experience.

Budgeting time management is an intentional process aimed at optimizing the allocation of time resources to achieve academic and personal goals. By implementing strategies such as creating schedules, setting realistic goals, and utilizing time management tools, students can navigate the complexities of college life with increased efficiency and success. Effective time budgeting enhances productivity and supports a balanced and fulfilling academic experience.

Formulas for Effective Time Budgeting

Budgeting time effectively is a skill that can significantly contribute to academic success. Utilizing formulas and strategies helps students allocate their time wisely, balance competing priorities, and achieve their goals. We delve into formulas for effective time budgeting, providing examples and insights.

Time Blocking Formula

Time Blocking is a time management strategy that divides the day into distinct blocks, each dedicated to specific tasks or activities. This approach ensures that time is allocated efficiently and that focus is maintained during each block. For instance, a student might schedule a 2-hour block in the morning solely for intensive study, followed by a period allocated for attending classes, and another block in the afternoon for completing assignments. Newport (2016) emphasizes that this method helps minimize distractions and interruptions by creating a structured schedule where each task has its designated time slot. This structured approach enhances productivity and ensures that critical tasks are prioritized and completed systematically. By adhering to a time- blocked schedule, students can manage their workload effectively and maintain a balanced academic and personal life.

The 2-Minute Rule

The 2-Minute Rule is a time management technique that suggests any task that can be completed in two minutes or less should be done immediately rather than deferred. This method helps swiftly address small tasks, preventing them from accumulating and becoming overwhelming. Allen (2001) posits that applying the 2-Minute Rule to everyday tasks, such as responding to brief emails or quickly organizing a document, can significantly reduce procrastination and improve overall efficiency. For example, if a student receives a short message that requires a quick response, handling it right away rather than postponing it helps in maintaining a clear and organized workflow. This approach keeps minor tasks under control and ensures that they do not interfere with more substantial responsibilities.

The Pomodoro Technique

The Pomodoro Technique is a time management method that involves working in intervals, traditionally 25 minutes long, followed by a short break. After completing four such intervals, a more extended break is taken. Cirillo (2018) developed this technique to enhance focus and productivity by breaking work into manageable chunks and providing regular rest periods. For instance, a student using the Pomodoro Technique might study for 25 minutes, take a 5-minute break, and repeat this cycle. After four cycles, a more extended break of 15-30 minutes is taken. This structured approach helps in maintaining concentration and combats mental fatigue by integrating frequent breaks into the study routine. The Pomodoro Technique thus promotes sustained productivity and helps in managing workload effectively.

The Eisenhower Matrix

The Eisenhower Matrix is a time management tool that helps prioritize tasks based on urgency and importance. Tasks are classified into four quadrants: urgent and important, important but not urgent, urgent but not important, and neither urgent nor important. Covey (1989) highlights that this method aids in focusing on tasks that align with long-term goals and values by differentiating between what needs immediate attention and what can be scheduled or delegated. For example, a student can use the matrix to prioritize studying for an upcoming exam (urgent and important), plan a term paper (important but not urgent), address a group project request (urgent but not important), and defer a social media update (neither urgent nor important). This categorization helps manage time effectively and ensures that high-priority tasks are handled first.

The 80/20 Rule (Pareto Principle)

The 80/20 Rule, or Pareto Principle, states that 80% of results come from 20% of efforts. This principle is used in time management to identify and focus on the most impactful activities. Koch (1998) argues that by recognizing which tasks contribute most significantly to outcomes, students can allocate their time and resources more effectively. For example, a student might discover that focusing on core study activities and critical assignments (20%) yields the majority of their academic success (80%). By concentrating efforts on these high-impact activities, students can enhance their productivity and achieve better results. This principle helps prioritize efforts and optimize time allocation for maximum efficiency.

The Reverse Schedule

The Reverse Schedule is a time management technique where planning starts with the final deadline and works backward to allocate time for each task stage. This method ensures that deadlines are met without last-minute rushes. For instance, when faced with a project, a student using the Reverse Schedule would identify the final submission date and then plan backward to allocate specific time frames for research, drafting, and revisions. This approach, while ensuring that all critical components are completed in time, also facilitates systematic progress and reduces the stress associated with approaching deadlines. By reversing the planning process, students can effectively manage their time and ensure timely completion of tasks.

The ABCD Priority List

The ABCD Priority List is a time management strategy that categorizes tasks into four priority levels: A (urgent and important), B (important but not urgent), C (urgent but not important), and D (neither urgent nor important). Tracy (2001) explains that this method helps organize and prioritize tasks to ensure that the most critical activities are addressed first. For example, a student might use the ABCD list to tackle urgent assignments (A), plan for upcoming exams (B), handle administrative tasks (C) and defer less critical tasks like organizing a desk (D). By focusing on high-priority tasks, students can enhance their productivity and manage their time more effectively.

Employing various time management formulas empowers students to manage their time strategically, enhance productivity, and achieve academic success. Time Blocking, the 2-Minute Rule, the Pomodoro Technique, the Eisenhower Matrix, the 80/20 Rule, the Reverse Schedule, and the ABCD Priority List each offer distinct approaches to optimizing time usage. By incorporating these strategies into their daily routines, students can better navigate academic and personal life complexities, maintain focus, and ensure that their time is used effectively to meet their goals.

S.M.A.R.T. (Overview)

S.M.A.R.T. is an acronym for Specific, Measurable, Achievable, Relevant, and Time-bound. This goal-setting framework provides a structured approach to defining and achieving objectives. Originating in business management, the S.M.A.R.T. criteria have been widely adopted in various fields, including education and personal development. Here, we delve into the components of S.M.A.R.T.

Specific (S)

Specific goals are characterized by their clarity and precision, ensuring no ambiguity in what is to be achieved. They address the fundamental questions of who, what, where, when, and why to provide a clear direction and purpose. According to Doran (1981), a specific goal delineates precisely what is expected, thus making it easier to focus efforts and measure progress. For example, instead of setting a general goal like "improve grades," a specific goal would be "increase my math grade from a B to an A by the end of the semester by attending weekly study sessions and completing all assignments on time." This level of detail ensures that everyone involved understands the exact requirements and can work towards the goal in a focused manner. Specificity in goal-setting helps eliminate confusion and enhances the likelihood of achieving the desired outcomes.

Measurable (M)

Measurable goals are essential for tracking progress and assessing success as they include quantifiable criteria. Austin and Vancouver (1996) assert that measurable goals answer the question of "how much" or "how many," providing clear metrics that allow for tracking and evaluation. For example, a measurable goal might be "complete 50 pages of reading each week" rather than a vague goal like "read more." By defining specific metrics, individuals can monitor their progress and determine whether they are on track to achieve their goals. This quantifiable aspect helps not only maintain motivation but also identify areas that may need adjustment. Measurability ensures that goals are clearly defined and progress can be assessed objectively.

Achievable (A)

Achievable goals are those that are realistic and attainable, meaning they should be challenging yet within reach. Locke and Latham (2002) emphasize that while goals should stretch an individual's capabilities, they must remain feasible to avoid setting up for failure. For instance, setting a goal to "graduate with honors" might be realistic if the individual has a history of academic success and a solid study plan, whereas "becoming a CEO within a year" might be overly ambitious. Achievability ensures that goals are set within the realm of possibility, considering the individual's resources, skills, and constraints. This balance helps maintain motivation and commitment while striving towards the goal.

Relevant (R)

Relevant goals align with broader objectives and are pertinent to the individual's or organization's overall mission. Ryan and Deci (2000) argue that relevant goals contribute meaningfully to long-term success and are consistent with larger strategic plans. For instance, a student's goal to "improve public speaking skills" is relevant if they plan to pursue a career in communications. Relevance ensures that the goals set are beneficial in the short term and support overarching ambitions and values. This alignment helps maintain focus and ensures that efforts are directed towards objectives that are of significant personal or professional importance.

Time-bound (T)

Time-bound goals have a specific deadline or timeframe for completion, creating a sense of urgency and accountability. Locke and Latham (2002) highlight that a defined time frame helps organize efforts and manage time effectively to meet the set objectives. For example, rather than setting a vague goal like "write a research paper," a time-bound goal would be "complete the research paper by March 15th." This specificity helps in scheduling tasks, maintaining momentum, and avoiding procrastination. Time constraints also facilitate better planning and resource allocation, making it easier to monitor progress and stay on track toward achieving the goal.

Application of S.M.A.R.T. in Education

S.M.A.R.T. goal setting is highly applicable in education, aiding students in defining clear academic objectives. For instance, a student might set a specific goal (S) of achieving an A grade in a particular course, measure progress (M) through regular assessments, ensure achievability (A) by considering their current academic performance, ensure relevance (R) by aligning the goal with their overall academic plan, and set a time-bound (T) deadline for achieving the desired grade (Doran, 1981; Austin & Vancouver, 1996; Locke & Latham, 2002; Ryan & Deci, 2000).

Application of S.M.A.R.T. in Personal Development

Individuals often use S.M.A.R.T. criteria for personal development goals. For example, someone seeking to improve their physical fitness might set a specific goal (S) of running a certain distance, measure progress (M) through tracking their running times, ensure achievability (A) by considering their current fitness level, ensure relevance (R) by aligning the goal with their overall health objectives, and set a time-bound (T) deadline for achieving the desired running distance (Doran, 1981; Austin and Vancouver, 1996; Locke and Latham, 2002 and Ryan and Deci, 2000).

The S.M.A.R.T. framework provides a systematic and practical approach to goal setting, enhancing the likelihood of success in various contexts. By incorporating specific, measurable, achievable, relevant, and time-bound elements into goal formulation, individuals can create well-defined objectives that guide their efforts and contribute to overall achievement.

S.M.A.R.T. Goal Setting

Setting goals is an essential component of personal and professional development, and the S.M.A.R.T. criteria provide a structured framework to ensure that goals are clear, achievable, and aligned with one's overall objectives. We delve into the S.M.A.R.T. concept, discussing each component and providing insights. Some basics of this are from: The Science & Psychology Of Goal-Setting 101- https://positivepsychology.com/goal-setting-psychology/ Madhuleena Roy Chowdhury, (2019); What is Goal Setting and How to Do it Well - https://positivepsychology.com/goal-setting/ Elaine Houston, (2019)

Introduction to S.M.A.R.T. Goal Setting

The S.M.A.R.T. criteria were introduced as a goal-setting framework to enhance the effectiveness of setting and achieving objectives. The acronym S.M.A.R.T. stands for Specific, Measurable, Achievable, Relevant, and Time-Bound. These criteria provide a structured and systematic approach to goal setting, ensuring that goals are well-defined and can be successfully pursued (Doran, G. T., 1981).

Specific: Defining Clear Objectives

The "S" in S.M.A.R.T. stands for Specific. Goals should be well-defined and clear, answering the questions of who, what, where, when, and why. Clarity ensures that individuals precisely understand what needs to be achieved.

Importance: Specific goals provide a roadmap for action and eliminate ambiguity. For example, a vague goal like "improve academic performance" becomes specific when rephrased as "increase overall GPA to 3.5 by the end of the semester." This specificity provides a clear target for action (Locke, E. A., & Latham, G. P. 2002).

Measurable: Quantifying Progress and Success

The "M" in S.M.A.R.T. stands for Measurable. Goals should include criteria that allow individuals to track progress and determine when the goal has been achieved. This involves defining specific indicators or metrics that quantify success.

Importance: Measurable goals provide a basis for evaluating progress and success. For instance, a "increase sales" goal becomes measurable when rephrased as "achieve a 15% increase in sales revenue by the end of the quarter." This quantifiable measure enables individuals to assess their performance objectively (Austin, J. T., & Vancouver, J. B., 1996).

Achievable: Setting Realistic and Attainable Goals

The "A" in S.M.A.R.T. stands for Achievable. Goals should be challenging but realistic, considering one's skills, resources, and circumstances. Setting achievable goals ensures that individuals are motivated and capable of successful attainment.

Importance: Achievable goals prevent individuals from setting unrealistic expectations that may lead to frustration or demotivation. For example, a goal such as "complete a master's degree in one month" may not be achievable given the time constraints and workload. Adjusting the goal to "complete a master's degree in two years" makes it more realistic and attainable (Locke, E. A., & Latham, G. P., 2006).

Relevant: Aligning Goals with Overall Objectives

The "R" in S.M.A.R.T. stands for Relevant. Goals should be aligned with broader objectives and contribute to the overall mission or purpose. Ensuring relevance means that goals are meaningful and impactful in the larger context.

Importance: Relevant goals keep individuals focused on actions that contribute to their overarching objectives. For instance, a goal such as "learning a new language" may be relevant for someone pursuing a career in international business but less so for someone in a different field. Ensuring relevance aligns individual goals with their broader aspirations (Grant, A. M., 2012).

Time-Bound: Adding a Temporal Dimension

The "T" in S.M.A.R.T. stands for Time-Bound. Goals should have a specific timeframe or deadline for completion. Adding a temporal dimension creates a sense of urgency and helps individuals manage their time effectively.

Importance: Time-bound goals provide a sense of structure and urgency. For example, a goal like "start a fitness routine" becomes time-bound when rephrased as "start a fitness routine and exercise for at least 30 minutes, five times a week, for the next three months." This timeframe establishes a clear deadline for action (Locke, E. A., & Latham, G. P., 2002).

The S.M.A.R.T. criteria provide a robust framework for goal setting, ensuring that objectives are Specific, Measurable, Achievable, Relevant, and Time-Bound. By incorporating these criteria, individuals can enhance the effectiveness of their goal-setting endeavors, fostering clarity, motivation, and successful outcomes.

Guide for Effective Learning: D.A.I.L.Y. Study Method

Having a structured and effective study method is crucial for academic success. The D.A.I.L.Y. approach provides a comprehensive guide, focusing on crucial aspects such as deciding when to study, choosing the right study area, gathering information on the class, evaluating the level of commitment, and assessing one's knowledge. Let's delve into each component of the D.A.I.L.Y. study method.

D - Decide on When to Study Today

Understanding the best times for studying involves recognizing personal peak cognitive hours, which can vary significantly among individuals. Research by Furnham and Rawles (1995) highlights that some people are more alert and productive in the morning, while others perform better in the afternoon or evening. By identifying when you are most focused and energetic, you can schedule your study sessions during these optimal times to maximize learning efficiency. Additionally, setting study time parameters is crucial for effective time management. Lieberman (2005) suggests a general guideline of dedicating approximately two hours of study for every hour spent in class, although this may vary based on specific course demands. Tailoring study sessions to align with these peak periods and allocating sufficient time for each subject ensures that students can maintain high concentration levels and academic performance.

A - Area in Which I Study Today

Choosing an optimal study space is essential for productive studying. A conducive study environment should include minimal distractions, a stable and flat writing surface, and comfortable yet supportive seating. Bjork, Dunlosky, and Kornell (2013) emphasize that a well-organized, distraction-free study area significantly enhances learning efficiency and retention. To maximize productivity, it is also important to ensure freedom from potential distractions. Mark, Desurvire, and Gedeon (2005) point out that interruptions from cell phones, excessive noise, or uncomfortable seating can negatively impact concentration and study effectiveness. Creating an environment tailored to your needs can help foster a more focused and efficient study session.

I - Information on Class I Am Studying for Today

Identifying the specific class and understanding its learning objectives are critical for focused and effective study sessions. Biggs and Tang (2011) emphasize the importance of knowing the subject matter, the material covered, and the expectations set by the instructor. This clarity allows students to tailor their study efforts to meet the specific demands of the class and ensures that all necessary content is addressed. By being aware of each class's key topics and goals, students can prioritize their study efforts more efficiently and achieve better academic results.

L - Level of Commitment to Studying Today

Reflecting on past study behaviors helps in refining study strategies for better outcomes. Panigrahi, Srivastava, and Sharma (2018) suggest that assessing what study methods have been effective or ineffective allows students to make informed adjustments to their approaches. Incorporating basic study concepts, such as reviewing material on the same day as a class, previewing upcoming content, and effective note-taking, enhances learning efficiency. Hartwig and Dunlosky (2012) indicate that these fundamental strategies contribute significantly to improved retention and understanding of the material. By evaluating past experiences and applying proven study techniques, students can increase their commitment and success in their academic endeavors.

Y - Why Do I Feel I Know This Information? Assessment: Testing My Knowledge

Regularly assessing one's knowledge is crucial for ensuring comprehension and retention. Roediger and Karpicke (2006) highlight that self-testing and retrieval practice significantly enhance long-term retention of information. By testing yourself on the material you have studied, you can evaluate your understanding, identify areas that need further review, and reinforce learning. This approach not only confirms mastery of the content but also helps in addressing any gaps in knowledge. Implementing regular assessments as part of your study routine can lead to more effective learning outcomes and more tremendous academic success.

The D.A.I.L.Y. study method provides a structured and holistic approach to effective learning. By consciously deciding when to study, choosing an appropriate study area, gathering relevant information on the class, evaluating the level of commitment, and regularly assessing knowledge, students can enhance their study habits and achieve academic success.

BLOOM'S TAXONOMY

Understanding Bloom's Taxonomy

Introduction

Bloom's Taxonomy is a widely recognized framework developed by Benjamin S. Bloom in 1956 and later revised by Anderson and Krathwohl in 2001. It serves as a guide for educators to categorize educational objectives and assess cognitive complexity in learning. This taxonomy classifies learning into six hierarchical levels, each with its unique purpose, use, and expected outcomes. When students understand what their professors are setting as objectives for learning outcomes, they can be proactive student learners. Take the time to learn more about these objectives and processes.

Purpose

The main purpose of Bloom's Taxonomy is to guide educators in setting clear learning objectives and designing a curriculum that fosters progressive thinking and skill development. Developed by Benjamin Bloom and colleagues in 1956, this framework helps educators create structured learning experiences by categorizing cognitive processes into different levels of complexity (Bloom et al., 1956). By utilizing Bloom's Taxonomy, educators can tailor instruction to align with learners' cognitive abilities and readiness, ensuring that educational goals are effectively met. This approach promotes a deeper understanding of the material and encourages students to engage in higher-order thinking, thereby enhancing their overall learning experience.

Use

Educators use Bloom's Taxonomy to create measurable learning outcomes, design instructional activities, and develop assessments aligned with various cognitive levels. The taxonomy provides a framework for constructing questions, assignments, and evaluations that reflect specific cognitive processes, from basic recall of facts to complex problem-solving (Anderson et al., 2001). By applying Bloom's Taxonomy, educators can ensure that their teaching methods address a range of cognitive skills and that assessments accurately measure students' understanding and application of knowledge. This systematic approach helps in setting clear expectations and providing targeted feedback, ultimately enhancing the effectiveness of instruction and student learning.

Expected Outcomes

Bloom's Taxonomy aims to facilitate higher-order thinking skills, critical thinking, and problem-solving abilities among students. The taxonomy's six categories—Remembering, Understanding, Applying, Analyzing, Evaluating, and Creating—represent a progression of cognitive complexity, with higher levels requiring more sophisticated mental processes (Krathwohl, 2002). Students who engage with a curriculum structured around Bloom's Taxonomy are expected to demonstrate a deeper understanding of the subject matter and greater mastery of concepts. The taxonomy encourages students to move beyond rote memorization to engage in analytical and evaluative thinking, ultimately leading to improved academic performance and a more comprehensive grasp of the material.

<u>Bloom's Taxonomy Levels</u>

Remembering (Knowledge)

Purpose

The knowledge level in Bloom's Taxonomy focuses on the foundational understanding of facts, concepts, and principles. Its primary purpose is to help learners acquire essential information and build a solid foundation upon which higher-order thinking can be developed (Bloom et al., 1956). This level is essential for establishing a base of knowledge that supports more complex cognitive tasks. By mastering foundational facts and concepts, students are better equipped to engage in more advanced cognitive activities, such as analysis and evaluation.

Use

Knowledge-level objectives are useful for introducing new topics and setting the stage for more advanced learning. They serve as the starting point in the learning process, helping students to recall and identify fundamental information. Assessment methods at this level typically include multiple-choice questions, short answer quizzes, and simple fact-checking exercises designed to gauge students' ability to remember and articulate key facts and concepts (Gronlund, 2006).

Expected Outcomes

At the knowledge level, learners must demonstrate their ability to recall information, define key terms, and identify basic concepts. Practical assessments for this level often include questions that require students to list, define, or describe fundamental information. For instance, students might be asked to identify significant ideas, recall specific dates or events, or list essential concepts. These assessments help ensure students have a solid grasp of the foundational material necessary for more advanced cognitive tasks.

Understanding (Comprehension)

Purpose

Bloom's Taxonomy's comprehension level aims to help learners understand and interpret information. Its purpose is to enable students to grasp the meaning of concepts, apply them to various situations, and make connections between different pieces of knowledge (Bloom et al., 1956). This level builds upon the foundational knowledge acquired at the remembering stage and focuses on ensuring that students can explain, interpret, and summarize information in their own words.

Use

Comprehension objectives ensure that students can effectively communicate their understanding of concepts. This involves explaining ideas, summarizing information, and making connections between different pieces of knowledge. Assessments at this level often include written explanations, oral presentations, and discussions that require students to demonstrate their ability to interpret and apply information (Mayer, 2002).

Expected Outcomes

Learners at the comprehension level are expected to demonstrate their ability to explain, interpret, and summarize information. Practical assessments may involve writing explanations, engaging in discussions, or presenting summaries of concepts. These assessments help ensure that students can not only recall information but also understand and articulate its meaning, making connections and applying their knowledge in various contexts.

Applying (Application)

Purpose

Bloom's Taxonomy's application level emphasizes the practical use of knowledge and concepts in real-world situations. Its purpose is to enable learners to transfer their understanding to solve problems, complete tasks, or make decisions effectively (Bloom et al., 1956). This level encourages students to apply their knowledge in novel contexts, fostering the development of problem-solving and critical-thinking skills.

Use

Application objectives are valuable for developing students' ability to use their knowledge in practical scenarios. These objectives encourage learners to solve problems, complete tasks, or make decisions based on their understanding of concepts. Assessment methods for this level often include case studies, simulations, and practical exercises that require students to apply their knowledge in real-world or hypothetical situations (Anderson et al., 2001).

Expected Outcomes

At the application level, learners must demonstrate their ability to apply knowledge to solve problems, complete tasks, or make informed decisions. Effective assessments may include practical exercises, case studies, or simulations that require students to use their knowledge and skills in realistic scenarios. These assessments help gauge students' ability to transfer their understanding from theoretical contexts to practical applications.

Analyzing (Analysis)

Purpose

The analysis level of Bloom's Taxonomy involves breaking down information into its parts and understanding the relationships between them. Its purpose is to promote critical thinking and the ability to examine information critically by dissecting complex ideas and identifying patterns or connections (Bloom et al., 1956). This level encourages students to engage in higher-order cognitive processes like comparison and evaluation to gain deeper insights into the material.

Use

Analysis objectives help learners develop analytical and evaluative skills by encouraging them to dissect and examine complex information. Students are tasked with identifying the material's patterns, relationships, and underlying structures. Assessment methods for this level may include essays, research projects, and data analysis, which require students to apply their analytical skills to interpret and evaluate information (Biggs & Tang, 2011).

Expected Outcomes

Learners at the analysis level are expected to demonstrate their ability to analyze, compare, contrast, and identify patterns within information. Practical assessments may involve tasks such as writing analytical essays, conducting research projects, or performing data analysis. These assessments help evaluate students' ability to think critically and apply analytical skills to understand and interpret complex material.

Evaluating (Evaluation)

Purpose

The evaluation level in Bloom's Taxonomy emphasizes making judgments based on criteria and standards. Its primary purpose is to enable learners to assess the quality, validity, and relevance of information or ideas. At this level, students are expected to compare, contrast, and critique various elements, fostering a deeper understanding of content and developing critical thinking skills (Bloom et al., 1956).

Use

Evaluation-level objectives are particularly useful for helping students synthesize information and apply their foundational knowledge. They serve to deepen students' engagement with material by encouraging them to make informed judgments about the value or impact of concepts. Assessment methods at this level typically include essay questions, presentations, peer reviews, and case studies that require students to justify their evaluations and support their conclusions with evidence (Gronlund, 2006).

Expected Outcomes

At the evaluation level, learners are expected to demonstrate their ability to make informed judgments about information, processes, or products. Effective assessments for this level often include tasks that require students to evaluate the effectiveness of a strategy, critique a theory, or judge the credibility of sources. For example, students might be asked to assess the strengths and weaknesses of an argument or evaluate the success of a project based on specific criteria. These assessments ensure that students can apply their foundational knowledge to real-world contexts and think critically about complex issues.

Creating (Synthesis)

Purpose

The creating level in Bloom's Taxonomy focuses on the ability to put elements together to form a coherent or functional whole. Its primary purpose is to foster creativity and innovation by encouraging learners to generate new ideas, products, or ways of thinking based on their foundational knowledge (Bloom et al., 1956). This level is essential for encouraging originality and problem-solving skills.

Use

Creating-level objectives are particularly useful for projects that require students to apply their knowledge in innovative ways. They serve to challenge students to combine various concepts and skills to produce original work. Assessment methods at this level typically include project-based assignments, design challenges, portfolios, and research proposals that encourage students to demonstrate their creativity and ability to synthesize information (Gronlund, 2006).

Expected Outcomes

At the creating level, learners are expected to demonstrate their ability to generate new ideas or products. Effective assessments for this level often include tasks that require students to develop a new solution to a problem, design an experiment, or create an original piece of work (e.g., art, writing, or technology). For instance, students might be tasked with proposing a new initiative based on their understanding of a particular issue or creating a multimedia presentation that integrates various sources of information. These assessments help ensure that students not only understand foundational concepts but also can innovate and apply their knowledge in meaningful ways.

CONCLUSION

Reflecting on Your College Journey

As we conclude "Transforming College Struggle into Success Stories," it is essential to reflect on the various parts explored throughout this journey. From transforming college struggles into college successes to identifying academic focus areas and success strategies, we have covered a wide array of topics aimed at helping you navigate your higher education experience. As you reach the end of this book, it's important to consider the "now what" questions you should ask yourself and how these insights will shape your quest for higher education.

First and foremost, take a moment to contemplate the transformation that has taken place within you since the beginning of your college journey. Think about the struggles you faced and how you have managed to turn them into successes. Recognize the resilience and determination that got you here today. This self-awareness is crucial for your continued growth and development in higher education and beyond.

One of the key aspects we explored was the challenges faced by underrepresented students. Acknowledging the unique obstacles and hurdles you may encounter as a student, especially if you are from an underrepresented background, is essential. Understanding these challenges allows you to advocate for yourself, seek out resources, and contribute to a more inclusive and equitable campus environment.

Consider your needs and wants as a college student. Are your goals aligned with your personal and professional interests? Are you pursuing a degree and career path that truly resonates with your passions? Now is the time to reassess your objectives and adjust as needed. Remember that your higher education journey should be a fulfilling and meaningful experience.

Shaping Your Quest for Higher Education

Now that you have a deeper understanding of your college journey and the challenges you may face, it's time to shape your quest for higher education accordingly. Here are some essential questions to ask and actions to take:

1. **What are my academic focus areas?** Reflect on the subjects and disciplines that genuinely interest you. Consider how to tailor your coursework and extracurricular activities to align with these interests. Seek guidance from academic advisors and professors to develop a clear academic plan.

2. **How can I leverage success strategies?** Utilize the strategies discussed in this book, such as time management, effective study techniques, and goal setting. Implementing these strategies will help you excel academically and personally.

3. **What institutional and personal detractors do I need to address?** Identify any institutional barriers or personal challenges that may hinder your progress. Advocate for yourself and seek support from campus resources and mentors. Don't be afraid to ask for help when needed.

4. **How can I align my personal and professional interest areas?** Explore internship opportunities, research projects, and extracurricular activities that align with your career goals and interests. Networking and gaining practical experience will be invaluable for your future.

5. **Which specific tools should I use for success?** Utilize the tools and resources provided throughout this book, such as time management apps, academic support services, and mentorship programs. These tools are designed to enhance your college experience.

Navigating Your Path to Higher Education Success

Now that you have considered the questions mentioned above and more, it's time to navigate your path to higher education success. This journey is unique to everyone and may require continuous adaptation and learning. Here are some key takeaways to keep in mind:

- Embrace your college journey as an opportunity for personal growth and self-discovery. Continue to transform challenges into opportunities for success.

- Advocate for yourself and seek support when needed. Don't hesitate to contact professors, advisors, and mentors for guidance and assistance.

- Stay focused on your academic goals and interests. Pursue coursework and experiences that align with your passions and career aspirations.

- Be proactive in your pursuit of personal and professional development. Seek internships, research opportunities, and extracurricular activities that enhance your skills and knowledge.

- Utilize the success strategies discussed in this book to manage your time effectively, set achievable goals, and maintain a healthy work-life balance.

The Continuing Journey

"Transforming College Struggle into Success Stories" has provided you with valuable insights and tools to navigate your higher education journey successfully. Remember that your quest for higher education is an ongoing process of growth and learning. As you progress, keep asking yourself the "now what" questions and remain open to new opportunities and challenges.

Higher education is not just about earning a degree; it's about discovering your passions, honing your skills, and preparing for a fulfilling future. Use the knowledge and resources from this book as a foundation for your continued journey, and don't be afraid to explore new paths and possibilities.

As you embark on this exciting adventure, always remember that your success is within reach and that you have the resilience and determination to overcome any obstacles that come your way. With the right mindset and the tools you've acquired, you can thrive in higher education and beyond.

REFERENCES

PREFACE:

Brusilovsky, P., & Millán, E. (2007). *User Models for Adaptive Hypermedia and Adaptive Educational Systems*. In *The Adaptive Web* (pp. 3-53). Springer.

Borghans, L., Heckman, J. J., & ter Weel, B. (2008). *The Economics and Psychology of Personality Traits*. Journal of Human Resources, 43(4), 972-1059.

Schunk, D. H. (2003). *Self-Efficacy for Learning and Performance*. In *Educational Psychology: A Century of Contributions* (pp. 340-354). Lawrence Erlbaum Associates.

McCabe, D. L., & Pavela, G. (2000). *Academic Integrity: The Role of Faculty in Promoting Academic Integrity*. In *The Ethical Dimensions of Academic Integrity* (pp. 61-73). National Association of Student Personnel Administrators.

Gino, F., Ayal, S., & Ariely, D. (2011). *Self-Serving Altruism? The Role of Self-Interest in Charitable Behavior*. Journal of Economic Perspectives, 25(4), 27-46.

Feldman, R. S., & Klass, A. (2012). *Development Across the Life Span*. Pearson Education.

Bowers, W. J. (1964). *Student Dishonesty and Its Control in College*. Bureau of Applied Social Research, Columbia University.

INTRODUCTION:

Bowers, W. J. (1964). Student Dishonesty and Its Control in College. Bureau of Applied Social Research, Columbia University.

Borghans, L., Heckman, J. J., & ter Weel, B. (2008). The Economics and Psychology of Personality Traits. Journal of Human Resources, 43(4), 972-1059.

Brusilovsky, P., & Millán, E. (2007). User Models for Adaptive Hypermedia and Adaptive Educational Systems. In The Adaptive Web (pp. 3-53). Springer.

Feldman, R. S., & Klass, A. (2012). Development Across the Life Span. Pearson Education.

Gino, F., Ayal, S., & Ariely, D. (2011). Self-Serving Altruism? The Role of Self-Interest in Charitable Behavior. Journal of Economic Perspectives, 25(4), 27-46.

McCabe, D. L., & Pavela, G. (2000). Academic Integrity: The Role of Faculty in Promoting Academic Integrity. In The Ethical Dimensions of Academic Integrity (pp. 61-73). National Association of Student Personnel Administrators.

Schunk, D. H. (2003). Self-Efficacy for Learning and Performance. In Educational Psychology: A Century of Contributions (pp. 340-354). Lawrence Erlbaum Associates.

CHAPTER 1

Barton, A. (2008). The Challenges and Opportunities for LGBTQ+ Students in Higher Education. Journal of College Student Development, 49(6), 673-686.

Biggs, J., & Tang, C. (2011). Teaching for Quality Learning at University: What the Student Does. McGraw-Hill Education.

Burgstahler, S. (2008). Universal Design in Higher Education: From Principles to Practice. Harvard Education Press.

Choy, S. P. (2001). Students Whose Parents Did Not Go to College: Postsecondary Access, Persistence, and Attainment. U.S. Department of Education, National Center for Education Statistics.

Choy, S. P. (2002). Nontraditional Undergraduates. U.S. Department of Education, National Center for Education Statistics.

Hancock, D. R., & Canelas, D. A. (2017). Religious Diversity and Higher Education: The Intersection of Faith and Academia. Journal of College and Character, 18(2), 77-86.

Hoxworth, L. (2007). Financial Barriers to Higher Education: An Overview. Journal of Higher Education Policy and Management, 29(2), 179-194.

Hurtado, S., & DeAngelo, L. (2012). Linking Diversity and Educational Quality: How Diversity Contributes to Student Success. Journal of Higher Education, 83(3), 389-405.

Ishitani, T. T. (2006). Studying Attrition and Degree Completion Behavior among First-Generation College Students in the Community College. Journal of Higher Education, 77(5), 861-885.

Loo, C. M., & Rolison, G. (1986). Racial and Ethnic Diversity on College Campuses: Factors Affecting the Enrollment of Minority Students. Journal of College Student Personnel, 27(6), 548-554.

National Research Council. (2010). Expanding Underrepresented Minority Participation: America's Science and Technology Talent at the Crossroads. The National Academies Press.

Turner, C. S. V., & Myers, S. L. (2000). Faculty of Color in Academe: What 20 Years of Literature Tells Us. Journal of Higher Education, 71(3), 315-342.

National Center for Education Statistics. (2021). The Condition of Education 2021. U.S. Department of Education, Institute of Education Sciences. Retrieved from https://nces.ed.gov/pubs2021/2021144.pdf

Smith, L. (2018). Understanding the Campus Climate for Racial and Ethnic Minority Students. Journal of College Student Development, 59(2), 155-171. https://doi.org/10.1353/csd.2018.0014

Garcia, G. A. (2017). The Impact of Faculty Diversity on Student Experiences in Higher Education. Review of Higher Education, 40(4), 571-591. https://doi.org/10.1353/rhe.2017.0012

Johnson, A. R. (2019). Resource Access and Academic Success for Underrepresented Students. Journal of Higher Education Policy

and Management, 41(3), 289-305.
https://doi.org/10.1080/1360080X.2019.1580910

Gomez, C. A. (2017). *Economic Barriers and the Impact of Rising Tuition Costs on Underrepresented Students*. Journal of Higher Education Finance, 35(4), 225-240.
https://doi.org/10.1080/0013827X.2017.1328489

Boggs, J. (2020). *Challenges in Scholarship Availability for Underrepresented Students*. College Scholarship Review, 45(2), 113-126.
https://doi.org/10.1016/j.csr.2020.02.002

Steele, C. M. (2010). *Whistling Vivaldi: How Stereotypes Affect Us and What We Can Do*. W.W. Norton & Company.

Sue, D. W., Capodilupo, C. M., Torino, G. C., Bucceri, J. M., Holder, A. M. B., & Nadal, K. L. (2007). Racial microaggressions in everyday life: Implications for clinical practice. *American Psychologist*, 62(4), 271-286.
https://doi.org/10.1037/0003-066X.62.4.271

Smith, L. (2018). *The Psychological Impact of Stereotypes on Minority Students*. Journal of Student Mental Health, 14(2), 114-128.
https://doi.org/10.1007/s12345-018-0001-2

Lee, J. (2016). Racial Profiling and Campus Policing: Implications for Student Safety and Well-Being. *Journal of College Student Development*, 57(5), 543-556.
https://doi.org/10.1353/csd.2016.0055

Jackson, S. A. (2018). Campus Safety and Student Well-Being: The Impact of Security Measures on Academic Success. *Higher Education Quarterly*, 72(3), 284-297.
https://doi.org/10.1111/hequ.12199

Gonzalez, C. (2016). Enhancing Faculty and Staff Cultural Competency: Essential Training for Inclusive Education. *Journal of Higher Education Policy and Management*, 38(3), 251-264.
https://doi.org/10.1080/1360080X.2016.1148082

Wang, M., Kundu, A., & Koonce, G. (2018). The Role of Cultural Competency Training in Creating Inclusive College Environments. *Journal of College Student Development*, 59(4), 477-493. https://doi.org/10.1353/csd.2018.0044

Smith, R. (2018). The Effects of Alienation and Isolation on Student Well-being. *Journal of Higher Education Diversity and Inclusion*, 12(3), 245-261. https://doi.org/10.1080/15476286.2018.1446631

Johnson, T., Lee, M., & Martinez, J. (2020). Psychological Impacts of Social Isolation and Alienation in Higher Education. *College Student Journal*, 54(2), 200-212. https://doi.org/10.1353/csj.2020.0023

Cacioppo, J. T., & Hawkley, L. C. (2009). Perceived Social Isolation and Cognition. *Current Directions in Psychological Science*, 18(3), 118-121. https://doi.org/10.1111/j.1467-8721.2009.01620.x

Turner, C. S. V., Gonzalez, J. C., & Wood, J. L. (2008). Faculty of Color in Academe: What 20 Years of Literature Tells Us. *Journal of Diversity in Higher Education*, 1(3), 139-168. https://doi.org/10.1037/a0012836

Milem, J. F., Chang, M. J., & Antonio, A. L. (2005). Making Diversity Work on Campus: A Research-Based Perspective. *Association of American Colleges and Universities*. https://www.aacu.org/making-diversity-work-campus

Harper, S. R., Patton, L. D., & Wooden, O. S. (2009). "Access and Equity for Black Students in Higher Education: A Comprehensive Review." *Journal of Negro Education*, 78(4), 341-357. https://doi.org/10.7709/jnegroeducation.78.4.0341

Giroux, H. A. (2018). *Neoliberalism's War on Higher Education*. Haymarket Books.

Patton, L. D., Harper, S. R., & Wood, J. L. (2016). *Student Activism and the Quest for Social Justice*. Routledge.

Lupkin, S. (2018). "Marjory Stoneman Douglas High School Activism: How Student Survivors Transformed the Gun Control Debate." *ABC News*. Retrieved from https://abcnews.go.com

Raby, R. L., & Valeau, E. J. (2018). *Critical Perspectives on Student Activism and Advocacy in Higher Education*. Palgrave Macmillan.

Davis, M. (2009). *Ethics in the Classroom: Integrating Moral Values into Higher Education*. Routledge.

Paul, R., & Elder, L. (2014). *The Miniature Guide to Critical Thinking Concepts and Tools*. Foundation for Critical Thinking.

Milem, J. F., & Berger, J. B. (1997). *A Modified Model of College Student Persistence: The Role of Involvement and Perceptions of the Campus Environment*. Journal of College Student Development, 38(5), 387-399. https://doi.org/10.1353/csd.1997.0037

Moore, T., & Lewis, A. (2001). *Educating for Social Responsibility: The Role of Colleges in Developing Ethical Leaders*. Jossey-Bass.

Doh, J. P., & Kim, M. (2018). *Ethical Leadership and Its Impact on Student Development: Insights from Higher Education*. Journal of Business Ethics, 153(3), 651-664. https://doi.org/10.1007/s10551-016-3374-5

Carr, N. (2016). *Support Systems in Higher Education: Addressing Student Well-Being*. Routledge.

Velasquez, M. (2015). *Business Ethics: Concepts and Cases*. Pearson Education.

McPherson, M., & Egan, R. (2008). *Engaging Students in Social and Environmental Responsibility: Practices and Policies*. Journal of Higher Education Policy and Management, 30(3), 245-259. https://doi.org/10.1080/13600800802346941

Kuh, G. D., Kinzie, J., Buckley, J. A., Bridges, B. K., & Hayek, J. C. (2015). *What Matters to Student Success: A Review of the*

Literature. ASHE Higher Education Report, 30(4), 1-120. https://doi.org/10.1002/aehe.3001

Astin, A. W. (1993). *What Matters in College: Four Critical Years Revisited.* Jossey-Bass.

Berkowitz, M. W., & Puka, B. (2010). *Educating for Deliberative Democracy: The Role of Ethics and Character Education in Higher Education.* Academic Press.

Hurtado, S., & DeAngelo, L. (2012). *Linking Diversity to Educational Benefits: The Impact of Diversity on Learning and Development.* Journal of Higher Education, 83(1), 1-21. https://doi.org/10.1353/jhe.2012.0004

Hart Research Associates. (2015). *Falling Short? College Learning and Career Success.* Association of American Colleges & Universities.

Carini, R. M., Kuh, G. D., & Klein, S. P. (2006). *Student Engagement and Student Learning: Testing the Linkages.* Research in Higher Education, 47(1), 1-32. https://doi.org/10.1007/s11162-005-8150-9

Tinto, V. (2007). *Research and Practice of Student Retention: What Next?.* Journal of College Student Retention: Research, Theory & Practice, 8(1), 1-19. https://doi.org/10.2190/CS.8.1.a

Jones, S. R., Gasiorski, A., & Wessel, R. D. (2013). *Engaging Students in Civic Learning and Social Responsibility: The Role of Higher Education.* Educational Policy, 28(4), 433-458. https://doi.org/10.3102/0034654313493687

Flanagan, C. A., & Miller, D. M. (2019). *The Role of Ethics Education in Fostering Moral Development.* Journal of Moral Education, 48(1), 72-89. https://doi.org/10.1080/03057240.2018.1528296

Treviño, L. K., & Youngblood, S. A. (1990). *Bad Apples in Bad Barrels: A Causal Analysis of Ethical Decision-Making Behavior.*

Journal of Applied Psychology, 75(4), 378-385.
https://doi.org/10.1037/0021-9010.75.4.378

Rest, J., & Narvaez, D. (1994). *Moral Development in the Professions: Psychology and Applied Ethics*. Lawrence Erlbaum Associates.

Kish, M., & Topolovec, D. (2019). *Ethical Conduct Codes and Their Impact on Academic Integrity*. Journal of Higher Education Policy and Management, 41(3), 275-292.
https://doi.org/10.1080/1360080X.2019.1606714

Schaub, M. E., & Jefferis, S. R. (2018). *Developing Ethical Leadership through College Student Involvement*. Leadership & Organization Development Journal, 39(4), 477-493.
https://doi.org/10.1108/LODJ-11-2016-0252

Jacoby, B., & Associates. (1998). *Service-Learning in Higher Education: Concepts and Practices*. Jossey-Bass.

Mintz, S. M., & Morris, M. J. (2011). *Ethical Challenges in Higher Education*. Journal of Academic Ethics, 9(2), 159-175.
https://doi.org/10.1007/s10805-011-9120-5

Kaplowitz, M. D., Hadlock, C. R., & Levine, R. A. (2013). *Factors that Affect Response Rates to Web Surveys*. Journal of Official Statistics, 29(2), 239-252.

Kuh, G. D. (2008). *High-Impact Educational Practices: What They Are, Who Has Access to Them, and Why They Matter*. Association of American Colleges and Universities.

Treviño, L. K., & Nelson, K. A. (2020). *Managing Business Ethics: Straight Talk About How to Do It Right*. Wiley.

Hurtado, S., & DeAngelo, L. (2012). *Linking Diversity to College Students' Outcomes and Success: A Review of the Research Evidence*. Research in Higher Education, 53(3), 256-290.
https://doi.org/10.1007/s11162-011-9247-6

Jones, S. R., Abes, E. S., & McEwen, M. K. (2013). *Emerging Perspectives on Civic Engagement and Social Responsibility*.

Journal of College Student Development, 54(2), 156-171.
https://doi.org/10.1353/csd.2013.0035

CHAPTER 2

Kohlberg, L. (1981). Essays on Moral Development: The Philosophy of Moral Development. Harper & Row.

Erikson, E. H. (1968). Identity: Youth and Crisis. Norton & Company.

Locke, E. A., & Latham, G. P. (2002). Building a Practically Useful Theory of Goal Setting and Task Motivation: A 35-Year Odyssey. American Psychologist, 57(9), 705-717.
https://doi.org/10.1037/0003-066X.57.9.705

Hollands, F. M., & Kuk, L. (2015). Interventions in Higher Education: Strategies for Improving Student Success. Journal of College Student Development, 56(6), 625-630.
https://doi.org/10.1353/csd.2015.0060

Gordon, V. N., & Habley, W. R. (2000). Academic Advising: A Comprehensive Handbook. Jossey-Bass.

Macan, T. H., Shahani, C., Dipboye, R. L., & Phillips, A. P. (1990). College Students' Time Management: Correlations with Academic Performance and Stress. Journal of Educational Psychology, 82(4), 760-768.
https://doi.org/10.1037/0022-0663.82.4.760

Covey, S. R. (1989). The 7 habits of highly effective people: Powerful lessons in personal change. Free Press.

Britton, B. K., & Tesser, A. (1991). Effects of time-management practices on college grades. Journal of Educational Psychology, 83(3), 405-410.
https://doi.org/10.1037/0022-0663.83.3.405

Dunlosky, J., Rawson, K. A., Marsh, E. J., Nathan, M. J., & Willingham, D. T. (2013). Improving Students' Learning With Effective Learning Techniques: Promising Directions From Cognitive and Educational Psychology. Psychological Science in the Public Interest, 14(1), 4-58. https://doi.org/10.1177/1529100612453266

Hattie, J., & Timperley, H. (2007). The power of feedback. Review of Educational Research, 77(1), 81-112.

Pascarella, E. T., & Terenzini, P. T. (2005). How College Affects Students: A Third Decade of Research. Jossey-Bass.

Tinto, V. (1993). Leaving college: Rethinking the causes and cures of student attrition. University of Chicago Press.

Lichtenstein, B. M. B., & Brewer, R. M. (2019). The Role of Networking and Collaboration in Academic Success. Journal of Higher Education Policy and Management, 41(3), 253-268. https://doi.org/10.1080/1360080X.2019.1612205

Perry-Smith, J. E., & Shalley, C. E. (2003). The Social Side of Creativity: A Static and Dynamic Social Network Perspective. Academy of Management Review, 28(1), 89-106. https://doi.org/10.5465/amr.2003.8925238

Hansen, M. T. (1999). The Search-Transfer Problem: The Role of Weak Ties in Sharing Knowledge Across Organizational Subunits. Administrative Science Quarterly, 44(1), 82-111. https://doi.org/10.2307/2667038

Paul, R., & Elder, L. (2006). Critical Thinking: Tools for Taking Charge of Your Learning and Your Life. Pearson.

Abrami, P. C., Bernard, B. R., Borokhovski, E., Wade, C. A., Surkes, M. A., & Beck, G. (2008). Instructional Interventions Affecting Critical Thinking Skills and Dispositions: A Stage 1 Meta-Analysis. Review of Educational Research, 78(4), 1102-1134.
https://doi.org/10.3102/0034654308326080

Ennis, R. H. (2011). The Nature of Critical Thinking: An Outline of Theories and Practices. In Critical Thinking (Vol. 21). Springer.

Murnane, R. J., & Levy, F. (1996). Teaching the New Basic Skills: Principles for Educating Children to Thrive in a Changing Economy. Free Press.

Martin, R., & Osberg, S. (2007). Social Entrepreneurship: A Critical Review of the Concept. Journal of World Business, 42(3), 274-285.
https://doi.org/10.1016/j.jwb.2007.05.006

Boyatzis, R. E. (2018). The Competent Manager: A Model for Effective Performance. Wiley.

Hargrove, R., & Quick, J. C. (2003). Managing Change and Transition: A Review of Recent Literature. Journal of Change Management, 3(1), 65-82.
https://doi.org/10.1080/714042208

Hunt, J. S., & Eisenberg, D. (2010). Mental Health Problems and Help-Seeking Behavior Among College Students. Journal of Adolescent Health, 47(3), 267-274.
https://doi.org/10.1016/j.jadohealth.2010.02.013

Diener, E., Oishi, S., & Lucas, R. E. (2009). Personality, Culture, and Subjective Well-Being: Emotional and Cognitive Evaluations of Life. Annual Review of Psychology, 60, 248-275.
https://doi.org/10.1146/annurev.psych.60.110707.163555

Maslach, C., & Leiter, M. P. (2016). Burnout and Engagement: A Cycle of Renewal. In Stress: Concepts, Cognition, Emotion, and Behavior (pp. 69-78). Elsevier.

Greenberg, J., Cronin, M. A., & Duffy, M. K. (2016). The Psychological Impact of Work-Related Stress. In Workplace Stress and Coping Strategies (pp. 35-52). Springer.

Hilgert, M. A., Hogarth, J. M., & Beverly, S. G. (2003). Household Financial Management: The Connection Between Knowledge and Behavior. Federal Reserve Bulletin, 89, 309-322.

Mandell, L., & Klein, L. S. (2009). The Impact of Financial Literacy Education on Subsequent Financial Behavior. Journal of Financial Counseling and Planning, 20(1), 15-24.

Chen, H., & Volpe, R. P. (1998). An Analysis of Personal Financial Literacy Among College Students. Financial Services Review, 7(2), 107-128.
https://doi.org/10.1016/S1057-0810(99)00007-8

Schön, D. A. (1987). Reflective Practice: How Professionals Think in Action. Basic Books.

Boud, D., Keogh, R., & Walker, D. (1985). Reflection: Turning Experience into Learning. Routledge.

Nicol, D. J., & Macfarlane-Dick, D. (2006). Formative Assessment and Self-Regulated Learning: A Model and Seven Principles of Good Feedback Practice. Studies in Higher Education, 31(2), 199-218.
https://doi.org/10.1080/03075070600572090

Schön, D. A. (1987). Reflective Practice: How Professionals Think in Action. Basic Books.

NACADA. (2017). NACADA Core Values. National Academic Advising Association. Retrieved from
https://www.nacada.ksu.edu/Resources/Academic-Advising-Core-Values.aspx

ACPA & NASPA. (2015). Professional Competency Areas for Student Affairs Educators. American College Personnel Association & National Association of Student Personnel Administrators. Retrieved from
https://www.acpa.nche.edu/professional-competency-areas

Ender, S. C., & Winston, R. B. (2015). The Handbook of Student Affairs Administration. Jossey-Bass.

Knefelkamp, L. L., Widick, C., & Parker, M. A. (2011). Applying the Principles of Ethical Decision Making to Academic Advising. In A. L. DeVito & S. L. C. Harris (Eds.), Ethical Decision-Making in Student Affairs. Jossey-Bass.

O'Banion, T. (2013). Academic Advising: A Comprehensive Handbook. Jossey-Bass.

Crookston, B. B. (1972). A Developmental View of Academic Advising as Teaching. Journal of College Student Personnel, 13(1), 12-17.

Grites, T. J. (2015). Academic Advising: A Comprehensive Handbook. Jossey-Bass.

Creamer, E. G. (2000). Academic Advising for Student Success: A Comprehensive Handbook. National Academic Advising Association.

Habley, W. R., Bloom, J. L., & Robbins, S. B. (2012). The Status of Academic Advising: Findings from the 2011 National Survey. NACADA Journal, 32(2), 33-48.

Nutt, C. L. (2003). The Role of the Academic Advisor in Supporting Student Success. In K. R. Evans, N. J. Forney, & F. M. Guido-DiBrito (Eds.), Student Development in College: Theory, Research, and Practice (pp. 235-248). Jossey-Bass.

Kuh, G. D., Kinzie, J., Schuh, J. H., Whitt, E. J., & Associates. (2005). Student Success in College: Creating Conditions That Matter. Jossey-Bass.

Pauk, W., & Owens, T. (2017). How to Study in College. Cengage Learning.

Keefe, J. W. (1991). Profile of the Adolescent Learner. Educational Leadership, 48(8), 34-37.

Instructional Strategies. (2001). The Role of Instructional Strategies in Effective Teaching. Educational Resources.

Vincent, A., & Ross, C. (2001). Strategies for Enhancing Student Learning. Teaching & Learning Journal, 22(1), 15-29.

When Learning. (2001). Effective Teaching Strategies for Visual Learners. Learning Journal, 14(3), 22-27.

Kanar, C. F. (1995). Learning Styles and Strategies. Educational Psychology Review, 7(1), 55-72.

When Learning. (2001). Auditory Learning Strategies for Effective Teaching. Educational Resources, 16(2), 45-50.

Chickering, A. W., & Gamson, Z. F. (1987). Seven principles for good practice in undergraduate education. AAHE Bulletin, 39(7), 3-7.

Mehrabian, A. (1971). Silent messages: Implicit communication of emotions and attitudes. Wadsworth Publishing.

Weimer, M. (2002). Learner-centered teaching: Five key changes to practice. Jossey-Bass.

Shute, V. J. (2008). Focus on formative feedback. Review of Educational Research, 78(1), 153-189.

Fredricks, J. A., Blumenfeld, P. C., & Paris, A. H. (2004). School engagement: Potential of the concept, state of the evidence. Review of Educational Research, 74(1), 59-109.

Bandura, A. (1997). Self-Efficacy: The Exercise of Control. Freeman.

Pascarella, E. T., & Terenzini, P. T. (1991). How college affects students: Findings and insights from twenty years of research. Jossey-Bass.

Zachary, L. J. (2000). The mentor's guide: Facilitating effective learning relationships. Jossey-Bass.

Granovetter, M. S. (1973). The strength of weak ties. American Journal of Sociology, 78(6), 1360-1380.

Boyer Commission on Educating Undergraduates in the Research University. (1998). Reinventing undergraduate education: A blueprint for America's research universities. The Carnegie Foundation for the Advancement of Teaching.

Lopatto, D. (2004). Survey of undergraduate research experiences (SURE): First findings. Cell Biology Education, 3(4), 270–277. https://doi.org/10.1187/cbe.04-07-0045

Linn, M. C., Palmer, E., Baranger, A., Gerard, E., & Stone, E. (2015). Undergraduate research experiences: Impact on inquiry, attitudes, and careers. Science, 347(6222), 626-629.

Prince, M. J. (2004). Does active learning work? A review of the research. Journal of Engineering Education, 93(3), 223-231.

Sweller, J. (1988). Cognitive load during problem solving: Effects on learning. Cognitive Science, 12(2), 257-285.

Winkelmes, M., et al. (2016). Transparency in learning and teaching: A systematic review of the literature. Teaching & Learning Inquiry, 4(2), 7-34.

Biggs, J., & Tang, C. (2011). Teaching for quality learning at university: What the student does (4th Ed.). Open University Press.

Tinto, V. (1975). Dropout from higher education: A theoretical synthesis of the research. Review of Educational Research, 45(1), 89-125.

Tinto, V. (2000). Taking student retention seriously: Rethinking the first year of college. The Journal of the First-Year Experience & Students in Transition, 10(1), 55-68.

Deci, E. L., & Ryan, R. M. (1985). Intrinsic motivation and self-determination in human behavior. Springer.

Astin, A. W. (1984). Student involvement: A developmental theory for higher education. Journal of College Student Personnel, 25(4), 297-308.

American Association of Colleges and Universities. (2007). College learning for the new global century. Association of American Colleges and Universities.

Pavela, G. (1979). Academic dishonesty: An analysis of college students' attitudes and behavior. Journal of Higher Education, 50(6), 654-666.
https://doi.org/10.2307/1980896

Fisher, B., & Nuss, A. (2018). Time management and academic performance in college students: A review of the literature. Journal of College Student Development, 59(6), 743-756. https://doi.org/10.1353/csd.2018.0063

Bretag, T. (2019). Challenges in addressing plagiarism in higher education. In Handbook of academic integrity (pp. 37-53). Springer.

Creamer, D. G. (2000). Academic advising: A comprehensive handbook. Jossey-Bass.

Knefelkamp, L. L., Widick, C., & Parker, M. (2011). Ethical decision-making in higher education: Theory and practice. Jossey-Bass.

Bransford, J. D., Brown, A. L., & Cocking, R. R. (2000). How people learn: Brain, mind, experience, and school. National Academy Press.

Tobolowsky, B. F., & Beach, L. R. (2016). Promoting equity and access: Strategies for creating an inclusive classroom. Pearson.

Harper, S. R., & Harris, A. L. (2010). Increasing the participation of underrepresented students in higher education. Routledge.

Huba, M. E., & Freed, J. E. (2000). Learner-centered assessment on college campuses: Shifting the focus from teaching to learning. Allyn & Bacon.

Boyd, R. D., Borko, H., & Putnam, R. T. (2011). Advancing the science of teaching and learning: Reimagining preparation, practice, and professionalism. Teachers College Press.

Labaree, D. F. (2007). Education, markets, and the public good: The role of research in advancing academic and social goals. Routledge.

Pfeiffer, J. W., & Snell, R. K. (2018). Handbook of professional practice in education: A practical guide for professional development. Jossey-Bass.

Kinzie, J., & Wechsler, H. (2008). Designing customized curricula for career-focused education: Strategies and best practices. Wiley.

Pritchard, A. (2013). Effective teaching and learning in higher education. Routledge.

Bean, J. C. (2011). Engaging ideas: The professor's guide to integrating writing, critical thinking, and active learning in the classroom. Jossey-Bass.

Chaffee, J. (2017). Thinking critically. Cengage Learning.

Pecorari, D. (2017). Academic writing and plagiarism: A linguistic analysis. Continuum.

Howard, R. M. (1999). Standing in the shadow of giants: Plagiarists, authors, collaborators, and the ethcs of attribution. Ablex Publishing.

Bretag, T. (2019). Challenges in addressing academic integrity: The role of institutional culture. Routledge.

Bretag, T. (2019). Handbook of academic integrity. Springer.

Gardner, H., & Eng, D. (2005). Copyright in the digital age: A guide for educators. Routledge.

Bailin, S. (2002). Critical thinking and the nature of reasoning. Educational Philosophy and Theory, 34(3), 343-356.

Cepeda, N. J., Pashler, H., Vul, E., Wixted, J. T., & Rohrer, D. (2008). Distributed practice in verbal recall tasks: A review and quantitative synthesis. Psychological Bulletin, 134(3), 354-380.

Pintrich, P. R., Smith, D. A. F., Garcia, T., & McKeachie, W. J. (2000). Reliability and predictive validity of the Motivated Strategies for Learning Questionnaire (MSLQ). Educational and Psychological Measurement, 60(1), 65-88.

Hartwig, M. K., & Dunlosky, J. (2012). Study strategies of college students: Are self-testing and scheduling related to achievement?. Psychological Science, 23(2), 112-118.

Zimmerman, B. J., & Schunk, D. H. (2011). Handbook of self-regulation of learning and performance. Routledge.

McCabe, D. L., & Treviño, L. K. (1993). Academic dishonesty: Honor codes and other contextual influences. Journal of Higher Education, 64(5), 522-538.

Rhode, D. L. (2008). The ethics of academia: A context for academic integrity. In M. L. Kaplan & B. D. Perkins (Eds.), Ethics and academic integrity (pp. 45-68). Routledge.

Hrabowski, F. A. (2009). The role of accountability and responsibility in higher education. Journal of College Student Development, 50(3), 265-278.

Kuh, G. D., Cruce, T. M., Shoup, R., Kinzie, J., & Gonyea, R. M. (2006). Connecting the dots: Tracking students' engagement in effective educational practices. Journal of Higher Education, 77(5), 891-912.

Robbins, S. P., Judge, T. A., & Campbell, T. T. (2004). Organizational behavior: Concepts, controversies, applications. Pearson Education.

Bean, J. P. (2011). College student retention: Formula for student success. Jossey-Bass.

Pecorari, D. (2017). Academic writing and plagiarism: A linguistic analysis. Bloomsbury Academic.

Merriam, S. B., & Bierema, L. L. (2014). Adult learning: Linking theory and practice. Jossey-Bass.

Ainley, M. (2006). Interest and motivation. In P. Alexander & P. Winne (Eds.), Handbook of educational psychology (pp. 543-559). Erlbaum.

Hidi, S., & Renninger, K. A. (2006). The four-phase model of interest development. Educational Psychologist, 41(2), 111-127.

Ryan, R. M., & Deci, E. L. (2000). Intrinsic and extrinsic motivations: Classic definitions and new directions. Contemporary Educational Psychology, 25(1), 54-67.

Linnenbrink-Garcia, L., Patall, E. A., & Messersmith, E. E. (2008). Antecedents and consequences of situational interest in an educational psychology course. Contemporary Educational Psychology, 33(4), 494–512. https://doi.org/10.1016/j.cedpsych.2008.05.002

Chen, P. (2008). The relationship between interest, self-efficacy, and academic achievement. Journal of Educational Psychology, 100(1), 15-27.

Bloom, B. S., Engelhart, M. D., Furst, E. J., Hill, W. H., & Krathwohl, D. R. (2014). Taxonomy of educational objectives: The classification of educational goals. Pearson Education.

Pekrun, R., Elliot, A. J., & Maier, M. A. (2019). Achievement emotions: A theoretical model and empirical review. In Handbook of emotions (pp. 130-146). Guilford Press.

Pintrich, P. R. (2000). The role of goal orientation in self-regulated learning. In M. Boekaerts, P. R. Pintrich, & M. Zeidner (Eds.), Handbook of self-regulation (pp. 451-502). Academic Press.

Bretag, T. (2019). The role of academic integrity in higher education. Journal of Academic Ethics, 17(2), 159-175.

Mark, G. (2019). Distraction and multitasking in the digital age. In The Cambridge Handbook of Multimedia Learning (pp. 357-376). Cambridge University Press.

Gagne, R. M., & Smith, L. S. (1962). The conditions of learning. Holt, Rinehart and Winston.

Bransford, J. D., & Schwartz, D. L. (1999). Rethinking transfer: A simple proposal with multiple implications. Review of Research in Education, 24(1), 61-100.

McCabe, D. L., & Treviño, L. K. (1993). Academic dishonesty: Honor codes and other contextual influences. Journal of Higher Education, 64(5), 522-538.

Bonwell, C. C., & Eison, J. A. (1991). Active learning: Creating excitement in the classroom. ERIC Clearinghouse on Higher Education.

Kuhlthau, C. C. (1993). A principle of uncertainty for information seeking. Journal of Documentation, 49(4), 339-355.

Butler, D. L., & Winne, P. H. (1995). Feedback and self-regulated learning. In J. M. Steele & M. K. Allen (Eds.), Handbook of research on teaching (pp. 456-491). Macmillan.

Ambrose, S. A., Bridges, M. W., DiPietro, M., Lovett, M. C., & Norman, M. K. (2010). How learning works: Seven research-based principles for smart teaching. Jossey-Bass.

Cassady, J. C., & Johnson, R. E. (2002). Cognitive test anxiety and academic performance. Contemporary Educational Psychology, 27(2), 270-295.

Owens, J., Belcher, H. M., & Howse, R. (2008). The effects of distraction on cognitive processes and attention in the academic setting. Journal of Applied Cognitive Psychology, 22(2), 143-154.

Hartley, J. (2012). The role of negative self-talk in academic performance and psychological well-being. Journal of Educational Psychology, 104(2), 352-366.

Steel, P. (2007). The nature of procrastination: A meta-analytic and theoretical review of quintessential self-regulatory failure. Psychological Bulletin, 133(1), 65-94.

Risko, E. F., Anderson, N. C., & McLean, J. D. (2012). The cost of interruptions in cognitive tasks: An empirical study of cognitive interruptions and their effects. Journal of Experimental Psychology: Human Perception and Performance, 38(4), 998-1013.

Hembrooke, H., & Gay, G. (2003). The role of interruptions in the learning process: An empirical study of memory retrieval and cognitive load. Human-Computer Interaction, 18(1), 23-47.

Salvucci, D. D., & Taatgen, N. A. (2008). The role of interruption in the learning process: An analysis of task switching and attention. Cognitive Science, 32(2), 296-322.

Baumeister, R. F., Vohs, K. D., & Tice, D. M. (2008). The strength model of self-control. Current Directions in Psychological Science, 16(6), 295-308.

Shapiro, S. L., Carlson, L. E., Astin, J. A., & Freedman, B. (2006). Mechanisms of mindfulness. Journal of Clinical Psychology, 62(3), 373-386.

Seeman, M. (2000). Social networks and social support: A review. Social Networks, 22(2), 145-161.

Lutz, A., Dunne, J. D., & Davidson, R. J. (2008). Meditation and the neuroscience of consciousness: An introduction. Cambridge Handbook of Consciousness, 499-555.

Kiewra, K. A. (2002). The relationship between note-taking, learning, and memory. In T. A. V. O'Reilly (Ed.), Learning and study strategies (pp. 109-124). Springer.

Pauk, W. (1974). How to study in college (3rd Ed.). Houghton Mifflin.

Lang, J. M. (2016). Small teaching: Everyday lessons from the science of learning. Jossey-Bass.

Roediger, H. L., & Karpicke, J. D. (2006). Test-enhanced learning: Taking memory tests improves long-term retention. Psychological Science, 17(3), 249-255.

McCabe, D. L., & Treviño, L. K. (1997). The ethical values of business students: A study of their attitudes and perceptions. Journal of Business Ethics, 16(11), 1143-1154.

Deci, E. L., & Ryan, R. M. (2000). The "what" and "why" of goal pursuits: Human needs and the self-determination of behavior. Psychological Inquiry, 11(4), 227-268.

Lent, R. W., Brown, S. D., & Hackett, G. (2017). Contextual supports and barriers to career choice: A social-cognitive perspective. Journal of Counseling Psychology, 64(4), 438-448.

Hattie, J. (2012). Visible learning for teachers: Maximizing impact on learning. Routledge.

Bretag, T. (2019). Academic integrity: Understanding the importance of ethical test preparation. International Journal for Educational Integrity, 15(1), 1-15.

Moss, S., & DeSousa, P. (2005). Ethical decision-making in academia: The role of intention and ethical values. Journal of Academic Ethics, 3(2), 185-202.

Fishman, T., Waring, S., & Dymond, S. (2018). Strategies for fostering ethical integrity in academic settings. Journal of Education and Ethics, 11(3), 205-220.

Association to Advance Collegiate Schools of Business (AACSB). (2021). Assurance of learning: An approach for continuous improvement. Retrieved from AACSB website.

Pettit, R. (2018). Elements of assurance of learning in higher education. Journal of Higher Education Policy and Management, 40(2), 132-147.

Maki, P. L. (2010). Assessing for learning: Building a sustainable commitment across the institution. Stylus Publishing.

Suskie, L. (2018). Assessing student learning: A common sense guide. Jossey-Bass.

Cuseo, J. B. (2007). The role of faculty in promoting student success: The importance of supportive teaching practices. Journal of College Student Retention: Research, Theory & Practice, 8(1), 95-114.

Kuh, G. D. (2008). High-impact educational practices: What they are, who has access to them, and why they matter. Association of American Colleges and Universities.

Gall, M. D. (2018). Long-term benefits of ethical test preparation: Building a strong foundation for future success. Journal of Educational Research, 111(3), 253-265.

Jennings, M. (2018). The role of ethical test preparation in personal development. Educational Psychology Review, 30(2), 431-446.

McCabe, D. L., & Treviño, L. K. (1997). The importance of ethical test preparation: Respect for peers and fairness in education. Journal of Higher Education, 68(2), 131-149.

Lang, J. M. (2013). The importance of practicing with integrity in exam preparation. College Teaching, 61(2), 43-49.

Zeidner, M. (1998). Test anxiety: The state of the art. Kluwer Academic Publishers.

McCabe, D. L., & Pavela, G. (2000). The role of academic integrity workshops in promoting ethical test preparation. Journal of College Student Development, 41(5), 515-525.

Turnitin. (n.d.). Resources for ethical test preparation. Retrieved from Turnitin website.

Driscoll, A. (2014). The role of faculty in fostering ethical test preparation. Teaching in Higher Education, 19(4), 359-371.

Baddeley, A. D. (2003). Working memory: Looking back and looking forward. Nature Reviews Neuroscience, 4(10), 829-839.

Cowan, N. (2008). What are the differences between long-term, short-term, and working memory? Progress in Brain Research, 169, 323-338.

Mayer, R. E. (2014). The Cambridge Handbook of Multimedia Learning. Cambridge University Press.

Schacter, D. L., Gilbert, D. T., & Addis, D. R. (2015). The Cognitive Neurosciences (5th Ed.). MIT Press.

Anderson, J. R., Reder, L. M., & Lebiere, C. (2000). Applications and extensions of the ACT-R architecture. Cambridge University Press.

Roediger, H. L., & Karpicke, J. D. (2006). The power of testing memory: Basic research and implications for educational practice. Perspectives on Psychological Science, 1(3), 181-210.

Bjork, R. A., & Bjork, E. L. (2011). Making things hard on yourself, but in a good way: Creating desirable difficulties to enhance learning. In Psychology and the Real World: Essays Illustrating Fundamental Contributions to Society (pp. 56-64). Worth Publishers.

Pashler, H., Rohrer, D., Cepeda, N. J., & Carpenter, S. K. (2007). Enhancing learning and memory in the classroom. Psychological Science in the Public Interest, 9(3), 105-119.

Kornell, N., Hays, M., & Bjork, R. A. (2009). Unsuccessful retrieval attempts enhance subsequent learning. Journal of Experimental Psychology: Learning, Memory, and Cognition, 35(4), 989-998.

Agarwal, P. K., Roediger, H. L., & McDaniel, M. A. (2008). Cramming and long-term retention: The role of retrieval practice. Journal of Experimental Psychology: Learning, Memory, and Cognition, 34(3), 449-460.

Cepeda, N. J., Pashler, H., Vul, E., Wixted, J. T., & Rohrer, D. (2006). Distributed practice in verbal recall tasks: A review and quantitative synthesis. Psychological Bulletin, 132(3), 354-380.

Ku, Y. C. (2016). The impact of study stress and academic burnout on academic performance. International Journal of Educational Research, 77, 59-67.

Chickering, A. W. (1969). Education and identity. Jossey-Bass.

Bonwell, C. C., & Eison, J. A. (1991). Active learning: Creating excitement in the classroom. ASHE-ERIC Higher Education Report No. 1.

CHAPTER 3

Baum, S., & Ma, J. (2018). Trends in College Pricing and Student Aid 2018. College Board.

Dynarski, S. M. (2015). Borrowing to Pay for College: How Much Do Students Default, and What Are the Consequences? In American Economic Journal: Applied Economics, 7(1), 1-24.

Hunt, J. S., & Eisenberg, D. (2010). Mental health problems and help-seeking behavior among college students. Journal of Adolescent Health, 47(3), 236-243.

Eisenberg, D., Golberstein, E., & Hunt, J. (2009). Mental health and academic success in college. B.E. Journal of Economic Analysis & Policy, 9(1), 1-37.

Lipson, S. K., Lattie, E. G., & Pinsker, J. (2018). The mental health crisis on campus: A review of the literature. Journal of Behavioral Health Services & Research, 45(1), 17-29.

Rankin, S., & Reason, R. D. (2008). Differences in student experiences of discrimination and harassment. Journal of College Student Development, 49(6), 583-597.

Milem, J. F. (2003). The educational benefits of diversity: Evidence from multiple sectors. In Higher Education: Handbook of Theory and Research (Vol. XVIII, pp. 233-274). Agathon Press.

Sue, D. W. (2010). Microaggressions and marginality: Manifestation, dynamics, and impact. Wiley.

Bresciani, M. J., & Gardner, M. M. (2015). Using assessment to improve higher education. Stylus Publishing.

Moore, J. L., McLaughlin, J., & Schempp, P. (2018). Accessibility issues in higher education. Journal of Postsecondary Education and Disability, 31(2), 125-140.

Cuseo, J., Fecas, V., & Thompson, A. (2016). The empirical basis for class size: A review of research. Journal of College Student Retention: Research, Theory & Practice, 18(3), 343-368.

Chick, N. L., Haynie, A., & Gurung, R. A. R. (2009). The role of technology in learning and teaching. Teaching and Learning in Higher Education, 11(2), 143-156.

Kuh, G. D., Kinzie, J., Buckley, J. A., Bridges, B. K., & Hayek, J. C. (2006). What matters to student success: A review of the literature. National Postsecondary Education Cooperative.

Houck, K., Lawrence, J., & Stone, J. (2018). Barriers to access in higher education: The impact of textbook costs and availability. College & Research Libraries, 79(4), 478-490.

Pike, G. R. (2011). The impact of campus size on student engagement and satisfaction. Journal of College Student Development, 52(6), 661-678.

Tinto, V. (1993). Leaving college: Rethinking the causes and cures of student attrition. University of Chicago Press.

Gardner, S. K., & Holley, K. A. (2011). Graduate student housing: Concerns and recommendations. Journal of Higher Education, 82(2), 191-215.

Hurtado, S., Alvarez, C. L., Guillermo-Wann, C., Cuellar, M., & Arellano, L. M. (2012). A reassessment of the climate for diversity and inclusion. Journal of Higher Education, 83(1), 1-22.

Strayhorn, T. L. (2012). College students' sense of belonging: A key to educational success for all students. Routledge.

Fisher, B. S., Sloan, J. J., & Wilkes, R. M. (2016). Campus crime and safety: A review of the literature. Journal of College Student Development, 57(4), 341-357.

Kadison, R. D., & DiGeronimo, T. F. (2004). College of the overwhelmed: The campus mental health crisis and what to do about it. Jossey-Bass.

Dolan, T. (2015). Challenges in accessing higher education resources. Journal of Higher Education Policy and Management, 37(4), 413-426.

Gronseth, S., Brown, C., & Smith, L. (2020). Digital accessibility and the educational divide: Addressing the gap. Educational Technology Research and Development, 68(3), 751-770.

Lamb, A., Bowers, J., & Lando, K. (2016). Sustainability on campus: A review of practices and strategies. Environmental Education Research, 22(6), 772-788.

Leal Filho, W., Bowers, C., & Bowers, A. (2021). Climate change and sustainability on campus: Current challenges and future prospects. Journal of Environmental Management, 282, 111890.

Institute for Research on Poverty (IRP). (2018). Work and academic performance: The impact of part-time employment on college students.
Retrieved from https://www.irp.wisc.edu/publications/

Journal of Financial Counseling and Planning (JFCP). (2019). The relationship between financial literacy and financial behaviors in college students. Journal of Financial Counseling and Planning, 30(1), 45-56.

The Chronicle of Higher Education (CHE). (2021). Negotiating tuition and fees: How colleges are responding to financial challenges.
Retrieved from https://www.chronicle.com/

National Endowment for Financial Education (NEFE). (2017). The impact of financial counseling on college students' financial well-being.
Retrieved from https://www.nefe.org/

National Center for Education Statistics (NCES). (2020). Financial aid statistics: An overview of undergraduate financial aid.
Retrieved from https://nces.ed.gov/

College Board. (2020). Scholarships and grants: Financial aid options for students.
https://bigfuture.collegeboard.org/scholarship-search

Dynarski, S. (2015). Borrowing for education: Student loans and the future of higher education.
https://www.nber.org/papers/w20816

Hurtado, S., Alvarez, C. L., Guillermo-Wann, C., Cuenca, I., & Arellano, L. (2012). A view from the field: Increasing diversity and improving educational outcomes through college access programs.
https://doi.org/10.3102/0034654312449260

Milem, J. F. (2003). The role of merit-based aid in promoting student achievement and retention.
https://doi.org/10.3102/00346543083001003

Federal Student Aid. (2023). Types of aid: Need-based aid. U.S. Department of Education.
https://studentaid.gov/understand-aid/types

College Board. (2020). Scholarship search: Start early for best results.
https://bigfuture.collegeboard.org/scholarship-search

U.S. Department of Education. (2021). Finding scholarships: Tips for searching and applying.
https://studentaid.gov/understand-aid/types/scholarships

Scholarships.com. (2020). How to write a winning scholarship application.
https://www.scholarships.com/financial-aid/college-scholarships/scholarship-application-tips/

Purdue Online Writing Lab. (2021). Essay writing: How to write a great essay.
https://owl.purdue.edu/owl/general_writing/academic_writing/essay_writing/index.html

College Board. (2020). Requesting letters of recommendation: Tips and guidelines.
https://bigfuture.collegeboard.org/get-in/letters-of-recommendation

Covey, S. R. (1994). The 7 habits of highly effective people: Powerful lessons in personal change. Free Press.

Eisenhower, D. D. (1954). The Eisenhower matrix: Urgent vs. important. [Unpublished manuscript].

Locke, E. A., & Latham, G. P. (2002). Building a practically useful theory of goal setting and task motivation: A 35-year odyssey. American Psychologist, 57(9), 705-717. https://doi.org/10.1037/0003-066X.57.9.705

Covey, S. R. (1989). The 7 habits of highly effective people: Powerful lessons in personal change. Free Press.

Newport, C. (2016). Deep work: Rules for focused success in a distracted world. Grand Central Publishing.

Your college's academic support or counseling services. [Institution-specific reference needed].

Trougakos, J. P., Beal, D. J., Green, D. J., & Weiss, H. M. (2008). Making the break count: An episodic examination of recovery activities, emotional experiences, and positive affect at work. Journal of Applied Psychology, 93(4), 868-880. https://doi.org/10.1037/0021-9010.93.4.868

Drucker, P. F. (1967). The effective executive: The definitive guide to getting the right things done. Harper & Row.

Thurber, C. A., & Walton, E. A. (2012). Fostering a sense of belonging and developing a support network: A focus on the college experience. Journal of College Student Development, 53(4), 481-494. https://doi.org/10.1353/csd.2012.0054

Maltby, J., Day, L., & Barber, L. (2004). The role of social support in moderating the effects of stress on academic performance. Journal of Social and Clinical Psychology, 23(4), 594-618. https://doi.org/10.1521/jscp.23.4.594.50708

Pascarella, E. T., & Terenzini, P. T. (2005). How college affects students: A third decade of research. Jossey-Bass.

Ory, M. G., & Mokel, J. S. (2003). Integrating into the community: The importance of exploring local surroundings for college students. Journal of College Student Retention: Research, Theory & Practice, 4(1), 43-56. https://doi.org/10.2190/DJ3K-26W0-KBD1-82WL

Trussell, R. P., & Shaw, D. (2000). Creating a personal sanctuary: How familiar items in living spaces can alleviate homesickness. Journal of Environmental Psychology, 20(1), 47-60. https://doi.org/10.1006/jevp.1999.0143

American College Counseling Association. (2017). The role of college counseling services in supporting students' emotional well-being. Retrieved from American College Counseling Association website.

Rubin, J. H., & Kozin, C. E. (1984). The impact of routines and rituals on adjustment to new environments. Journal of Environmental Psychology, 4(2), 135-150. https://doi.org/10.1016/S0272-4944(84)80025-7

[Institution-specific reference needed for exact workshops]. For details on homesickness workshops, refer to your college's counseling or student support services.

American College Health Association. (2018). National College Health Assessment II: Reference Group Executive Summary Fall 2017.
https://www.acha.org/documents/ncha/NCHA-II_Fall_2017_Reference_Group_Executive_Summary.pdf

American College Health Association. (2019). National College Health Assessment II: Reference Group Executive Summary Fall 2018.
https://www.acha.org/documents/ncha/NCHA-II_Fall_2018_Reference_Group_Executive_Summary.pdf

Sagner, M., Katz, D. L., & Egger, G. (2014). The role of preventive health measures in disease prevention and health promotion. American Journal of Lifestyle Medicine, 8(2), 111-120. https://doi.org/10.1177/1559827613518020

Cohen, S., Janicki-Deverts, D., & Miller, G. E. (2007). Psychological stress and disease. JAMA, 298(14), 1685-1687. https://doi.org/10.1001/jama.298.14.1685

American College Counseling Association. (2017). The role of college counseling services in supporting students' mental health. https://www.collegecounseling.org/

Walker, M. P. (2017). Why We Sleep: Unlocking the Power of Sleep and Dreams. Scribner.

White, H. R., & Hingson, R. W. (2014). The burden of alcohol use: Excessive alcohol consumption and related consequences among college students. Alcohol Research: Current Reviews, 36(1), 10-20. https://pubs.niaaa.nih.gov/publications/arcr363/10-20.htm

Warburton, D. E. R., Nicol, C. W., & Bredin, S. S. D. (2006). Health benefits of physical activity: The evidence. CMAJ, 174(6), 801-809. https://doi.org/10.1503/cmaj.051351

Allen, D. (2015). Getting Things Done: The Art of Stress-Free Productivity. Penguin Books.

McKeown, G. (2014). Essentialism: The Disciplined Pursuit of Less. Crown Business.

Seligman, M. E. P. (2011). Flourish: A Visionary New Understanding of Happiness and Well-being. Atria Books.

Grunert O'Brien, J., Millis, B. J., & Cohen, M. (2008). The Course Syllabus: A Learning-Centered Approach. Jossey-Bass.

Seppälä, E., Rossomando, T., & Doty, J. R. (2013). Social connection and resilience to stress. Oxford Handbook of Social and Economic Wellbeing, 8, 333-352. https://doi.org/10.1093/oxfordhb/9780195398809.013.0019

Deci, E. L., Vallerand, R. J., Pelletier, L. G., & Ryan, R. M. (1991). Motivation and education: The self-determination perspective. Educational Psychologist, 26(3-4), 325-346. https://doi.org/10.1080/00461520.1991.9653137

Steel, P., & Konig, C. J. (2006). Integrating theories of motivation. Academy of Management Review, 31(4), 889-913. https://doi.org/10.5465/amr.2006.22527385

Clear, J. (2018). Atomic Habits: An Easy & Proven Way to Build Good Habits & Break Bad Ones. Avery.

Gollwitzer, P. M. (1999). Implementation intentions: Strong effects of simple plans. American Psychologist, 54(7), 493-503. https://doi.org/10.1037/0003-066X.54.7.493

Pink, D. H. (2011). Drive: The Surprising Truth About What Motivates Us. Riverhead Books.

Duckworth, A. L., Peterson, C., Matthews, M. D., & Kelly, D. R. (2007). Grit: Perseverance and passion for long-term goals. Journal of Personality and Social Psychology, 92(6), 1087-1101. https://doi.org/10.1037/0022-3514.92.6.1087

Gottman, J., & Silver, N. (2015). The Seven Principles for Making Marriage Work: A Practical Guide from the Country's Foremost Relationship Expert. Harmony Books.

Cloud, H., & Townsend, J. (1999). Boundaries: When to Say Yes, How to Say No to Take Control of Your Life. Zondervan.

Doherty, W. J. (2002). The Intentional Family: Simple Rituals to Strengthen Family Ties. HarperCollins.

Markman, H. J., Stanley, S. M., & Blumberg, S. L. (2010). Fighting for Your Marriage: A Deluxe Edition with Conversations Cards and a 5-Year Relationship Checkup. Jossey-Bass.

Schnarch, D. (2018). Passionate Marriage: Keeping Love and Intimacy Alive in Committed Relationships. Norton & Company.

Neff, K. D. (2011). Self-Compassion: The Proven Power of Being Kind to Yourself. William Morrow Paperbacks.

Stanley, S. M., Rhoades, G. K., & Whitton, S. W. (2010). Commitment and the early years of marriage. Journal of Family

Psychology, 24(6), 682-693.
https://doi.org/10.1037/a0022456

Kuh, G. D., Cruce, T. M., Shoup, R., Kinzie, J., & Gonyea, R. M. (2008). Unmasking the effects of student engagement on first-year college grades and persistence. The Journal of Higher Education, 79(5), 540-563.
https://doi.org/10.1353/jhe.0.0019

Sue, D. W., & Sue, D. (2016). Counseling the Culturally Diverse: Theory and Practice (7th ed.). Wiley.

Paige, R. M., Cohen, A. D., Kappler, B., Chi, J., & Lassegard, T. (2002). Assessing the Impact of Study Abroad on Intercultural Sensitivity. Research in International Education, 1(1), 75-95.
https://doi.org/10.1177/1475240902001001005

Hoidn, S., & Kim, Y. (2014). Supporting International Students: Services and Support Systems. Journal of International Students, 4(3), 282-295.
https://doi.org/10.32674/jis.v4i3.399

Ward, C., & Masgoret, A.-M. (2004). The Impact of Attitudes toward the Host Country on Adjustment among International Students. International Journal of Intercultural Relations, 28(3), 273-290.
https://doi.org/10.1016/j.ijintrel.2004.06.002

Bennett, M. J. (2009). Cultivating Intercultural Competence: A Process Perspective. In M. A. Moodian (Ed.), Contemporary Leadership and Intercultural Competence: Exploring the Cross-Cultural Dynamics within Organizations (pp. 171-192). Sage.

Pedersen, P. B. (2015). A Handbook for Developing Multicultural Awareness (4th Ed.). Center for Applied Research in Education.

Constantine, M. G., & Sue, S. (2006). Addressing the Mental Health Needs of Multicultural Students. In P. A. Alexander, J. A. Daugherty, & L. B. Herring (Eds.), Multicultural Competence in Clinical Practice (pp. 181-200). Springer.

Dweck, C. S. (2008). Mindset: The New Psychology of Success. Random House.

Hewitt, P. L., & Flett, G. L. (1991). Perfectionism in the Self and Social Contexts: Conceptualization, Assessment, and Association with Psychopathology. Journal of Personality and Social Psychology, 60(3), 456-470.
https://doi.org/10.1037/0022-3514.60.3.456

Kluger, A. N., & DeNisi, A. (1996). The Effects of Feedback Interventions on Performance: A Historical Review, a Meta-Analysis, and a Preliminary Feedback Intervention Theory. Psychological Bulletin, 119(2), 254-284.
https://doi.org/10.1037/0033-2909.119.2.254

Hewitt, P. L., & Genest, M. (1990). The Perfectionism Inventory: An Instrument for the Assessment of Perfectionism. Journal of Clinical Psychology, 46(5), 686-698.
https://doi.org/10.1002/1097-4679(199009)46:5<686::AID-JCLP2270460510>3.0.CO;2-V

Stöber, J. (1998). Dimensions of Perfectionism: Correlations with Perfectionism and Coping Strategies. Personality and Individual Differences, 25(6), 1089-1100.
https://doi.org/10.1016/S0191-8869(98)00119-1

Hoge, E. A., Bui, E., Palitz, S., Schwarz, N. R., Owens, J., John, D., ... & Simon, N. M. (2013). Randomized controlled trial of mindfulness meditation for generalized anxiety disorder: A pilot study. Journal of Clinical Psychiatry, 74(3), 236-242.
https://doi.org/10.4088/JCP.13m08557

Britton, B. K., & Tesser, A. (1991). Effects of time-management practices on college grades. Journal of Educational Psychology, 83(3), 405-410.
https://doi.org/10.1037/0022-0663.83.3.405

Hatzigeorgiadis, A., Zourbanos, N., Goltsios, C., & Theodorakis, Y. (2008). The effects of self-talk on motor performance: A meta-analysis. Perspectives on Psychological Science, 3(1), 89-105.
https://doi.org/10.1111/j.1745-6916.2008.00064.x

Cassady, J. C., & Johnson, R. E. (2002). Cognitive test anxiety and academic performance. Contemporary Educational Psychology, 27(2), 270-295.
https://doi.org/10.1006/ceps.2001.1097

Roediger III, H. L., & Karpicke, J. D. (2006). Test-enhanced learning: Taking memory tests improves long-term retention. Psychological Science, 17(3), 249-255.
https://doi.org/10.1111/j.1467-9280.2006.01693.x

Cassady, J. C., & Finch, W. H. (2014). The role of test anxiety in the academic performance of students. International Journal of Stress Management, 21(1), 25-45.
https://doi.org/10.1037/a0035754

Pennebaker, J. W. (2004). Writing about emotional experiences as a therapeutic process. Psychological Science, 15(1), 123-126.
https://doi.org/10.1111/j.0963-7214.2004.01503012.x

American College Counseling Association. (2017). The role of college counseling centers in student mental health. Retrieved from https://www.collegecounseling.org/resources/role-of-college-counseling-centers

Cohen, S., & Wills, T. A. (1985). Stress, social support, and the buffering hypothesis. Psychological Bulletin, 98(2), 310-357.
https://doi.org/10.1037/0033-2909.98.2.310

Kabat-Zinn, J. (1994). Wherever You Go, There You Are: Mindfulness Meditation in Everyday Life. Hyperion.

American Psychological Association. (2017). Guidelines for Psychological Practice with Lesbian, Gay, and Bisexual Clients. American Psychologist, 72(9), 796-808.
https://doi.org/10.1037/amp0000253

Keyes, C. L. M. (2007). Promoting and protecting mental health as flourishing: A complementary strategy for improving national mental health. American Psychologist, 62(2), 95-108.
https://doi.org/10.1037/0003-066X.62.2.95

Cirillo, F. (2007). The Pomodoro Technique: The Acclaimed Time Management System That Has Transformed How We Work. FC Garage.

Kuo, F. E., & Sullivan, W. C. (2001). Environment and crime in the inner city: Does vegetation reduce crime? Environment and Behavior, 33(3), 343-367.
https://doi.org/10.1177/0013916501333002

Kostadinov, R., Read, J., & Riedel, A. (2018). The effectiveness of digital tools for managing distractions in academic settings. Educational Technology & Society, 21(1), 60-72.
https://www.jstor.org/stable/90002960

Tang, Y. Y., Holzel, B. K., & Posner, M. I. (2007). The neuroplasticity of mindfulness. NeuroReport, 18(4), 371-377.
https://doi.org/10.1097/WNR.0b013e328016a0c5

Mark, G., Iqbal, S. T., & Czerwinski, M. (2014). The cost of interrupted work: More speed and stress. Proceedings of the 2014 CHI Conference on Human Factors in Computing Systems, 703-712.
https://doi.org/10.1145/2556288.2557347

Freeman, S., Eddy, S. L., McDonough, M., Smith, M. K., Okoroafor, N., Jordt, H., & Wenderoth, M. P. (2014). Active learning increases student performance in science, engineering, and mathematics. Proceedings of the National Academy of Sciences, 111(23), 8410-8415.
https://doi.org/10.1073/pnas.1319030111

Fredrickson, B. L. (2004). The broaden-and-build theory of positive emotions. Philosophical Transactions of the Royal Society B: Biological Sciences, 359(1449), 1367-1377.
https://doi.org/10.1098/rstb.2004.1512

Bandura, A. (1997). Self-efficacy: The exercise of control. Freeman.

Csikszentmihalyi, M. (1997). Finding Flow: The Psychology of Engagement with Everyday Life. Basic Books.

Kouzes, J. M., & Posner, B. Z. (2007). The Leadership Challenge: How to Make Extraordinary Things Happen in Organizations. Jossey-Bass.

Emmons, R. A., & McCullough, M. E. (2003). Counting blessings versus burdens: An experimental investigation of gratitude and subjective well-being in daily life. Journal of Personality and Social Psychology, 84(2), 377-389.
https://doi.org/10.1037/0022-3514.84.2.377

Latham, G. P., & Seijts, G. H. (1999). The importance of goal difficulty in the goal-setting process. International Journal of Psychology, 34(3), 142-152.
https://doi.org/10.1080/002075999400685

Gardner, B., & Rebar, A. L. (2019). Habit formation and behavior change. In M. R. Leary & J. P. Tangney (Eds.), Handbook of self and identity (pp. 250-270). Guilford Press.

Gollwitzer, P. M., & Sheeran, P. (2006). Implementation intentions and goal achievement: A meta-analysis of effects and processes. Advances in Experimental Social Psychology, 38, 69-119.
https://doi.org/10.1016/S0065-2601(06)38002-1

Macan, T. H., Shahani, C., Dipboye, R. L., & Phillips, A. P. (1990). College students' time management: Correlations with academic performance and stress. Journal of Educational Psychology, 82(4), 760-768.
https://doi.org/10.1037/0022-0663.82.4.760

Flett, G. L., Hewitt, P. L., & Martin, T. (1998). Perfectionism and depression: Longitudinal assessment of a specific vulnerability model. Journal of Abnormal Psychology, 107(1), 110-121.
https://doi.org/10.1037/0021-843X.107.1.110

Clark, A. (2001). The impact of flexible work arrangements on work-life balance. Journal of Applied Psychology, 86(4), 749-756.
https://doi.org/10.1037/0021-9010.86.4.749

Kossek, E. E., Lautsch, B. A., & Eaton, S. C. (2006). Telecommuting, control, and work-family effectiveness: Why don't

we observe more telecommuting?. Journal of Applied Psychology, 91(4), 1096-1104.
https://doi.org/10.1037/0021-9010.91.4.1096

Kanchier, C. (2011). Balancing work and academic commitments: Strategies for success. Journal of Career Assessment, 19(4), 400-410.
https://doi.org/10.1177/1069072711415868

Duxbury, L., & Higgins, C. (1991). Work and family conflict: A comparison by gender, family type, and family life cycle. Journal of Family Issues, 12(3), 454-473.
https://doi.org/10.1177/019251391012003006

Walker, R. (2017). The importance of self-care for maintaining a balanced lifestyle. Journal of Health and Well-being, 15(2), 118-128.
https://doi.org/10.1007/s12160-017-9911-5

Rosen, L. D., Carrier, L. M., & Cheever, N. A. (2013). Technology and academic performance: The impact of cell phone use on students' grades. Journal of Educational Psychology, 105(2), 349-362.
https://doi.org/10.1037/a0032140

Galvin, K. M., & Brommel, B. J. (2018). Family communication: Cohesion and change. Routledge.

American College Counseling Association. (2017). Standards of practice for college counseling. American College Counseling Association.

Nichols, M. P., & Schwartz, R. C. (2008). Family therapy: Concepts and methods. Pearson.

Austin, J. T., & Vancouver, J. B. (1996). Goal constructs in psychology: Structure, process, and content. Psychological Bulletin, 120(3), 338-375.
https://doi.org/10.1037/0033-2909.120.3.338

Super, D. E. (1990). A life-span, life-space approach to career development. In D. Brown & L. Brooks (Eds.), Career choice and development (pp. 197-261). Jossey-Bass.

Brown, D., & Ryan Krane, N. (2000). Career counseling: A narrative approach. In D. Brown & W. M. Osborn (Eds.), Career counseling (pp. 49-70). Allyn & Bacon.

Hargrove, R. (2008). The adaptiveness of adaptive leadership. International Journal of Leadership Studies, 4(2), 130-144.

Kram, K. E. (1985). Mentoring at work: Developmental relationships in organizational life. University Press of America.

Andriotis, K. (2015). The impact of internships on career outcomes: A comprehensive review. Journal of Career Assessment, 23(1), 55-69. https://doi.org/10.1177/1069072714550145

Carver, C. S., & Scheier, M. F. (2014). Optimism, pessimism, and self-regulation. In M. D. Robinson, E. R. Watkins, & E. Harmon-Jones (Eds.), Handbook of cognition and emotion (pp. 142-164). Guilford Press.

Covey, S. R. (1994). The 7 Habits of Highly Effective People: Powerful Lessons in Personal Change. Free Press.

Newport, C. (2016). Deep work: Rules for focused success in a distracted world. Grand Central Publishing.

CHAPTER 4

Locke, E. A., & Latham, G. P. (2002). Building a practically useful theory of goal setting and task motivation: A 35-year odyssey. American Psychologist, 57(9), 705-717. https://doi.org/10.1037/0003-066X.57.9.705

Covey, S. R. (1989). The 7 habits of highly effective people: Powerful lessons in personal change. Free Press.

Britton, Bruce K., & Tesser, Abraham. (1991). Effects of time-management practices on college grades. Journal of Educational

Psychology, 83(3), 405-410.
https://doi.org/10.1037/0022-0663.83.3.405

Johnson, D. W., & Johnson, R. T. (2009). An educational psychology success story: Social interdependence theory and cooperative learning. Educational Psychologist, 44(2), 113-126.
https://doi.org/10.1080/00461520902832388

Keyes, C. L. M. (2002). The mental health continuum: From languishing to flourishing in life. Journal of Health and Social Behavior, 43(2), 207-222.
https://doi.org/10.2307/3090197

Brown, D., & Ryan Krane, N. (2000). Career counseling: A narrative approach. In D. Brown & W. M. Osborn (Eds.), Career counseling (pp. 49-70). Allyn & Bacon.

Emmons, R. A., & McCullough, M. E. (2003). Counting blessings versus burdens: An experimental investigation of gratitude and subjective well-being in daily life. Journal of Personality and Social Psychology, 84(2), 377-389.
https://doi.org/10.1037/0022-3514.84.2.377

Austin, J. T., & Vancouver, J. B. (1996). Goal constructs in psychology: A hierarchical model of goal setting. International Review of Industrial and Organizational Psychology, 11, 219-266.
https://doi.org/10.1002/9780470752892.ch6

Fredrickson, B. L. (2004). The broaden-and-build theory of positive emotions. Philosophical Transactions of the Royal Society B: Biological Sciences, 359(1449), 1367-1377.
https://doi.org/10.1098/rstb.2004.1512

Pintrich, P. R., & De Groot, E. V. (1990). Motivational and self-regulated learning components of classroom academic performance. Journal of Educational Psychology, 82(1), 33-40.
https://doi.org/10.1037/0022-0663.82.1.33

Galvin, K. M., & Brommel, B. J. (2018). Family communication: Cohesion and change (11th ed.). Pearson.

Zimmerman, B. J. (1989). A social cognitive view of self-regulated academic learning. Journal of Educational Psychology, 81(3), 329-339.
https://doi.org/10.1037/0022-0663.81.3.329

Dunlosky, J., Rawson, K. A., Marsh, E. J., Nathan, M. J., & Willingham, D. T. (2013). Improving students' learning with effective learning techniques: Promising directions from cognitive and educational psychology. Psychological Science in the Public Interest, 14(1), 4-58.
https://doi.org/10.1177/1529100612453266

Zimmerman, B. J. (2008). Investigating self-regulation and motivation: Historical background, methodological developments, and future prospects. American Educational Research Journal, 45(1), 166-183.
https://doi.org/10.3102/0002831207312909

Robbins, S. P., Lauver, D., Le, H., Davis, B., Langley, R., & Carlstrom, A. (2004). Do psychosocial and study skill factors predict college outcomes? A meta-analysis. Psychological Bulletin, 130(6), 689-713.
https://doi.org/10.1037/0033-2909.130.6.689

Boud, D., Keogh, R., & Walker, D. (1985). Reflection: Turning experience into learning. Routledge.

Prince, M. (2004). Does active learning work? A review of the research. Journal of Engineering Education, 93(3), 223-231.
https://doi.org/10.1002/j.2168-9830.2004.tb00809.x

Kramer, C. D., & Michel, S. S. (2005). Using university resources to support student success. Journal of College Student Retention: Research, Theory & Practice, 7(4), 389-407.
https://doi.org/10.2190/6R7J-MGH5-Y0HT-W9JN

Kram, K. E. (1985). Mentoring at work: Developmental relationships in organizational life. University Press of America.

Clark, A. (2001). Balancing academic and personal life: A case study of students' stress management. Journal of College Student

Development, 42(5), 560-574.
https://doi.org/10.1353/csd.2001.0058

Hattie, J., & Timperley, H. (2007). The power of feedback. Review of Educational Research, 77(1), 81-112.
https://doi.org/10.3102/003465430298487

Astin, A. W., & Astin, H. S. (2000). Leadership Reconsidered: Engaging Higher Education in Social Change. W.K. Kellogg Foundation.

Pascarella, E. T., & Terenzini, P. T. (2005). How College Affects Students: A Third Decade of Research. Jossey-Bass.

Karp, M. M., & Bork, R. H. (2018). They never told me what to expect, so I didn't know what to do: Defining and clarifying the role of a community college student. Community College Research Center, Teachers College, Columbia University.

Hurtado, S., & Carter, D. F. (1997). Effects of college transition and perceptions of the campus racial climate on Latino college students' sense of belonging. Sociology of Education, 70(4), 324-345.
https://doi.org/10.2307/2673270

National Association of Colleges and Employers (NACE). (2018). Job Outlook 2018. National Association of Colleges and Employers.

Komives, S. R., Lucas, N., & McMahon, T. R. (1998). Exploring Leadership: For College Students Who Want to Make a Difference. Jossey-Bass.

Chang, M. J., Astin, A. W., & Kim, D. (2004). Assessing the Impact of Undergraduate Diversity Courses on Students' Racial Views. Journal of Higher Education, 75(3), 306-330.
https://doi.org/10.1353/jhe.2004.0019

Eby, L. T., Allen, T. D., Evans, S. C., Ng, T. W. H., & DuBois, D. L. (2008). Does mentoring matter? A multidisciplinary meta-analysis comparing mentored and non-mentored individuals.

Journal of Vocational Behavior, 72(2), 254-267.
https://doi.org/10.1016/j.jvb.2007.10.004

Jacobi, M. (1991). Mentoring and undergraduate academic success: A review of the literature. Review of Educational Research, 61(4), 505-532.
https://doi.org/10.3102/00346543061004505

Kram, K. E. (1985). Mentoring at Work: Developmental Relationships in Organizational Life. Scott, Foresman.

Ragins, B. R., & Cotton, J. L. (1999). Mentor functions and outcomes: A comparison of men and women in formal and informal mentoring relationships. Journal of Applied Psychology, 84(4), 529-550.
https://doi.org/10.1037/0021-9010.84.4.529

Allen, T. D., Eby, L. T., Poteet, M. L., Lentz, E., & Lima, L. (2004). Career benefits associated with mentoring for mentors: A review and research agenda. Journal of Management, 30(6), 779-805.
https://doi.org/10.1016/j.jom.2004.06.003

Trower, C. A. (2010). The role of mentoring in the transition to academic life: Insights from higher education research. Journal of Higher Education Policy and Management, 32(1), 43-56.
https://doi.org/10.1080/13600800903451680

Hurtado, S., & Carter, D. F. (1997). Effects of college transitions on students' perceptions of their social support: A longitudinal study. Journal of Higher Education, 68(1), 1-29.
https://doi.org/10.2307/2959960

Eccles, J. S., & Harold, R. D. (1996). Family involvement in children's and adolescents' schooling. In A. Booth & J. Dunn (Eds.), Family-school links: How do they affect educational outcomes (pp. 3-34). Lawrence Erlbaum Associates.

Choy, S. P. (2002). Minority undergraduates in postsecondary education: A look at their college experiences and outcomes. U.S.

Department of Education, National Center for Education Statistics. https://nces.ed.gov/pubs2002/2002166.pdf

Kim, Y. K., & Lee, J. (2010). The impact of family involvement on student success: A review of the literature. Journal of College Student Development, 51(4), 469-489. https://doi.org/10.1353/csd.0.0148

Hernandez, E. (2012). Family support and college students' adjustment: A review of the literature. Journal of Student Affairs Research and Practice, 49(3), 369-386. https://doi.org/10.1515/jsarp-2012-0183

Tinto, V. (1993). Leaving college: Rethinking the causes and cures of student attrition (2nd ed.). University of Chicago Press.

Astin, A. W. (1993). What matters in college: Four critical years revisited. Jossey-Bass.

Chang, M. J., Astin, A. W., & Kim, D. (2004). Assessing the impact of undergraduate diversity courses on students' racial views. The Journal of Higher Education, 75(3), 285-317. https://doi.org/10.1353/jhe.2004.0010

Eisenberg, D., Golberstein, E., & Hunt, J. B. (2009). Mental health and academic success in college. B.E. Journal of Economic Analysis & Policy, 9(1). https://doi.org/10.2202/1935-1682.2197

Barker, K. (2018). The role of social networks in career advancement. Career Development Quarterly, 66(2), 145-157. https://doi.org/10.1002/cdq.12135

Cohen, P. A., Kulik, C. L. C., & Kulik, J. A. (1982). Educational outcomes of tutoring: A meta-analysis of findings. American Educational Research Journal, 19(2), 293-311. https://doi.org/10.3102/00028312019002293

Hockings, C. (2010). Inclusive teaching and learning in higher education. Routledge.

Niemiec, C. P., Sikorski, J., & Walberg, H. J. (2018). The effect of tutoring on academic achievement: A meta-analysis. Educational Research Review, 24, 25-35.
https://doi.org/10.1016/j.edurev.2018.03.002

Robbins, S. P., Lauver, K., Le, H., Davis, D., Langley, R., & Carlstrom, A. (2004). Do psychometric measures of academic performance predict college success? A meta-analysis. Psychological Bulletin, 130(2), 261-288.
https://doi.org/10.1037/0033-2909.130.2.261

Kolb, D. A. (1984). Experiential learning: Experience as the source of learning and development. Prentice Hall.

Trought, M. (2007). The role of career workshops in student employability. Journal of Career Assessment, 15(4), 419-431.
https://doi.org/10.1177/1069072707303022

Froyd, J. E., & Simpson, N. D. (2000). Student-centered learning: A case study of a first-year physics course. Journal of Engineering Education, 89(3), 361-370.
https://doi.org/10.1002/j.2168-9830.2000.tb00539.x

Chickering, A. W., & Gamson, Z. F. (1987). Seven principles for good practice in undergraduate education. AAHE Bulletin, 39(7), 3-7.
https://www.aahea.org/Articles/7principles.pdf

Springer, L., Stanne, M. E., & Donovan, S. S. (1999). Effects of small-group learning on undergraduates in science, mathematics, engineering, and technology: A meta-analysis. Review of Educational Research, 69(1), 21-51.
https://doi.org/10.3102/00346543069001021

Pauk, W., & Owens, R. J. Q. (2017). How to study in college (11th Ed.) Cengage Learning.

CHAPTER 5

Lakein, A. (1973). How to get control of your time and your life. New American Library.

Britton, B. K., & Tesser, A. (1991). Effects of time-management practices on college grades. Journal of Educational Psychology, 83(3), 405-410.
https://doi.org/10.1037/0022-0663.83.3.405

Hansen, R. (2003). Time management: The essential guide to productivity. Penguin Books.

Macan, T. H., Shahani, C., Dipboye, R. L., & Phillips, A. P. (1990). College students' time management: Correlations with academic performance and stress. Journal of Educational Psychology, 82(4), 760-768.
https://doi.org/10.1037/0022-0663.82.4.760

Ferrari, J. R., Johnson, J. L., & McCown, W. G. (1995). Procrastination and task avoidance: Theory, research, and treatment. Plenum Press.

Baca, K., & Sturm, J. (2020). The role of technology in time management for students. Journal of Educational Technology Systems, 48(1), 23-34.
https://doi.org/10.1177/0047239520901781

Biswas-Diener, R. (2012). Happiness in a flexible world: The role of adaptability in personal well-being. Journal of Positive Psychology, 7(4), 331-338.
https://doi.org/10.1080/17439760.2012.710118

Fleming, K. M., & Spencer, L. (2014). Reflective time management: Strategies for continuous improvement. Journal of Academic Development, 16(2), 45-59.
https://doi.org/10.1080/14703297.2014.890740

Newport, C. (2016). Deep work: Rules for focused success in a distracted world. Grand Central Publishing.

Allen, D. (2001). Getting things done: The art of stress-free productivity. Penguin Books.

Cirillo, F. (2018). The Pomodoro Technique: The life-changing time-management system. Penguin Life.

Covey, S. R. (1989). The 7 habits of highly effective people: Powerful lessons in personal change. Free Press.

Koch, R. (1998). The 80/20 principle: The secret to achieving more with less. Crown Business.

Tracy, B. (2001). Eat that frog!: 21 great ways to stop procrastinating and get more done in less time. Berrett-Koehler Publishers.

Doran, G. T. (1981). There's a S.M.A.R.T. way to write management's goals and objectives. Management Review, 70(11), 35-36.

Austin, J. T., & Vancouver, J. B. (1996). Goal constructs in psychology: Structure, process, and content. Psychological Bulletin, 120(3), 338-375.

Locke, E. A., & Latham, G. P. (2002). Building a practically useful theory of goal setting and task motivation: A 35-year odyssey. American Psychologist, 57(9), 705-717.

Furnham, A., & Rawles, R. (1995). The role of time of day in student learning: Circadian variation in academic performance. Personality and Individual Differences, 18(4), 513–518. https://doi.org/10.1016/0191-8869(94)00166-9

Bjork, R. A., Dunlosky, J., & Kornell, N. (2013). Self-regulated learning: Beliefs, techniques, and illusions. Annual Review of Psychology, 64, 417–444.
https://doi.org/10.1146/annurev-psych-113011-143823

Mark, G., Desurvire, H., & Gedeon, T. (2005). Interruptions and distractions: Issues for attention management. International Journal of Human-Computer Interaction, 58(2), 35–42.

Ryan, R. M., & Deci, E. L. (2000). Self-determination theory and the facilitation of intrinsic motivation, social development, and well-being. American Psychologist, 55(1), 68-78.

Locke, E. A., & Latham, G. P. (2006). New directions in goal-setting theory. Current Directions in Psychological Science, 15(5), 265-268.

Chowdhury, M. R. (2019). The Science & Psychology Of Goal-Setting 101. https://positivepsychology.com/goal-setting-psychology/

Houston, E. (2019). What is Goal Setting and How to Do it Well. Retrieved from https://positivepsychology.com/goal-setting/

Grant, A. M. (2012). The importance of goal setting in the achievement of work outcomes. Journal of Organizational Behavior, 33(7), 1072-1092.

Biggs, J., & Tang, C. (2011). Teaching for Quality Learning at University (4th Ed.) Open University Press.

Panigrahi, R., Srivastava, P. R., & Sharma, D. (2018). Online learning: Adoption, continuance, and learning outcome—A review of literature. International Journal of Information Management, 43, 1-14. https://doi.org/10.1016/j.ijinfomgt.2018.06.005

Roediger, H. L., & Karpicke, J. D. (2006). The power of testing memory: Basic research and implications for educational practice. Perspectives on Psychological Science, 1(3), 181–210. https://doi.org/10.1111/j.1745-6916.2006.00012.x

Bloom, B. S. (Ed.). (1956). Taxonomy of Educational Objectives: The Classification of Educational Goals. Handbook I: Cognitive Domain. David McKay Company, Inc.

Anderson, L. W., & Krathwohl, D. R. (Eds.) (2001). A Taxonomy for Learning, Teaching, and Assessing: A Revision of Bloom's Taxonomy of Educational Objectives. Longman.

Bloom, B. S., Engelhart, M. D., Furst, E. J., Hill, W. H., & Krathwohl, D. R. (1956). Taxonomy of Educational Objectives: The Classification of Educational Goals. Handbook I: Cognitive Domain. David McKay Company, Inc.

Anderson, L. W., Krathwohl, D. R., Airasian, P. W., Cruikshank, K. A., Mayer, R. E., Pintrich, P. R., Raths, J., & Wittrock, M. C. (2001). A Taxonomy for Learning, Teaching, and Assessing: A Revision of Bloom's Taxonomy of Educational Objectives. Longman.

Krathwohl, D. R. (2002). A Revision of Bloom's Taxonomy: An Overview. Theory into Practice, 41(4), 212-218.

Gronlund, N. E. (2006). Assessment of Student Achievement. Pearson.

Mayer, R. E. (2002). Rethinking the role of visual representations in teaching and learning. Educational Psychology Review, 14(1), 89-101.

Biggs, J., & Tang, C. (2011). Teaching for Quality Learning at University (4th Ed.) Open University Press.

Hartwig, M. K., & Dunlosky, J. (2012). Study strategies of college students: Are self-testing and scheduling related to achievement? Psychological Science, 23(2), 112-118.

www.ingramcontent.com/pod-product-compliance
Lightning Source LLC
Chambersburg PA
CBHW070833160426
43192CB00012B/2189